Owen Wister
and the West

The Oklahoma Western Biographies
Richard W. Etulain, General Editor

Owen Wister. Library of Congress Prints and Photographs Division.

Owen Wister
and the West

Gary Scharnhorst

University of Oklahoma Press : Norman

Also by Gary Scharnhorst

Bret Harte: Opening the American Literary West (Norman, Okla., 2000)

Kate Field: The Many Lives of a Nineteenth-Century American Journalist (Syracuse, N.Y., 2008)

Literary Eats: Emily Dickinson's Gingerbread, Ernest Hemingway's Picadillo, Eudora Welty's Onion Pie and 400+ Other Recipes from American Authors Past and Present (Jefferson, N.C., 2014)

Julian Hawthorne: The Life of a Prodigal Son (Champaign, Ill., 2014)

Library of Congress Cataloging-in-Publication Data

Scharnhorst, Gary.
    Owen Wister and the West / Gary Scharnhorst.
        pages cm. — (The Oklahoma western biographies ; 30)
    Includes bibliographical references and index.
    ISBN 978-0-8061-4675-1 (hardback)
    ISBN 978-0-8061-9409-7 (paperback)
    1. Wister, Owen, 1860–1938. 2. Authors, American—19th century—Biography. 3. Western stories—History and criticism.
4. West (U.S.)—In literature. I. Title.

    PS3346.S33 2015
    813'.52—dc23
    [B]   2014032715

The paper in this book meets the guidelines for permanence and durability of the Committee on Production Guidelines for Book Longevity of the Council on Library Resources, Inc. ∞

Owen Wister and the West is Volume 30 in The Oklahoma Western Biographies.

For Heather, Nick, Alex, Charlie,
Olivia, Sage, Ryan, Rachel,
and other friends at my own
Last Chance Saloon

He could have been a very great writer and the combination of circumstances that prevent that are always tragic.

Ernest Hemingway to Maxwell Perkins,
December 29, 1929

Contents

Illustrations

Series Editor's Preface

Stories of heroes and heroines have intrigued many generations of listeners and readers. Americans, like people everywhere, are captivated by the lives of military, political, and religious figures and intrepid explorers, pioneers, and rebels. The Oklahoma Western Biographies series endeavors to build on this fascination with biography and to link it with two other abiding interests of Americans: the frontier and the American West. Although volumes in the series carry no notes, they are prepared by leading scholars, are soundly researched, and include a discussion of the sources used. Each volume is a lively synthesis based on thorough examination of pertinent primary and secondary sources.

Above all, the Oklahoma Western Biographies aim at two goals: to provide readable life stories of significant westerners, and to show how their lives illuminate a notable topic, an influential movement, or a series of important events in the history and cultures of the American West.

Gary Scharnhorst's biographical-literary study of Owen Wister makes major contributions to understanding that writer's links to the American West. Scharnhorst has dug deeper and more widely than any previous writer in examining Wister's West. Mining the most important Wister manuscripts in the Library of Congress and the American Heritage Center at the University of Wyoming, as well as Wister materials in other libraries and archives, Scharnhorst fills his probing account with numerous illuminating quotations from firsthand Wister sources.

This work likewise provides thorough discussions of Wister's personal-historical experiences in the West. Scharnhorst shows how Wister used (or changed) these experiences in his western stories and novels. Particularly extensive are Scharnhorst's comments about people and incidents that became central emphases in Wister's western fiction.

Scharnhorst's abundant talents as a widely published literary historian and critic shine through in every section of this literary biography. The evaluations of Wister's stories and novels provide numerous insights into Wister's adroit uses of his sources. In addition, we get revealing comparisons between Wister's western works and the writings of other authors treating the West.

Also of much value is Scharnhorst's extensive chronology of Wister's travels and the writings that emanated from these western journeys. These important connections are clarified in the prefatory chronology as well as in later chapters.

Altogether, this well-written study makes clearer than any previous biography or literary analysis the length and breadth of Owen Wister's strong links to the American West. Scharnhorst clearly traces Wister's western ties up to and through the publication of his classic work, *The Virginian* (1902); he shows too, as others have failed to do, that Wister maintained his western connections after the appearance of that notable novel. Clearly, in this revealing study of Owen Wister and the West, Gary Scharnhorst achieves the major goals of volumes in the Oklahoma Western Biographies series.

Acknowledgments

As ever, I am indebted to friends and librarians across the country for their help and encouragement in this project, most important among them Mike Kelly, Fales Library, New York University; Stephen Crook and Tal Nadan, New York Public Library; Louis Tanner, University of New Mexico; Claude Zachary, University of Southern California Library; and Pranita Amatya, Doe Library, University of California at Berkeley. Thanks, too, to Dick Etulain and Chuck Rankin of the University of Oklahoma Press; and Edmund Harley, Khaled Khiyar, and Kelvin Neosu for their encouragement as I've completed the project. For the record, I have deposited a fully documented copy of the manuscript of this biography in the English Department library at the University of New Mexico, should interested scholars wish to consult my sources.

Chronology

1860

July 14   Born in Germantown, Pennsylvania

1882

June 18   Graduates from Harvard

1885

Early June   Diagnosed with neurasthenia by S. Weir
                        Mitchell

June 30   Leaves Philadelphia for Wyoming via
                        Pittsburgh, Chicago, and Omaha

July 3   Arrives in Cheyenne. Spends the summer on
                        Major Frank Wolcott's ranch in Converse
                        County, Wyoming.

July 18   Meets the physician and future Wyoming
                        Governor Amos Barber

July 19   First visit to Medicine Bow

Early September   Returns to Philadelphia

Chronology

1887

July 1	Leaves Philadelphia for Wyoming via Albany, Niagara Falls, Toronto, Qu'Appelle, Vancouver, Victoria, Seattle, Portland
July 23	Leaves San Francisco
Late July	Fort Washakie, Wyoming. Hires George West as hunting guide.
August 6–11	Hunting and fishing in the Wind River Mountains
August 25–31	Travels through Yellowstone National Park
September 1	Leaves Wyoming for Boston via Cinnabar, Billings, St. Paul, and Chicago
September 8	Arrives in Boston

1888

June 27	Graduates from Harvard Law School
July 16	Leaves Philadelphia for Wyoming via Chicago and Omaha
Mid-July to mid-September	Hunts with George West in vicinity of Fort Washakie, Wind River, and Snake River
September 18	Leaves Wyoming for Philadelphia

1889

October 9	Leaves Philadelphia for Wyoming via Pittsburgh, Valparaiso, Fort Wayne, Chicago, and Omaha
October 11	Arrives in Laramie
October 12	Arrives in Rawlins
October 15	Joins George West at Fort Washakie
November 26	Departs from Rawlins for Philadelphia via Chicago and Columbus

Chronology

1891

June 4	Leaves Philadelphia for Wyoming via Boston and Detroit
June 10	Chadron, Nebraska
June 11	Douglas, Wyoming
June 13–20	D. R. Tisdale's ranch
June 25–27	Buffalo, Wyoming
July 2–3	Casper, Wyoming
July 9–11	Fort Washakie
August 4–September 9	Yellowstone National Park
September 4	Meets Captain Frank Edwards
September 18	Departs for Philadelphia
November	Completes "Hank's Woman"

1892

January	Completes "How Lin McLean Went East"
April	Johnson County War
June	Completes "Balaam and Pedro," first story written featuring the Virginian
July 6	Leaves Philadelphia for nine-day round trip to Wyoming via Chicago and St. Paul
July 10	Arrives in Cinnabar, Wyoming, and pays George West for canceling three-month hunting trip. Departs on return trip.
July 14	Arrives in Philadelphia
August 27	"Hank's Woman" published in *Harper's Weekly*
October 1	Leaves Philadelphia for Washington State via Chicago

Chronology

Chronology

Chronology

October 8–15	Fort Bowie, Arizona. Meets Charles Skirdin.
October 16–30	San Carlos, Arizona
November	"Em'ly" published in *Harper's Monthly*. First published appearance of the Virginian.
November	Writes "Little Big Horn Medicine"
November 4–14	Fort Grant, Arizona
November 16	Leaves Yuma bound for Los Angeles
November 17	San Joaquin Valley
November 17–December 11	San Francisco
December	"The Winning of the Biscuit-Shooter" published in *Harper's Monthly*
December 13	Portland, Oregon
December 18	Leaves Portland for Philadelphia via Ogden, Cheyenne, Omaha, and Chicago
December 23	Arrives in Philadelphia

1894

January	"Balaam and Pedro" published in *Harper's Monthly*
January	Writes "Specimen Jones"
February	Writes "The General's Bluff"
March	Writes "The Serenade at Siskiyou" and "Salvation Gap"
April	"The Promised Land" published in *Harper's Monthly*
April–May	Writes "Lin McLean's Honeymoon"
April 28	Leaves Philadelphia for the Southwest via Columbus, Cincinnati, Louisville, and Memphis

Chronology

May	"A Kinsman of Red Cloud" published in *Harper's Monthly*
May 2	Fort Worth
May 3	El Paso
Mid-May	Fort Bayard, Silver City, and Deming, New Mexico
Late May– June 21	Forts Grant and Bowie, Arizona
June	"Little Big Horn Medicine" published in *Harper's Monthly*
June 22	Copper Queen mine, Bisbee, Arizona
June 23–24	Tombstone, Arizona
June 25	Benson, Arizona
June 26	Start of the Pullman strike
June 27	Tucson, Arizona
June 28	Los Angeles
July	"Specimen Jones" published in *Harper's Monthly*
June 29–July 1	Sails from Los Angeles to San Francisco via San Luis Obispo
July 1–26	San Francisco
July 18	California Midwinter International Exposition
July 26	Leaves San Francisco for Philadelphia via Sacramento, Cheyenne, Omaha, and Chicago
July 29	Visits Amos Barber in Cheyenne
August	"The Serenade at Siskiyou" published in *Harper's Monthly*
Early August	Arrives in Philadelphia

Chronology

September	"The General's Bluff" published in *Harper's Monthly*
September	Writes "The Second Missouri Compromise"
October	"Salvation Gap" published in *Harper's Monthly*
November	Writes "La Tinaja Bonita"

1895

January	"Lin McLean's Honeymoon" published in *Harper's Monthly*
January	Writes "The Evolution of the Cow-Puncher"
February–April	Writes "A Boom in Tucson" aka "A Pilgrim on the Gila"
March	"The Second Missouri Compromise" published in *Harper's Monthly*
May	"La Tinaja Bonita" published in *Harper's Monthly*
May 9	Leaves Philadelphia for the Southwest via New Orleans and San Antonio
May 13	Meets Dean Duke in El Paso
May 31–June 11	Apache Tejo, New Mexico
June 13–23	Los Angeles and San Francisco
June 24–30	Yosemite National Park
July 5	En route from Salt Lake to Denver
Last three weeks in July	Denver, Boulder, Fort Logan, and Estes Park
August 3	Cheyenne
August 6	Denver
August 8	Fort Logan
August 11	Fort Meade

Chronology

August 18	Milwaukee
Circa August 20	Arrives in Philadelphia
September	"The Evolution of the Cow-puncher" published in *Harper's Monthly*
September	Writes "His Own Family" aka "A Journey in Search of Christmas"
November	"A Pilgrim on the Gila" published in *Harper's Monthly*
November	Revises "The Bear Creek Barbeque" aka "Concerning Children" and "Where Fancy Was Bred"
November 8	*Red Men and White* published
December 14	"A Journey in Search of Christmas" published in *Harper's Weekly*

1896

March	"Where Fancy Was Bred" published in *Harper's Monthly*
July 18	Leaves Philadelphia for Wyoming with Grant La Farge and Jack Mitchell via Buffalo, New York, Chicago, and Omaha
July 20	Dines at Cheyenne Club with U.S. Senator Francis E. Warren of Wyoming
Late July	Joined by George West at Fort Washakie for a hunt along Wind River
September	Jackson's Hole, Wyoming. Writes "The Passing of Ute Jack."
Late September	Departs from Cinnabar
Early November	Completes "Separ's Vigilante"
November 13–30	Writes "Grandmother Stark"
December 7–22	Writes "Sharon's Choice"

| December 29 | "How Ute Jack Was Taken" aka "Napoleon Shave-Tail" published in *Harper's Round Table* |

1897

January–February	Writes "The Jimmyjohn Boss"
March	Decides to divide the narratives of Lin McLean and the Virginian
March	Revises "How Lin McLean Went East"
March	"Separ's Vigilante" published in *Harper's Monthly*
April	Revises "The Winning of the Biscuit-Shooter"
May 19–June 1, July 19–August 5	Writes "Destiny at Drybone"
June	"Grandmother Stark" published in *Harper's Monthly*
June	"The Jimmyjohn Boss" published in *Pocket Magazine*
August	"Sharon's Choice" published in *Harper's Monthly*
December	"Destiny at Drybone" published in *Harper's Monthly*
December 7	*Lin McLean* published

1898

April 21	Marries his second cousin Mary (Molly) Channing Wister
July–October	Wedding journey to Pacific Northwest
Late July–September	Methow Valley, Washington

Chronology

Late September	Yellowstone National Park
Early October	Returns to Philadelphia

1899

March	Writes "The Game and the Nation"
August	Writes "Twenty Minutes for Refreshments"
December	Writes "Padre Ignazio"

1900

January	"Twenty Minutes for Refreshments" published in *Harper's Monthly*
January 4–8	Writes "The Patronage of High Bear" aka "Happy Teeth"
March	Rewrites "Hank's Woman"
April	"Padre Ignazio" published in *Harper's Monthly*
May	"The Game and the Nation" published in *Harper's Monthly*
May 3	*The Jimmyjohn Boss and Other Stories* published
Circa August 8	Leaves Philadelphia for California and Oregon via Nebraska and Colorado
August 14	Denver and Colorado Springs
Mid-August	Palace Hotel in San Francisco
Late August– end of September	Oregon
October 4	Capitol Hotel in Boise
October	Returns to Philadelphia

1901

January	"The Patronage of High Bear" published in *Cosmopolitan*

May	Writes "In a State of Sin"
Spring–winter	Works on a dramatization of *Lin McLean*
Summer	Writes "Superstition Trail" in Saunderstown, Rhode Island
October 26 and November 2	"Superstition Trail" published in the *Saturday Evening Post*

1902

January	Moves temporarily to Charleston, South Carolina, to finish *The Virginian*
February	"In a State of Sin" published in *Harper's Monthly*
May 3 and 10	"With Malice Aforethought" published in *Saturday Evening Post*
May 30	*The Virginian* published
Early summer	Writes "How the Energy Was Conserved" aka "In the Back"
September	Writes "The Vicious Circle" aka "Spit-Cat Creek"
December 13	"The Vicious Circle" published in *Saturday Evening Post*

1903

February 21	"How the Energy Was Conserved" published in *Collier's Weekly*
September 30	*The Virginian* (stage version) premieres in New Haven
October 10	*The Virginian* opens in Boston
October– December	Out-of-town tryouts of *The Virginian* in upstate New York and Pennsylvania

Chronology

1904

January 5   *The Virginian* opens at the Manhattan Theater in New York

Late May   *The Virginian* closes for the season at the Garrick Theater in Chicago

1907

June 19   Awarded an honorary Doctor of Laws degree by the University of Pennsylvania

1908

March 7   "Timberline" published in *Saturday Evening Post*

June 9   Sarah Butler Wister dies

July 18   "The Gift Horse" published in *Saturday Evening Post*

1909

February 27   "Extra Dry" published in *Saturday Evening Post*

1910

January 26   Leaves Philadelphia for California via New Orleans

March 25   El Paso

April 5   Leaves Tucson for Maricopa, Phoenix, and Yuma, Arizona. Spends three weeks in the Loma Linda Sanatorium near San Bernardino.

April   Hotel del Coronado near San Diego

May 26   Alvarado Hotel, Albuquerque

Late May– early June   El Ortiz Hotel, Lamy, New Mexico

Early June	Returns to Philadelphia
August 4	Leaves Philadelphia for Wyoming via Chicago, St. Paul, and Fargo, North Dakota
August 13	Cody, Wyoming
August 16– December 9	Ishawooa, Wyoming. Writes "The Drake Who Had Means of His Own."
December 10	Departs Cody for Billings, Montana
December 12	St. Paul
December 14	Chicago
December 15	Arrives in Philadelphia

1911

January	Revises "Happy Teeth"
February 19– March 1	Writes "Where It Was"
March 11	"The Drake Who Had Means of His Own" published in *Saturday Evening Post*
April 22	"Where It Was" published in *Saturday Evening Post*
May 11	*Members of the Family* published
Mid-June	Departs for West with family
Early July	Hotel del Coronado near San Diego
July 7–30	Salt Lake City
August 1	Leaves Salt Lake City for Medicine Bow, Jackson's Hole, and the Yellowstone
August	Jackson's Hole. Buys a 160-acre ranch near Jackson's Hole.
October 13	Leaves his ranch for a short hunting trip. Denies rumors of his ill health and death.
October 15	Leaves Wyoming for Philadelphia via Denver
November 1	Arrives in Philadelphia

Chronology

1912

March	Elected to American Academy of Arts and Sciences
June	Awarded Honorary Doctor of Letters degree by Williams College
June	Leaves Philadelphia
Early July	Santa Barbara
July 15	Hotel del Coronado, San Diego. Buys half-interest in 3,298 acres of Rancho El Cajon in La Mesa, California, for $25,000.
July 19	En route from San Diego to his Wyoming ranch
September 9	Moxum Hotel, Salt Lake City
Late September	En route back to Philadelphia

1913

August 24	Molly Wister dies

1915

Circa July 1	Leaves Philadelphia for the West
July 4	Pace Hotel, Gallup, New Mexico
July 11–12	El Tovar, Grand Canyon
July 16–21	Hotel del Coronado near San Diego
July 29–August 5	Fairmont Hotel, San Francisco
August 9	Arrives in Philadelphia

1916

July 1	Leaves Philadelphia for British Columbia
July 8	Seattle. Leaves for East via Wyoming and last visit to Yellowstone National Park.
Circa August 1	Returns to Philadelphia

Chronology

1917

Summer   At Trapper Lodge, Shell, Wyoming, with son Owen

1918

July 15   Leaves Philadelphia for Wyoming with son Owen

September 3   Trapper Lodge, Shell, Wyoming

September 10   Nebraska en route back to Philadelphia

1919

August 1–21   Visits Dean Duke at his ranch in Modoc county, California

Early September Returns east

1920

February   Sells his Wyoming ranch to the R Lazy S. Wister, Kirke La Shelle's widow, and Famous Players-Lasky Corporation sell movie rights to *The Virginian* to Douglas Fairbanks for $55,000; Wister receives two-ninths, or about $12,000.

1924

July   "Sun Road" aka "Bad Medicine" published in *Cosmopolitan*

September   "Captain Quid" published in *Cosmopolitan*

1925

August 25   Completes "Once Around the Clock"

1926

July   "Once Around the Clock" published in *Cosmopolitan*

November	"The Right Honorable the Strawberries" published in *Cosmopolitan*

1928

January 23–30	Completes "Skip to My Loo" in Palm Beach, Florida
February	"At the Sign of the Last Chance" published in *Cosmopolitan*
May	"Molting Pelican" published in *Cosmopolitan*
June	"Little Old Scaffold" published in *Cosmopolitan*
Last week of June	*When West Was West* published
July–August	Trapper Lodge, Shell, Wyoming
Late August	Meets Ernest Hemingway
Early September	Returns to Philadelphia

1929

October 27	Receives Roosevelt Medal for Distinguished Service

1930

June	*Roosevelt: The Story of a Friendship, 1880–1919* published

1936

March	"Old Yellowstone Days" published in *Harper's Monthly*

1938

July 21	Dies from cerebral hemorrhage in Saunderstown, Rhode Island

Owen Wister
and the West

Introduction

Westerns are rarely only about the West. From Fenimore Cooper to Gary Cooper, stories set in the American West have been vehicles for topical commentary. More than any other pioneer of the genre, moreover, Owen Wister turned the western into a form of social and political critique, touching on such issues as race, environment, women's rights, labor rights, tourism, and immigration. Put another way, the West was the crucible in which Wister imaginatively tested and expressed his political opinions.

Like his friend Theodore Roosevelt, Wister was the sickly scion of a privileged eastern family and graduate of Harvard College who recuperated in the West before returning to his eastern home and inherited social position. Whereas Roosevelt ventured to the Dakota Territory for the "West cure," however, Wister went to Wyoming. By 1895 he had traveled in every contiguous U.S. state and territory, "in trains, stage coaches, on horses; sleeping in important hotels, log cabins, and blankets out in the open." In all, between 1885 and 1928 he made twenty-five trips west of the Missouri River, ten of them after 1910.

Unfortunately, his western travels after 1895, and especially after his marriage in 1898, are relatively undocumented: they became rather routine vacations, not hunting and camping trips in the American outback. But his biographer Darwin Payne overstates the case for ignoring this period and these trips. After publishing three early collections of western local-color stories and achieving his great success with the novel *The Virginian* (1902), according to Payne, Wister "largely abandoned the West as a theme." On the contrary, Wister was interested in the West until his death, even if he expanded his literary interests to include other topics and regions late in life. To be sure, he was always a literary tourist, more a man of leisure than a man of letters. But he collaborated on a critically and commercially successful theatrical version of his novel in 1903, and he published enough western stories after *The Virginian* to fill two additional volumes, the second issued when he was sixty-eight years old.

In all, Wister wrote six books of western fiction (two novels and four collections totaling thirty-three stories), as well, of course, as the theatrical version of *The Virginian*. His brand of fiction went hand in glove with the old triumphal model of western American history, the narrative of conquest or "the winning of the West," told from the point of view of the hardy Anglo-Saxon pioneer. Wister featured the character of the Virginian in thirteen separate stories, almost all published originally in magazines. Eight of these were folded into the novel *The Virginian*, plus the 1900 version of "Hank's Woman"; two were folded into the novel *Lin McLean* (1897); and two stories were reprinted in *Members of the Family* (1911). Wister continued to correspond with western friends and to reminisce about his western travels until his death.

This biography focuses on Wister's West, his life there and his writings about the region. In it, such figures as Roosevelt, Frederic Remington, Rudyard Kipling, and author Hamlin Garland make cameo appearances, and I chronicle the composition and reception of his most important western stories.

Though he has long been relegated to the attic of American letters, Wister was a remarkably versatile writer: poet, playwright, essayist, lecturer, writer of westerns and novelist of manners, author of children's books, journalist, foreign correspondent, book critic, biographer, historian, satirist, and musical composer. Though he never wrote an autobiography, he kept copious diaries of his early western travels. Because he suffered from a series of (psychosomatic?) illnesses throughout his adulthood, however, he was never prolific. As he explained to an interviewer in 1894, years before achieving his greatest literary successes, even when healthy he wrote

> very slowly, and often the stories are written over two or three times. I write first in pencil, and then change, cut out and turn about in such a way that the original draft would scarcely be recognized. As a general thing it takes from two to five weeks for me to write a story of 6,000 to 8,000 words.

Wister developed the habits of a professional writer, always working "in the early part of the day, usually from 9 o'clock in the morning to lunch time. . . . I find my brain is clear in the morning, and usually otherwise, at least not exactly what I could wish, later." By his own admission he was an anguished stylist. "I get so wrapped up in my story and am oftentimes so dissatisfied with my first drafts," he allowed, "that I am really in pain to get it down in the shape I desire." After dining in August 1895 with Captain Charles King, the author of some sixty books, including *Campaigning with Crook and Stories of Army Life* (1890), Wister confided to his journal that for once he had enjoyed conversing with a fellow writer because King

> talks of other matters and raises no pet arguments upon style & the manipulation of the parts of speech. Those things are better left behind with your foolscap and other apparatus. I think it is chiefly

the unsuccessful who discuss their tools. . . . The recording angel knows how I worry over my words. In fact I have chiseled at my last two writings with just as much deliberation as I ever gave to verse. That is too much I think, and bad for prose. In my case it has produced an artificial effect that I was blind to at the time. . . . Perhaps I had to pass through this experimenting to learn my lessons. Anyhow, the next ventures shall be limbered from all such shackles. And some happy day we may achieve style!

Three months later, in a letter to his mother, Wister conceded that "the only thing I know about [style] is that it's something I haven't got myself."

Paradoxically, Wister was an elitist who invented a folk hero, the "Cowboy Superman," as the novelist Ford Madox Ford called him. "He was intuitively wise, naturally gentle, physically supreme, practically gifted with infallible tact, a God-sent leader of men, tamer of colts, rounder-up of cattle, and wielder" of a gun. Wister's hero, said Ford, typified the best "that America could produce or emulate." *The Virginian*, Wister's best and best-known work, is often credited with establishing the standard formula of the twentieth-century western, his lasting legacy in American letters. Among the well-known critics of the novel, Marcus Klein has called it the "essential Western," John Cobbs deemed it the "prototype for the modern Western," and, as John Cawelti noted, "its characters and the chief incidents of its plot have been repeated in countless novels and films." Much as Bret Harte invented the stock character of the eastern schoolmarm, Wister invented the character of the eastern dude. In short, more than any other western writer of the past century and a half, he merits resurrection from the footnote. "I value accuracy more than any other quality in such stories as I write," he insisted. "I don't care how effective they are, if they're false, they're spoiled for me."

Yet Wister always viewed the West narrowly, through the blinders of his social class and the rose-colored lens of nostalgia. His West, according to historian David Brion Davis, was hardly "the realistic, boisterous, sometimes monotonous West" of Andy Adams's *The Log of a Cowboy* (1903). On the contrary: Wister asserted in 1897 that the West was "the only greatly romantic thing our generation has known, the last greatly romantic thing our Continent holds; indeed the poetic episode most deeply native that we possess." Or as the western literature scholar Ben Merchant Vorphal has fairly concluded, "When Wister first went west in 1885, he was a romantic. When he wrote his last western story in 1928, he was still a romantic."

1

1885–1893

On June 30, 1885, Owen Wister boarded a train at Broad Street station in Philadelphia for his first trip west and a holiday from the banking job he loathed. Within half an hour he was "further West than ever before" in his twenty-five years. He had been diagnosed a few days earlier with neurasthenia, a debilitating nerve disease, by the leading American nerve specialist of the period, his cousin S. Weir Mitchell. Although Mitchell prescribed a "rest cure" for women with the ailment, he recommended the "West cure" to men. As the western literary historian Jennifer Tuttle explains, this therapy required a male patient to recharge his vital energies by subscribing to "a western model of manliness." In the West he would regain his strength and vigor "through contact with 'uncivilized' men and participation in some form of outdoor sport," such as camping, fishing, or hunting. As the critic Barbara Will adds, at Mitchell's urging "a whole generation of nervous men accordingly journeyed westward to recuperate not only by working on ranches and hunting game in the Rockies, but also by writing about their experiences."

"I went West that July day to cure a headache I had waked and slept with since February," Wister allowed later. "I was very near despair—I hope what my cup still holds for me may not be in any part of that bitterness I knew between 1883 and 1885. . . . I do not think the mental and spiritual dregs I tasted then poisoned me, but they made a beginning."

On July 3, after traveling more than fifteen hundred miles, Wister was introduced to the comforts of the Cheyenne Club, the headquarters of the Wyoming Stock Growers Association and "the pearl of the prairies" by Dick Trimble, a Harvard graduate who had emigrated west to make his fortune in cattle. "No other cow-country capital had anything like it," according to historian Helena Huntington Smith. "It boasted of having the best steward and the best chef of any club in the United States, a wine cellar second to none . . . and servants imported from Ottawa." Wister was impressed by the immensity of the West—"it is a very much bigger place than the East"—and despite the sparse population of Wyoming (a total of about forty-five thousand in a territory of about a hundred thousand square miles) he was delighted to discover that, so far as he could tell, it was settled predominantly by easterners: "Every man, woman and cowboy I see comes from the East—and generally from New England, thank goodness—if that's the stock that is going to fill these big fields with people." With his assumption of patrician privilege and blind to the ethnic pluralism of the West, Wister had hardly yet left home.

Two days later, he arrived at Major Frank Wolcott's VR Ranch, some ninety-six square miles of land on Deer Creek, a tributary of the North Platte River, in Converse County. The model for the wise and genial Judge Henry in *The Virginian*, Wolcott was a former Civil War officer, justice of the peace, and U.S. marshal as well as a Wister family friend. He was also, according to various sources, "a fire-eater," a bully, "quite possibly a briber of juries," a "rabid Republican with a complete absence of tact," and a "hardboiled rascal who would cheat his men out of their wages." Still, Wister noted in his diary, "Major and Mrs. Wolcott are delightful hosts," and their house was "a sort of miracle for these parts—so clean—comfortable—pretty." Wister was infatuated with Wyoming from the first. Even the air, he thought, was "better than all other air. Each breath you take tells you no one else has ever used it before you." Two weeks after his arrival he added that

> the details of the life here are interesting. Wish I could find out all about it—and master it—theoretically. It's a life as strange as any the country has seen, and it will slowly make room for Cheyennes, Chicagos, and ultimately inland New Yorks—everything reduced to the same flat prairie-like level of utilitarian civilization. [The cattle barons] will give way to Tweeds and Jay Goulds—and the ticker will replace the rifle.

Within a century, he predicted, the West would be "the true America with thought, type, and life of its own kind." He wished he might "come back in two hundred years and see a townful of real Americans."

Nevertheless, he was initially ambivalent about the character of the common folks he met. On the one hand, he thought, "a finer looking lot of men than the cowboys & ranch foremen of the region I have seen nowhere." But on the other, he was informed by a longtime rancher in the region that "a worse lot cannot be imagined." Still, Wister concluded, "if they are savages they seem to have the Barbaric Virtues—courage—a man whose occupation means holding his life in his hand daily—indeed only by the slim tenure of a pony's legs—must be brave—a reckless generosity—& a certain kind of tenderness bred of a wild life." In the end, Wister decided to split the difference: "as specimens of the human race these lively nomads only strike the average in all the important things." Most of them, he thought, were too attracted to populism, the farmers' alliances, and free silver to be trusted.

He spent most of the next two months working on the ranch and roughing it on hunting and camping trips—or, as he put it, he "did a great deal of camping and a good deal of shooting big game and missing still more big game." He toured the cattle company founded in 1879 by his Harvard friends Hubert E. Teschemacher and Frederic O. de Billier—this in the days when, as one ranch owner put it, "we had only to brand our calves when dropped and ship our beeves when fat." With free grass available on public lands, no expenses except wages for a few low-paid cowhands, and no investment except for some cows and bulls, the ranchers during the cattle boom faced minimal business risk. But as John W. Davis avers in *Wyoming Range War*, "Without all that free rangeland, the operations of large ranchers could not continue." Wister met the army surgeon Amos Barber, a fellow Pennsylvanian and future Wyoming governor, on Wolcott's ranch, and in mid-July Wister and Wolcott made a 180-mile round-trip journey to Medicine Bow, nineteen hours each way by carriage. One night in Medicine Bow, Wister "slept from ten to twelve thirty on the counter of the store," much as the tenderfoot narrator sleeps on the counter of the local general store in the opening chapters of *The Virginian*. While helping out during the cattle roundup in early August, Wister overheard a woman ask Tom King, the foreman of the VR, what happens to cowboys "when you get old?" With "wide eyes of mild amazement," King answered, "Madam, we don't live long enough for that." Wister was so struck by the line that he not only jotted it in his journal but quoted a version of it three different times in his fiction over the years.

Never before had he kept a journal. But on his first expedition west he began to keep a full, faithful, realistic diary, with details about packhorses, camps in the mountains, camps on the sagebrush, nights in town, card games with cavalry officers, meals with cowpunchers, roundups, scenery, Yellowstone National Park, fishing for trout, and hunting for "antelope, white tail deer, black tail sheep, elk, bear, mountain sheep—and missing these same animals."

"I don't know why I wrote it all down so carefully," he noted later. "I had no purpose in doing so, or any suspicion that it was driving Wyoming into my blood and marrow, and fixing it there." He could not have known at the time, but after 1891, when he began to write about the West, Wister often milked his journal for story ideas. More than forty years later, he bluntly allowed that the summer of 1885 had been a turning point in his life. As he told his daughter Fanny, "I was different after Wyoming."

Wister had, in fact, been born to privilege in July 1860. A descendant of Pierce Butler of South Carolina, a signer of the U.S. Constitution, and the renowned Shakespearean actress Fanny Kemble, he was the only child of an aloof Philadelphia physician, Owen Jones Wister, and his imperious wife, Sarah Butler Wister. Educated in Europe and the exclusive St. Paul's School in Concord, New Hampshire, Wister was admitted to Harvard in 1878. Always clubbable, he was active there in the Porcellian and Hasty Pudding Clubs, and he socialized with the scions of the Holmes and Roosevelt families. A gifted musician, he aspired as a Harvard undergraduate to become a composer, and at the age of twenty-two he performed on the piano for Franz Liszt, who declared he had "*un talent prononcé.*" Wister also exhibited an early talent for authorship: he was a regular contributor to the *Harvard Crimson* and published both a poem in the *Atlantic Monthly* and a short novel, *The New Swiss Family Robinson: A Tale for Children of All Ages*, before graduating in June 1882. No doubt he initially aspired to be a realistic novelist. His first long fiction, "A Wise Man's Son," was never published, however, because it was "altogether too plain spoken" for American readers, author and literary critic W. D. Howells explained to Wister. "Were it a translation from the Russian, there would be no objection to such a book; coming from a young American, it is certain to shock the public; it is full of hard swearing, hard drinking, too much knowledge of good and evil, and a whole fig tree would not cover the Widow Taylor." Wister became a charter member of the Tavern Club in Boston in 1884, along with such professionals as Howells, Henry Lee Higginson, Frederick Prince, and Arthur Rotch. Meanwhile, at the insistence of his father, he earned his living neither as a composer nor as a writer but as a bank clerk. He reluctantly agreed to attend Harvard Law School, as he put it, "since American respectability accepted lawyers, no matter how bad, which I was likely to be, and rejected composers, even if they were good, which I might possibly be." Little wonder that he began to suffer from the neurasthenia that drove him to Wyoming in 1885.

Wister returned to the West during the summer of 1887 to escape the drudgery of his law school studies. On July 1 he embarked on the newly completed Canadian Pacific Railway for British Columbia and was joined en route by his friends Copley Amory (Harvard class of '88) and George Norman. In a letter to his socialite mother Sarah Butler Wister, he exulted in their rustic pleasures. "I keep thinking how you would hate nearly all" the trip were she with him, he teased. "The only way you could ever come West and enjoy yourself would be inside a large party of friends who would form a hollow square whenever a public place was to be entered."

He was still so unaware of distances in the West that he left his party at Victoria, British Columbia, early under the delusion that in two days he could visit his Harvard classmate Guy Waring, son of the famous civil engineer Colonel George Waring, at his ranch in the Okanogan Valley of Washington. He caught up with his traveling companions in Portland, Oregon, and joined them for "seven glorious days and nights in San Francisco" and "the High Jinks of the Bohemian Club among the great redwoods." At the age of twenty-eight, he later remembered, "I was a freakish bachelor" and "I could play all night and go on playing in the morning."

In late July Wister and his friends Amory and Norman arrived at Fort Washakie, a frontier post in western Wyoming 150 miles from any railroad. (Wister carried a letter from General Phil Sheridan "recommending me to all officers of the Army.") There they hired a full-blooded Shoshone guide (Tighee), a native New Englander to cook (George West), and a cantankerous packer (Jules Mason) to accompany them on a month-long hunting trip for bear and elk through the Wind River mountains. This took them ninety miles across the Continental Divide along the Sheridan Trail—the route blazed four years earlier by Sheridan and his hunting party—to the Gros Ventre wilderness and from there to Jackson's Hole, Wyoming. Wister was especially impressed by West, who was "about twenty-four and much too good looking," as he noted at the time. "He is much better looking than any of us" and "a real brick." Wister hired West so often in ensuing years that he eventually modeled his character Lin McLean on him. West was "my cook, packer, and horse-wrangler." In fact, Wister based both his tale "How Lin McLean Went East" and a part of his aborted novel "Chalkeye" on "a personal experience [West] told me" during their first trip together in 1887.

The six men spent the final week of August in Yellowstone National Park, where hunting was prohibited. "We were merely five white men and one Indian, on six horses, with eight packs, in single file, riding at a walk, perfectly harmless, and as new to the Park as were the tourists who leaped from the stage coaches to snapshot us," Wister remembered. He was occasionally mistaken for an Englishman during the trip because he dressed like a dandy. He traveled in "a loose comfortable flannel shirt," trousers, and a coat from London like the one worn by the narrator of *The Virginian*, whose English clothes earned him the title "the Prince of Wales." The men camped one night near the geysers—"Old Faithful, the Castle, the Giant, the Beehive

Owen Wister's hunting party in camp (1887). Wister at upper right. Owen Wister Papers, American Heritage Center, University of Wyoming.

& several more"—much to Wister's disgust. "I did not like them or their neighborhood. The air has drafts of stenches through it sometimes like sulphur, sometimes like a stale marsh. The ground is drilled with hissing puddles & sounds hollow as you walk, and all healthy plants & grass keep at a prudent distance"—details he worked into his story "Sun Road," also titled "Bad Medicine," thirty-seven years later. He was also vexed by tourists who, "with that fetid vulgarity that is innate in our American race," carved their initials into rocks and trees. "I hope they'll have to write their names in Hell with a red hot pen holder," as he put it. On another day, however, he was charmed by the Lower Yellowstone Falls, which he thought "the most beautiful thing I have ever seen." At the end of the week he caught a Northern Pacific train in Cinnabar, Montana, a few miles from the park gates, and spent the night in Billings—"a pretty good town" where "you can buy kid gloves & whiskey in several places" and "the electric light has come." He arrived back in Philadelphia on September 8. Six years later he declared that this journey "settled my destiny as a writer, though I did not know it then."

Unmentioned in all of his accounts of the trip is the dramatic change that had occurred in the Wyoming economy since his visit two years earlier. The beef bonanza was over, the consequence of drought, overgrazing, and the severe winter of 1886–87 (aka "the Big Freeze") when entire herds of cattle died. Frank Wolcott was bankrupted when the bubble burst and lost ownership of his ranch, although he remained as manager under the new owner, the Tolland Company of Scotland. Wister noted in his journal that "ranches, after the VR, have but few attractions for me." At the same time, the competition between the cattle barons and the small ranchers became increasingly cutthroat. The population of Wyoming tripled during the decade, from about twenty thousand in 1880 to sixty-two thousand in 1890, the year Wyoming was admitted to the Union, with burgeoning settlement (and thus fencing) of what had been open range. Moreover, cattle-rustling or the theft of unbranded mavericks from unfenced pasture flourished "during the era of bad feeling which came in after 1887, and for several years convictions were impossible to obtain," according to historian Smith.

In response, the Wyoming Stock Growers Association (WSGA) imposed rules on the industry that safeguarded the cattle barons' patrician privileges. As the cultural historian Christine Bold has explained, "the WSGA was a financial cartel that enforced its monopoly on grazing lands in particularly violent ways." Under the infamous maverick law—"one of the worst pieces of legislation ever inflicted on the West," according to Smith—unbranded calves belonged to the association, which distributed them exclusively to its members. The association also regulated the issuing of brands. No member of the association was permitted to employ a cowhand who owned a brand or a herd; should any member do so, he was blacklisted. This made it virtually impossible for a typical cowpuncher to own land and prosper as an independent rancher. Mere ownership of a small herd was considered evidence of cattle-rustling or the intent to rustle. As Wister observed in the manuscript fragment "Chalkeye," few cowboys "got any land claims, and stock, and such like." By 1890, the few dozen association members owned 85 to 90 per cent of the cattle and the WSGA "had increasingly assumed the aspect of a rich man's club."

On July 16, 1888, three weeks after graduating from law school, Wister left Philadelphia for his third trip to Wyoming. Joined by his friend Bob Simes, a fellow Harvard Law alumnus, he arrived at Fort Washakie where, as the year before, the officers were "most cordial." For a two-month hunt along the Wind and Snake Rivers, Wister again hired George West, as well as the mixed-blood Paul La Rose and Dick Washakie—the son of Chief Washakie and therefore "the Crown Prince of the Shoshones"—a former student at the Carlisle Indian Industrial School in Pennsylvania. The trip was largely uneventful, save only for an electrical storm the men experienced atop the Washakie Needles on August 30. As the men approached the summit, the temperature dropped, hail began to fall "at a rate to chip pieces off one's ear," and "the lightning was constant and getting nearer." Wister huddled beneath his horse and "every now and then a particularly ugly crash of thunder would happen. . . . And then a thing happened" in the ionized atmosphere

which must seem incredible to any but the man who has knowledge of it by theory or experience. I was wandering about with

George, noting the decrease of the storm, when something near my head set up a delicate hissing or spitting. I listened and found it was in my hat. . . . The hail came very fine and gently now, but it began stinging behind my ear worse than it had done at all. Getting tired of this, I turned my face to the wind that was left, and found the hail perfectly harmless, while the stinging behind grew a little sharper. My hat continued to hiss. Feeling very uncanny, I called out to George to know if anything was the matter with his head, explaining what was going around mine. He nodded uneasily, and drew away from me as if I were an explosive. I connected my hat with the stinging somehow, and pulled it off. The hissing was in the brim, and died out as I stared at the leather binding and the stitching. The pricking behind my ears stopped too. George, a little below me on the hill, complained with his hand up to his head that it was getting unbearable. "Take off your hat," I said. He did, but relief not coming at once. "Take off your spectacles," I added. These measures were successful, and we discussed what had ailed us. According to George, our hats, becoming damp, had been charged like Leyden jars and, growing overcharged, had unloaded into our heads.

Wister recounted these events twenty years later in his essay "An Electric Storm on the Washakie Needles" in *Science* and depicted them the same year in his story "Timberline."

Wister followed much the same pattern when he next returned to Wyoming in the fall of 1889. He left Philadelphia on October 9 and arrived in Laramie alone on the 11th for a hunt. The range war had by then begun to percolate, and during the last leg of the train trip, he rode in the smoking car with one of the men who had been indicted for lynching "Cattle Kate" Watson and James Averell in July for alleged cattle-rustling, the first skirmish in what became the Johnson County War that pitted the oligarchs of the Wyoming ranching industry against the homesteaders. Wister privately betrayed his class bias more than two years before the Johnson County War made national news. The vigilante "seemed a good solid citizen," Wister noted in his journal, "and I hope he'll get off." Sheriff Frank Hadsell assured him that it was only the *wayward* classes that complain." Hadsell failed to mention the four eyewitnesses either to the abduction or the lynching who disappeared or died mysteriously before the trial of those indicted.

On October 15, Wister again met George West at Fort Washakie—all the people there as usual "were very pleasant and cordial"—for a six-week hunt in the mountains. However, he found little to shoot during this trip except grouse. "I don't believe that if you dragged this whole country with a sieve net you would catch game enough to cover a piece of toast," he grumbled on October 29. He was resigned to disappointment by mid-November. "It will be ludicrous to have come 2000 and odd miles hunting, and got a few birds," he conceded, "but camping and mountains are 3/4 what I came for, and I shall not at all regret it." He left Rawlins, Wyoming, on November 25 and was back in Philadelphia by the end of the month, stopping in Omaha for the sixth time on his four trips west. (As the narrator remarks in *The Virginian*, "Our continent drained prismatically through Omaha once.")

Wister tentatively planned to camp in Wyoming for most of the summer of 1890. "That is what I have done for a number of years, as it agrees with my necessities for air and exercise & puts me in good condition for winter duties," he wrote to John Osborne Sargent in May. Instead, he was chained to his desk in Philadelphia all summer.

Since graduating from college, he had published a few vagrant poems and essays in such parlor magazines as *Lippincott's* and the *Atlantic Monthly*, but nothing to indicate he was considering a change of career. Before leaving Philadelphia on June 4, 1891, for his fifth trip to Wyoming, however, Wister started a story about the West. He had been inspired by the western fiction of Mary Hallock Foote who, he wrote, "clothed the civilian frontier with serious and tender art" in such novels as *The Led-Horse Claim* (1883), and by the western memoirs of Captain Charles King, who "brought spirited army scenes to our ken" in *Campaigning with Crook* (1890) and other works. He was also influenced by the journals of Lewis and Clark, the western histories of Washington Irving, and the school of western humorists— Petroleum V. Nasby, Artemus Ward, Bret Harte, Josh Billings, Bill Nye, and particularly Mark Twain, whose *Roughing It* (1872) he first read in prep school at St. Paul's. Years later, when he was invited to attend Twain's sixty-seventh birthday celebration, Wister wrote him that there was "no living American of which I'm quite so proud as I am of you. I promise not to say this when I see you."

Wister was especially indebted for literary inspiration to his Harvard chum Theodore Roosevelt and his "vivid, robust accounts" of strenuous life in Montana and the Dakotas in such books as *Hunting Trips of a Ranchman* (1885). Wister recounted years later how the "wonderful and then unknown life of the cattle country made a great impression" on TR, who in turn "made known to the rest of the country these things that he had seen upon the frontier" and "preserved for posterity one of the most vital and at the same time romantic episodes in the life of our nation." Long before Roosevelt recruited his Rough Riders from the West, he was a real rancher and "whatever work the men did he did too, roughing it with them; and the zest of his prose makes plain his complete participation and enjoyment of the life."

During the winter of 1890–91, Wister had drafted three chapters of a tale titled "Chalkeye," set in the Wind River valley, about two easterners on a western hunting expedition; and between early June and mid-September he hoped to gather enough material to finish it: "I am bound on this trip to lose nothing," he observed. "Former experience has taught that you can hardly make a journal too full. I hope

I shall be able to keep it up, & get down in notes, anyhow, all the things that are peculiar to this life and country." He wrote his mother from Wyoming on June 21 that he had been filling his journal with "all shreds of local color and all conversations and anecdotes decent or otherwise that strike me as native wild flowers. After a while I shall write a great fat book about the whole thing." For the first time, too, he carried a camera to document scenes and events. Unfortunately, he never completed "Chalkeye," though he kept the manuscript in a desk drawer to the end of his life. Wallace Stegner speculates that Wister "realized he had made a wrong beginning in making Chalkeye a small landholder, a sort of nester," the type targeted by the cattle barons in the Johnson County War. Wister also contemplated several other story projects: "Raymond and His Three Lives," a collection of non-western stories; a novel called "The Tenderfoot"; and a series of sketches titled "The Adventures of a Bad Shot." He thought the latter title so appealing "a magazine might take it." He even conceived an opening sentence for the series: "No man tells the truth about himself and his gun."

As it happened, his 1891 trip was both his longest and most eventful excursion west to date, and he unearthed an abundance of material. In Riverside, Wyoming, on June 17 he jotted in his journal a pair of anecdotes that he later adapted to his fiction. The first was a tale about a rider who bragged to a stable of cowboys that he could break any wild horse by riding him at full speed before suddenly throwing him to the ground.

So he got on one, and they watched him fly over the grass for 200 yards or so. Then he leaned, seized the hackamore [bridle] on the right side of the pony's mouth, and jerked it hard down, swinging the pony to the right who instantly rolled over and up with the man still sitting in the saddle. But as they looked, he sat strangely, & tilted backwards, crooked, with his head on the horse's rump, his spur caught in the single cinch of the California saddle, & so holding him on. They took him into the cabin where he died, in 12 hours, never speaking. His whole insides seemed to have been crushed to pieces, for when they came to put him in a coffin 36 hours later, he was so swollen that he had to be jammed in and packed down.

Five years later, Wister worked the incident into his story "Separ's Vigilante." He also heard about a cowhand who "wanted a woman" but "couldn't get none in this country as was willin'," so the cowboy traveled to England and "fetched one along back." Not only had she "been raised under a wharf there in Liverpool," and so had no home to which she might return, but the cowboy told her "he had a large interest in the Powder River Cattle Company. Well she came, & learned he had an interest. Had a cookin' interest in the roundup sometimes. But she couldn't find her way out of the country. Had to stay." Here Wister found the germ of his first published western story, "Hank's Woman," a "sad and terrible drama" about a distraught wife's murder of her cowboy husband and her own accidental death.

On June 18, while an accidental guest at D. R. Tisdale's ranch on Willow Creek in far southern Johnson County, Wister witnessed a grisly incident that became the basis for one of his most famous short stories. He watched helplessly as the infuriated Tisdale gouged out the eye of an unruly horse.

Tisdale dismounted and kicked his poor quiet beast, who stood quite patient. He kicked his ribs, its legs, its jaw, and I saw that red foam was running from the bit. I saw Tisdale was insane with rage. "I'll have to ask you to swap horses for a time," he said to me. "This———brute's given out on me. They'd never got away if he hadn't given out. Just refused to go, for no reason whatever. No call to give out." Then he resumed his kicking the animal and jerking its head. I jumped off as soon as he said "swap," very anxious he should do so and leave his wretched horse in peace. Beyond urging him to take my horse at once and go, I said nothing. I felt like remonstrating, but I failed to do so. Tisdale seemed to forget about his intention of swapping. He continued to swear at his horse and kick it, and then I noticed him make several vicious grabs at its eye. Then he got into the saddle again, and the brute walked slowly forward with him some twenty yards in the direction of the vanished sorrel, leaving me dismounted and watching Tisdale's heels and fists beat the horse without pause. It stood still, too weak to move, and I saw Tisdale lean forward with his arm down on its forehead. He had told me that he would kill it if he had a gun, but he hadn't.

I watched him, dazed with disgust and horror. Suddenly the horse sank, pinning him to the ground. He could not release himself, and I ran across to him and found only his leg caught. So I lifted the horse and he got his leg out. I asked him if he was hurt. He said "No" and got up, adding "I've got one eye out all right." The horse turned where he lay, and I caught a sight of his face where there was no longer any left eye but only a sinkhole of blood. I was utterly stunned and sickened at this atrocious cruelty, and walked back to my own horse and sat down, not knowing very well what I was doing.

"Nothing disgraceful an acquaintance of mine has ever done has nauseated my soul like this," Wister confided to his journal two days later. But his description of the abuse—the staccato dialogue, the detail ("red foam running from the bit," "the sinkhole of blood"), and his own timid response ("I remain the moral craven who did not lift a finger or speak a word," he added on June 20)—hints at the skills he might have developed as a writer of realistic fiction. While on a hunting trip in mid-July, Wister witnessed another act of cruelty. One of the pack horses "marched into the Yellowstone [R]iver" and "showed no signs of returning" until one of the men "fired his six shooter twice," only to discover that he had accidentally "shot Baldy in the right hind leg," though the animal was not seriously injured. The incidents were reminiscent, Wister thought, of the biblical account of Balaam and his ass, and Wister eventually worked both of them into his story "Balaam and Pedro."

Put another way, Wister's experiences in Wyoming in 1891 reinforced his resolve to write about the West, to record rustic life on the frontier before it disappeared forever.

> I begin to conclude from 5 seasons of observation that life in this negligent irresponsible wilderness tends to turn people shiftless, incompetent, and cruel. I noticed in Wolcott in 1885, and I notice today a sloth in doing anything and everything that is born of the deceitful ease with which make-shifts answer here. Did I believe in the efficacy of prayer I should petition to be the hand that once for all chronicled and laid bare the virtues and the vices of this extraordinary phase of American social progress. Nobody has done it. Nobody has touched anywhere near it. A few have described external sights and incidents but the grand total thing—its rise, its hysterical unreal prosperity & its disenchanting downfall. All this & its influence on the various sorts of human character that has been subjected to it has not been hinted at by a single writer that I, at least, have heard of. The fact is, it is quite worthy of Tolstoi, or George Eliot, or Dickens.

The remainder of his 1891 trip was hardly less memorable. He spent a few days in Buffalo, Wyoming, ("a shade better in its appearance than most of these towns"); a few in Johnson County, Wyoming, near Fort McKinney, the epicenter of the looming cattle war; a few days more with his friends at Fort Washakie, and more than a month in Yellowstone National Park. He had again hired Dick Washakie as a guide, though to his dismay "the Crown Prince of the Shoshones" quit before they reached the park. Wister did not understand the reason until years afterward—Washakie's trepidation about the geysers. Ironically, Wister wrote his mother on August 11 that the sulfur springs there were "admirably interesting" but "they smell bad—very bad—and I mostly pass them by." He met Captain Frank Edwards, who would become one of his best friends and most valuable military sources, in the park on September 4. Edwards was "more patient and good natured over my endless questioning than it seemed possible for a man to be," Wister recalled, and later he reiterated that he was indebted to Edwards for "countless events and details of that old frontier military life, and endless hospitality at the old frontier posts where I was his guest." In 1903, Wister successfully lobbied President Theodore Roosevelt to appoint Edwards, who by then suffered from ill health, to be the military attaché in Rome in lieu of a government pension.

Back in Philadelphia in the fall, Wister began to earn his subsequent reputation as an expert on all things western. Years later he recorded an apocryphal account of his decision that completely ignores his earlier, unfinished "Chalkeye." One evening at the Philadelphia Club, "fresh from Wyoming and its wild glories" and while dining with Walter Furness, son of the Shakespearean scholar Horace Howard Furness, Wister wondered why no writer of fiction was preserving "that epic which was being lived at a gallop" in the West before it disappeared entirely. He declared that he would chronicle it, if no one else would, and retired to the library where, "by midnight or so, a good slice of 'Hank's Woman' was down in the rough."

Whether or not Wister composed "Hank's Woman" exactly as he claimed, he had certainly finished a draft of the story by November 1891. Formally, he modeled the "traveler's tale" upon Prosper Mérimée's "Carmen," a copy of which he had carried to Wyoming the summer before. As in the anecdote he heard in Riverside in June, the eponymous cowpuncher marries a foreign woman, in this case a German maid named Willomene who is abandoned by her employer during a visit to Yellowstone National Park. The marriage is an unhappy one, however, and Willomene kills Hank during a quarrel and plunges to her own death when she slips while dumping his body into a ravine. Wister revised the manuscript heavily at the urging of his friend Harry Mercer, a Harvard alumnus (class of '79) and one of the managers of the Museum of Science and Art at the University of Pennsylvania. "I can't remember a single story," Wister later allowed, "that has not gained by my adopting the criticism" of readers prior to publication. Lin McLean, who relates the story-within-a-story to the unnamed tenderfoot narrator who appears in many of Wister's western tales, alludes in passing to a cattle rustler named Ed Rogers who will "be dealt with one of these days. He's a-growin' bold, the way he takes calves." Wister again registers the simmering issues brought to a boil in the Johnson County War the next spring.

In January 1892, he finished the manuscript of a second western story, "How Lin McLean Went East," told by an omniscient narrator and based on the anecdote George West told him in 1887 about an ill-considered trip he had made to the "States" to visit his family. In Wister's aborted novel, the character Chalkeye had returned east to see his sisters, who had married "chaps I don't value. . . . They didn't care and I didn't care. I couldn't stand life there any more with no freedom to it." But Wister most fully explored the humorous situation in the story featuring the mischievous Lin McLean. After squandering his seven hundred dollars in spring pay at cards, mostly at the Drybone hog-ranch (that is, the brothel across a ravine from Fort Fetterman), McLean lights out for his old stomping grounds around Boston and New York. However, as in the parable of the prodigal son, his brother spurns him and, in a comic twist, McLean returns west to the far country harboring "a deep hatred of the crowded, scrambling East." "I know where my home is," he realizes, "and I wouldn't live nowheres else." (Wister thought about using the biblical verse Luke 15:20

as an epigraph to the story: "And he arose, and came to his father. But when he was yet a great way off, his father saw him, and had compassion, and ran, and fell on his neck, and kissed him.")

Wister distinguished between "Hank's Woman" and "How Lin McLean Went East" in a letter to Sarah Wister by comparing them to differing musical styles. "Hank's Woman," he wrote, "makes its effect by means of loud orchestration, cymbals, kettle drum, etc." On the other hand, "How Lin McLean Went East" was "andante sostenuto, generally p[iano] never ff [fortissimo], and without a single brass instrument." He assured his mother, with her delicate sensibilities, that the "second story is harmless & you can read it." Still, he was initially reticent to submit either of them to an editor, given the stigma often attached to western writing. "I didn't send them anywhere," he admitted, but "read them to one or two ranch friends. They stayed in my lawyer's desk, although the ranch friends were good enough to say that they were like the thing." Then Weir Mitchell, a part-time novelist as well as a physician, suggested that he send both of them to the publisher Harper & Brothers. Mitchell also gave him a letter of introduction to Henry Mills Alden, the editor of *Harper's New Monthly Magazine*. In his cover letter to Alden, Wister explained that the western experiences

I am trying to write about [don't] seem to me to have been treated in fiction so far—seriously at least. The cattle era in Wyoming is nearly over, and in the main unchronicled, though its brief existence created a life *permeated with eccentricity, brutality, and pathos* not only of the most vivid local color, but of singular moral interest. Its influence upon the characters of all grades of men—from Harvard graduates to the vagrants from the slums[—]has been potent and very special. I should say the salient thing it did was to produce in educated and uneducated alike more moral volatility than was ever set loose before.

Alden accepted both stories and paid Wister four hundred dollars for them. "Hank's Woman" appeared in *Harper's Weekly* in August 1892 and "How Lin McLean Went East" in *Harper's Monthly* for December 1892. Neither story attracted much attention except among Wister's western friends and acquaintances. But as a result of their publication, Wister remembered, when he next traveled west "every second or third person that I met promptly said, 'I'll tell you a thing you ought to write up.' It became a familiar spectacle—me, passive in the clutches of a determined narrator; so that my companions used to poke each other's ribs, and say 'Look at Wister. So-and-so has got him now!' And I became a brilliant listener:—yet more often than not, it wasn't what they told me" but "something else that drifted accidentally into sight or hearing, and which seemed worthless to them, but flashed on me as the true nugget in the tailings."

Meanwhile, Wister's ardor for Wyoming had begun to wane as a result of the violence there. As Smith recounts in *The War on Powder River*, in the wake of the crash in beef prices in the late 1880s, the small ranchers, mostly sheepmen and grangers, believed the cattle barons and their "regulators" were trying to bankrupt them by restricting their right to graze their herds on public land. Yet from the perspective of the cattle barons, specifically the members of the Wyoming Stock Growers Association, the small ranchers and their allies were little better than squatters and cattle rustlers. In early April 1892, an assassination squad of twenty-five ranchers including Wolcott, D. R. Tisdale, Hubert E. Teschemacher, W. C. Irvine (another Pennsylvanian by birth), the Philadelphia physician Charles B. Penrose, and other wealthy men whom Wister knew, along with twenty-one gunmen from Texas they had hired, planned to raid the homes of some seventy "cattle thieves" and kill them. According to Smith, "The ringleaders without exception belonged to the little coterie of early comers who had been running the affairs of Wyoming since the dawn of the beef bonanza in 1879." Max Westbrook bluntly states that the Johnson County War "was an illegal attack on homesteaders. The attack was financed and led by cattle barons who wanted to keep the open range, government-owned land, as their private property."

Wolcott in particular was "handicapped by the shortcomings of a military martinet" and despite his war experiences was "temperamentally unfit to lead men," Smith declares. The acting governor, Amos Barber, according to Smith a "weak-kneed ass" and lackey of the Stock Growers Association, was "plainly determined to avoid interfering with his friends' program of liquidation." He contacted President Benjamin Harrison for help "in suppressing the insurrection" on April 12 because the cattlemen and their Texas gunmen, after killing several "rustlers," were threatened with their own liquidation by another posse of two hundred men led by the sheriff of Johnson County. The "Invaders," as they were soon termed in the national press, were rescued by soldiers from Fort McKinney and arrested, but no charges against them were ever filed. They posed for a group photograph during their minimum-security incarceration at Fort D. A. Russell near Cheyenne the next month, and a reproduction of the photo accompanied an article about the War in *Frank Leslie's Illustrated Newspaper* for June 2, 1892. Wister kept a copy in his scrapbook. "Of all the various articles coming out of Cheyenne and pushing the line of the big cattlemen," according to John W. Davis, this one in *Leslie's Weekly* "may have been the most extreme" and was, at the least, "profoundly misleading" about events in Wyoming.

Predictably, Wister sided with his friends in their class war. He closely followed news of the conflict in papers across the country—he subscribed to the Buffalo (Wyoming) *Bulletin*, among others—and filled a scrapbook with

Johnson County War "Invaders." American Heritage Center, University of Wyoming, Photofile: Wyo – Johnson County War.

clippings. He wrote an article for the *Philadelphia Times* in late April—his first publication about the West—in which he favorably compared the "war of extermination" conducted by the Montana ranchmen with the less successful and more public war run by "these gentlemen in Johnson County. . . . In Montana it happened like a visit from the Destroying Angel. The ringleaders among the cattle thieves suddenly died, as it were, in one night." In both cases, however, the "extermination of thieves was most wholesome."

He may have approved such wars, but he declined to be exposed to them personally. He had planned a three-month hunting trip to Wyoming that summer, hired West to guide him, and even shipped his saddle ahead. But he was forewarned by a Cheyenne Club friend, Richard Repath, that his safety could not be guaranteed because his allegiances in the range war were too well known: "If any of the beggars were to run across you they would consider it a fitting climax to their nefarious deeds to put a shot or two through you." In the end, Wister compromised: he made a hurried, nine-day trip to Wyoming—from July 6 to 15—to retrieve his saddle and to pay West what he had promised. "The thought of this long hot journey for nothing in a way amuses me," he wrote in his journal the day of his departure.

> Making the decision was not amusing, but once made, there is something modern and globetrotting in traveling 2500 miles to say you're sorry you can't come. What is going to happen at the other end, I give up. . . . The only thing I don't like is that [some people may] think that the reason for my giving this summer up is personal fear for my carcass. Well, I can stand that probably.

He had hardly arrived in Cinnabar, Wyoming, on July 11 when, in the evening of the same day, he caught a train headed back home. But while there he paid West three hundred dollars for three months' work—the equivalent of several thousand dollars today, apparently too much money for Wister to entrust to the mail. Coincidentally, it was the same amount he earned from his next two stories combined, the first ones to feature the Virginian.

In "Balaam and Pedro," based on the eye-gouging incident Wister witnessed at Tisdale's ranch in June 1891 and written a year later, the Virginian is a comparatively minor figure, unworthy even of a proper name. In his first appearance, he is simply a "tall man" wearing "battered overalls." In a nod to *Uncle Tom's Cabin*, Wister described the villain Balaam as though he were a latter-day Simon Legree: "squat and strong, with little fat hands and a bullet head." Like Legree, Balaam is a native New Englander, though unlike Legree he abuses horses rather than slaves. He buys a pony named Pedro from a "lost dog" cowhand named Shorty for "forty dollars, a striped Mexican blanket, and a pair of spurs." While Balaam is returning a pair of borrowed horses to Judge Henny at Sunk Creek, escorted by the Virginian, who in this story is Henny's hired man, the horses stampede and Balaam exhausts Pedro trying to catch them.

He beats Pedro until he finally says to the Virginian that he will "have to take your horse; mine's played out on me" and the Virginian replies, "You ain' goin' to touch my hawse." The story continues:

[T]he words seemed not entirely to reach Balaam's understanding, so dulled by rage were his senses. He made no answer, but mounted Pedro, and the failing pony walked mechanically forward, while the Virginian, puzzled, stood looking after him. Balaam seemed without purpose of going anywhere, and stopped in a moment. The cow-puncher was about to advise him to get off, when he saw him lean over Pedro's neck and reach a hand down between his ears. The ranchman's arm and shoulder worked fiercely and twisted, when suddenly Pedro sank motionless, and his head rolled flat on the earth. Balaam, flung sharply on the ground, was jammed beneath him, and the cow-puncher ran, and taking the saddle-horn, shifted the horse's dead weight a little from the prisoner's body.

"Are you hurt?" he said, as Balaam raised himself and stood up slowly, looking sullenly at the fallen Pedro.

"No. But I got an eye out on him."

The cowboy heard these words without at first realizing their import; but the horse lifted his head and turned it piteously round, and he saw the ruined eye that Balaam's finger's had blinded.

Then Balaam was rolled to the ground again by the towering Virginian, in whose brawn and sinew the might of justice was at work; and, half stunned, the ranchman felt for his pistol, keeping one arm over his face till the weapon came out, and, together with his hand, was instantly stamped into the dust.

"Don't try that," said the Virginian, and lifted him, not able to struggle. He slung him so that he lay as though his skull were cracked, his crushed hand bleeding where it hung fallen across Pedro's saddle.

For several reasons this version is less impressive than Wister's original journal account. The gory details have been omitted, the realism muted, and the focus has shifted from the rancher's cruelty to the Virginian's heroic response. The craven Wister had merely observed and reported the abuse in his journal, but he reimagines the scene in the story so that his heroic alter ego exacts revenge. Or as biographer Darwin Payne explains, in this version "The Virginian acted as Wister wished he had been able to act."

By the end of the story, Balaam shoots Pedro inadvertently, much as the hunter Wister mentions in his 1891 journal accidentally shoots a pack horse. While still tracking the strays, the Virginian rides ahead into the mountain woods, and Balaam in the rear watches Pedro plunge into a river,

> evidently intending to cross. Fearing he would escape to the opposite meadow and add to their difficulties, Balaam, with the idea of turning him round, drew his six-shooter and fired in front of the horse. . . . His bruised hand had stiffened, marring his aim, and he saw Pedro fall over in the water, then rise and struggle up the bank on the further shore, where he now hurried also, to find he had broken the pony's leg.

Whereas the real pack horse had been only injured slightly, Balaam kills Pedro to spare him further misery and, despite his promise to wait for the Virginian and the runaway horses, he hurries ahead to Judge Henny's ranch out of fear of marauding Indians.

The final page of the original version of "Balaam and Pedro" is significant if only because the Virginian does not reappear. In fact, he apparently has been ambushed and killed. Balaam might return to his own ranch but, as the narrator notes, only at great cost to his reputation. If he returned "prematurely and without Pedro," his men would be curious, whereas a visit to the judge "might possibly conceal the most humiliating part of the story."

> Balaam reached the Judge's ranch late in the next afternoon, and after telling how he came to arrive alone, he went to bed with stiff joints and a blinding pain in his head.

A search party immediately started out. The Virginian was a man much valued by the Judge, much loved by his fellow-cowboys, and the search party hunted for him with a will in the valley where he had disappeared into the woods; but they hunted vainly. His last word to Balaam, that he might not "get back right away," haunted the ranchman during the three days he lay sick. Balaam was not always incapable of feeling, and now he could think of his tall travelling companion without hatred, and with a man's respect for a better man than himself. He returned to his ranch while the search party was still away in the Bow-Leg Mountains.

The tale concludes the following November when Balaam breaks the news to Shorty that Pedro is dead, killed by Indians. They also "got after me and that Virginia man," he says. "But they didn't get *me*." Balaam wags his head "to imply that this escape was due to his own superior intelligence." That is, the original version of "Balaam and Pedro" ends not with a cliffhanger, but with the Virginian buzzard food after appearing in the story as a nameless character. As Wister explained later, "'Balaam and Pedro' was not a story about *him*, but about the *horse*." The Virginian "was merely auxiliary." Until Henry Esling, a clerk in Wister's Philadelphia law office, read the story in manuscript and expressed his dismay at the hero's apparent death, the author "never contemplated bringing the Virginian out of that wood." Still, in "Balaam and Pedro" Wister found his métier: "I know that I have never done anything so good, or that contains so big a swallow of Wyoming."

Wister submitted the manuscript of "Balaam and Pedro" to Horace Scudder, editor of the *Atlantic Monthly*, who rejected it. He then sent it to W. D. Howells, who accepted it in June 1892 during his short-lived editorship of *Cosmopolitan*, but who soon left the magazine with the story unpublished. In December, several months after Howells resigned, Wister contacted John Brisbane Walker, the owner of the magazine, and "getting no answer" he requested "the

MS to be sent me, & it was, with a note that 'hoped I had not suffered inconvenience'!" Frustrated, he pigeon-holed the manuscript for a year.

Soon after writing "Balaam and Pedro," Wister made a few notes for stories he never wrote entitled "Lin McLean Becomes a Rustler," "Grand Opera in Drybone," and "How Lin McLean Went West." He also planned a backstory about the pitiful Shorty entitled "For Lack of Evidence" (working title "Left Afoot"). He failed to finish it, though a fragment survives among his working notebooks:

> Shorty, emigrant to Wyoming, and originally native of the great Eastern gutter, did not know his name, nor was there anyone to tell it to him. This deficiency left him undisturbed; for the grocery-man, whose errands & petty sales had been his education since the time when his memory began, had not taught him pride of prejudice or anything moral and intellectual. He did teach him to read & write & cipher a little, because thus was the grocery-boy rendered competent to sack five pounds of sugar and enter it in the ledger while his patron was helping arrange ward politics in a place round the corner. It never occurred to Shorty to criticize his anonymous begetters for assigning him to the Forlorn Hope because he was without imagination, amiable, and perfectly well all the time. By & by he came to be seventeen years old, and after acquiring the vices, fell in love with a girl who told him nothing further about herself than that she would marry him the day he should amass twelve hundred dollars. I do not know why she fixed that sum. A few months after this, the grocery-man made some investigations, & Shorty listened to the results.
>
> "You are a thief," commented the patron; "and a fool thief at that." Then he indulged in some laughter at tow-headed Shorty, who stood before him. "Did you expect you could work the baby-trick on me? Now, I'll tell you one thing. It aint any use to steal if you haven't the head for it." There was some more silence. "Do you know that I could put you in jail, my friend? But I wont. I'll give you another chance to do something for yourself— only, you

quit my shop this afternoon, & if I ever see you round here again I *will* put you in jail."

The grocery-man was aware of his own goodness throughout the transaction, & as a climax he presented Shorty with fifty dollars, & Shorty wept.

Before departing, he kissed the girl good bye, & at her suggestion deposited twenty-five dollars with her. He kissed another friend also—the grocery cat! She had been a better companion for him than the girl, and had she known that this embrace signified farewell would have been truly grieved. In her youth Shorty had removed her from the street and with his patron's permission brought her to a home & opulence, & she liked him. From what source his heart had learned this pity it is difficult to ascertain.

Wister referred to this backstory a decade later in chapter 31 of *The Virginian*.

The Johnson County War required Wister to rearrange but not cancel his plans for a western hunting trip in 1892. He left Philadelphia on October 1 and paused in Wyoming long enough to dine at the Cheyenne Club with Amos Barber on October 4. They gossiped about their mutual friend Frank Wolcott, "utterly bankrupt" and living alone "at his forlorn decaying ranch." His wife had left him two years earlier. Wister pitied him. "Barber seemed to think he [Wolcott] realized he had made a failure of his life, then said that a bullet from a rustler would probably be a welcome solution to Wolcott. This too is melancholy." After the violence of the spring, Wister averred, "there is tragedy in the air of Wyoming, tragedy over these lonely sagebrush plains."

He left Cheyenne for Spokane, thence to Coulee City, Washington, at the end of a trunk line of the Northern Pacific. The town was so poor, Wister joked, that the only prostitute—"a forlorn old wreck, so unsightly that even her monopoly brings her no profit"—had left for greener pastures. "I do not think the world has seen any greater degradation of shoddy ugliness than these Western towns," he added, "where a shiftless helter-skelter enterprise has out-run all solid prosperity." Then he traveled by stagecoach across the Grand Coulee to Bridgeport, Washington, on the Columbia—"a restless rapid river with rapid current, flowing among dismal hills." On October 11, he crossed the river "on a raft geared to a wire by a trolley, and so steered as to be propelled by the current. The current was fierce, and the river wide," and the wire he thought "rather unsafe." (Or as a character puts it in Wister's story "Where It Was," "I'd crossed the stinkin', vicious Columbia on a chain ferry.")

Two days later, after spending a night in Ruby, Washington, he finally reached his destination—Guy Waring's log cabin in the Methow valley, near Winthrop, Washington, ninety miles from any railroad. Waring had recently moved to the fork of the Chewack and Methow Rivers and, instead of ranching, opened a general store where he sold groceries, dry goods, hardware, candy, and ammunition. He had been ostracized by polite social circles in the East because, over the objections of his parents, he had married the sister of his stepmother, a woman eleven years his senior. For a month, from mid-October to mid-November, Wister hunted mountain goats and antelope in the isolated valley. He recalled later that "in those rocky and almost perpendicular circumstances, to carry a Kodak and a Winchester 45–90 (the latest and best model in 1892) was not entirely simple." One day he and his guide stumbled across the mountain cabin of an old fiddler whom they plied with

plenty of whiskey, and he played to us till late, all sorts of old fashioned airs and dances. He apologized for a sluriness in his tone, as the airs of his bars [presumably, the hairs of his bow] were much gone. We promised to bring him some if we passed soon again, and he spoke of the tail of a white horse as being superior. He had fiddled his way across the continent and taken his life time to do so, had seen the days of Indians, buffalo and the days in California, when for a night's fiddling in a mining camp his fee was $100, and he always got it. He was perfectly blithe hearted and penniless, though by his stories, he must have handled millions.

Wister celebrated Thanksgiving with Waring's family before returning to Philadelphia in early December. He was forced to travel through snow for three days in a buckboard and a freight wagon to catch the train at Coulee City, Washington. As G. Edward White has observed, after 1892 Wister "was not again to find in the West the frolicsome adventure he had found" during his earlier trips there.

He left Philadelphia again in mid-February 1893 for a month at the Seven Springs Ranch forty miles from Brownwood, Texas, owned by his Philadelphia friend Fitzhugh Savage. He was first exposed to Jim Crow laws during this trip through the segregated South. "The railroads present a new feature," he observed. "Each car is marked either 'For Whites' or 'For Negroes.'" Far from objecting, however, he tolerated and even approved of legal segregation and the "separate but equal" doctrine of racial separation that would be sanctioned by the *Plessy v. Ferguson* decision of the U.S. Supreme Court three years later. "The cars have special compartments for colored people, equally clean but separate," Wister noted. Yet the practice seemed to him nothing more serious than a benign regional custom: "Common sense dictated such an arrangement in certain parts of our country." Or as Wister's narrator observes in the story "Skip to My Loo" (1928), "some of my Massachusetts relations were trying to have [Jim Crow railcars] abolished by law. Directly I saw them, I saw the sense in them."

During his month at the ranch, strangely enough, Wister learned to play polo. Savage raised polo ponies for sale in the East, and the sport—not hunting or fishing—was one of the few forms of recreation available to Wister in west Texas during a drought. He also reunited with Frank and

Dick Conover, his classmates at St. Paul's School, who lived on a nearby ranch, and he recorded in his journal the lyrics of "a unique song" popular among the local cowboys entitled "Get Along Little Dogies"—its earliest known transcription anywhere. In late March, en route east, he paused in Austin and San Antonio, where he stayed at the historic Menger Hotel, toured the Alamo ("Its ornamented façade with shapely curved roof is not to be forgotten"), and attended a cockfight. He also stopped in New Orleans, where by chance he crossed paths with George Waring, Guy's father, and supped with him at Antoine's, the famous creole restaurant in the French Quarter where, he wrote, "one would easily suppose oneself at Tours or Dijon." Over dinner, the elder Waring disparaged his son's wife, the former Helen Clarke Green. "Waring spoke only once" of Helen "and then only in passing," Wister noted, "but he made it evident what opinion he holds of her. I expressed none, and though he talked quite freely, I said only good things about her and the children. And about them I had plenty to say and plenty as to her kindness to me. If she did a wicked thing" in marrying Guy, "she has surely reaped the consequences. I know of no woman belonging to society that has encountered the horrors of hardships which she has gone through."

Wister had already started to write a story entitled "Em'ly"—perhaps a sardonic reference to the eccentric poet Emily Dickinson, whose first book of poetry had been published posthumously in November 1890—based on an anecdote he heard at the Seven Springs ranch. The tale of an addled, "manly-lookin'" hen who tries to hatch chicks from potatoes, onions, and balls of soap and to raise a litter of puppies, "Em'ly" is a type of anti-feminist parable satirizing women's independence and "unnatural motherhood." The Virginian jokes that she "ought to wear knickerbockers," so confused was she about her gender. Em'ly "was a real hen," Wister wrote later. "She did everything I have told about her, and she actually lived in Texas where I did not meet her because she was dead already. It was her sorrowing owner who told me her tragic story. All that I did was to mix her up with the Virginian," in whose character he had begun to discover latent possibilities. In "Em'ly," he introduces a chorus of cowboys who "bore names of various denominations" such as Honey Wiggin, Nebrasky, and Dollar Bill; and he narrates the story from the point of view of his unnamed eastern tenderfoot, who according to critic Sanford Marovitz is "a somewhat effeminate fop." To solve the temporal problem posed by the Virginian's death towards the close of "Balaam and Pedro," Wister simply set "Em'ly" before the events that transpire in that story.

In neither of the first two tales in which the Virginian figures is he a paladin of justice in chaps and spurs on the side of the cattlemen. In "Em'ly," however, Wister hints at the underlying conflict between Wyoming cattle barons and homesteaders. He had not alluded in the least to the Johnson County War in "Balaam and Pedro." On the contrary, the villainous Balaam in that story is a cattle boss, one of the privileged ranchers whose cause Wister later championed. But in the original version of "Em'ly," written a year after "Balaam and Pedro," the Virginian remarks wistfully that, no longer an open range, "the land's bein' took up all over now [by homesteaders], and I expect they'll be runnin' their wire fences acrossed everywhere. I'm hopin' they ain't goin' to spoil a cow-puncher's business; but us or wire fences has sure got to go." Whereas the large cattle outfits turned their herds onto the open range until round-up, the small ranchers and farmers fenced their land with barbed wire to protect their cattle from poachers. Wister deleted the Virginian's comment from the version of the story incorporated into *The Virginian* several years later, obscuring his criticism of the homesteaders. Though his scorn for barbed wire may seem innocuous today, it was at the time a coded condemnation of the farmers who were occupying pastures formerly available free of charge to the cattle companies, under federal laws allowing unrestricted use of public lands.

Wister revised the original printed version of "Em'ly" prior to its reappearance in *The Virginian* in another telling way. Judge Henny, the Virginian's employer and the narrator's host, belongs to the privileged class. In the mid-1880s, when the story is set, Wyoming ranchers were claiming, if not actually realizing, a profit on their herds of upwards of 25 percent, and the judge is no exception. He is also a Babbitt-like civic booster. Unlike the more prescient Virginian, who foresees the danger of the wire fence, the judge in the original version of the story "was an optimist concerning cattle ranches. He saw an endless vista of range pasture never to be exhausted, and a steady twenty per cent upon his venture." In revising "Em'ly" for inclusion in his novel a decade later, however, Wister omitted the judge's expression of faith in the future of cattle ranching. Such optimism by then had proven to be extravagant and vain.

In June 1893, Wister submitted the manuscripts of both "Balaam and Pedro" and "Em'ly" to Harper's editor Henry Alden, who initially balked at the bloodiness of the former tale. "If 'Balaam & Pedro' strikes you as incredible," Wister assured the editor, he knew even "more heart rending things than that, not that in writing the story my problem was not to paint a true picture that should remain within the domain of Art." Alden eventually accepted both stories and paid the author three hundred dollars for them. "Em'ly" was subsequently published in *Harper's Monthly* for November 1893 and "Balaam and Pedro" two months later. That is, Alden printed the two stories not in the order in which they were written but in the temporal sequence in which they are set. The *New York Tribune* praised "Em'ly" and its author when it appeared: "Owen Wister's is a new name in current literature, but it is one with which one would fain become better acquainted. His little Western sketch, 'Em'ly' . . . is a winsome bit of work, full of humor and even softened by pathos, though its heroine is only a woolly-brained and inconsequent hen."

In spring 1893, Wister also planned a pair of Texas stories, one for publication at Christmas 1894 titled "The Partners," the other a comic tale titled "The Proximate Cause," ridiculing the intellect of the denizens of the Lone Star state. Its opening paragraph survives in his notebook:

> Brady City is in Texas, fifty miles from Brownwood where the railroads are, and its inhabitants are not deliberately metaphysical by habit or by nature. They have cattle and sheep to sell that are often their own property, and they play cards; also, when it comes to judging whiskey, they are easily pleased. One noon, however, when the court adjourned in the middle of the case of Wellman vs. Bisbee, there were metaphysics going hard in each of the three saloons. All Brady was riveted upon the question whether or not Bisbee was legally bound to pay for Dr. Wellman's cork leg. The customary mental attitude of the town was shaken from its uninterested bovine cynicism into a refined alertness of intellectuality which aptly proved what things the Western brain can do when it tries.

Neither story was ever completed.

Wister now began to contemplate a long novel that would feature the adventures of both the Virginian and his friend Lin McLean. Such a narrative would be a study in social caste, contrasting the two characters like the genteel and lesser heroes of James Fenimore Cooper's *The Prairie*, Duncan Middleton and Paul Hover. (Much as Cooper completed *The Prairie* in a Paris hotel, moreover, Wister wrote many of his western tales in the comfort of his Philadelphia, Charleston, South Carolina, and Saunderstown, Rhode Island, homes.) Wister thought that the nomadic life of the cowboy was well-suited to "a picaresque novel about the West," and he discussed his plans with Howells, who approved the idea. Wister began to plan "a long book made of short episodes, each complete in itself, but composing a sustained whole when taken together." So far he had written two tales in which the Virginian figured and two other stories about Lin, but he had not yet composed a tale in which they appeared together. While in Texas in February 1893, he had also recorded in his journal an anecdote about

> one of the regulation dances where the babies are all brought and piled in a corner while their parents jump about to music. After the thing had got going full swing, some unknown person got the babies and changed all their clothes—putting the linen of Mrs. Jones's little boy upon Mrs. Smith's little girl, and so on. In the dim light nobody noticed, and all went home with the wrong baby. Next morning there was the devil to pay, and for a week the whole country side was busy exchanging and identifying babies.

On June 6, Wister began a story entitled "The Bear Creek Barbeque," in which Lin and the Virginian perpetrate this practical joke. The barbeque is hosted by the Swinton brothers, owners of the Goose Egg Ranch at the height of the cattle boom of the mid-1880s. The Swintons had bought their spread in 1879 when cattle were at twenty dollars, and cattle prices had since skyrocketed to seventy-five dollars a head. More surprisingly, as Wister tells the tale, the brothers bought the brand, the ranch, and the entire herd from an honest broker. As he allowed, "People have upon occasions made the painful discovery that the cattle a man's books call for will materialize very partially indeed,—so partially sometimes that the man has been known to go away, and not be found when he was wanted"—another source of the range war.

In the tale, he introduced a pair of new characters. The first, a fiddler named Arkansaw, was based on the colorful "old vagrant" Wister had met in the Cascade Mountains in

October 1892. The geezer slurs his speech and requests tail hairs from a white horse to re-string his bow. He disappears from subsequent versions of the story, but on the original manuscript Wister glossed a reminder to "consult this MS. for good suggestions about a musician." The other new member of Wister's ensemble cast is the Vermont school-marm, the epitome of True Womanhood, known only as "Miss Wood" in her début. The type who taught school in the West, according to Wister, "was apt to be a cut above the mothers of the children she instructed. I decided that when the time came, my southerner should wed a New England schoolmarm." The object of Lin's and the Virginian's desires, Miss Wood seems to have wandered into the story from Bret Harte's "The Idyl of Red Gulch" (1869). She arrives at the barbeque with Lin, though she has rebuffed his advances en route. He has been "ridin' out with her afternoons, and she askin' me questions all the time, and me answerin' whenever I knowed, and lyin' when I didn't," so "I figured she wouldn't mind" if he kissed her. "Lots of 'em like it," Lin says, but not Miss Wood, who also snubs the Virginian.

Wister also laid the groundwork in this story for a further satire of feminism. The Wyoming territorial legislature had extended the vote to women in 1869, and when the so-called "Equality State" was admitted to the Union in 1890, its constitution included an equal-suffrage clause. In "The Bear Creek Barbeque," Lizzie Westfall, the wife of a common farmer, poses the rhetorical question: "What does Wyoming stand for? Equal rights, ladies and gentlemen! In Wyoming a woman's vote is as good as any man's." Wister here explicitly acknowledged the legal equality of women in Wyoming for the first and only time in his fiction. But make no mistake: he opposed women's suffrage, and he depicted Miss Wood in a way that many male chauvinists would have approved. In effect, the Virginian tames Molly. Though she is apparently an independent-minded woman and an enfranchised voter upon her arrival in Wyoming, the reader is assured that she is "not a New Woman" and, as if to prove the point, she increasingly defers to the hero in subsequent installments of their romance.

The Virginian's horse, Monte, though mentioned in "Balaam and Pedro, is first named, too, in "The Bear Creek Barbeque." That the heroine and horse are both christened in the same story is hardly a coincidence. As David Brion Davis long ago suggested, in the formulaic western "the Eastern belle's role is that of a glorified horse." Though some scholars have suggested that Wister named Monte after Monticello or Mount Vernon—or even the confidence game three-card monte—the most likely source is Montezuma, the emperor of Mexico when the Spanish introduced horses to the New World. In spring 1889 Wister had worked on a comic opera entitled *Montezuma*, and in his essay "The Evolution of the Cow-puncher" (1895) he observed that whether or not the ancestors of the "horse of the plains . . . looked on when Montezuma fell, they certainly hailed from Spain." In addition, "Monty" was the name of a horse owned by one of Wister's friends in Wyoming.

Unlike both the heroine and the horse, the hero who "started nameless" in "Balaam and Pedro" and "Em'ly" continued to be nameless because, as Wister explained, "I desired to draw a sort of heroic circle about him, almost a legendary circle, and thus if possible create an illusion of remoteness. . . . Leaving him nameless was my chief device to produce this effect." Not that he thought calling him simply "the Virginian" would be particularly evocative: Wister conceded to Richard Harding Davis that there was "nothing typically Virginian about him, save some accent, some bad grammar, and some apparent laziness; and he was meant by me to be just my whole American creed in flesh and blood."

Wister's work on "The Bear Creek Barbeque" was complicated, as was becoming the norm for Wister, by illness.

"I have been sleeping so badly and so many aches of neuralgia or gout or some devilish thing have been troubling my head night and day that writing has been a slow process," he complained. While he was able to write at least two hours a day, after eight days he had completed only about six thousand words. On June 14 he laid the manuscript aside long enough to take a whirlwind, four-day trip to Chicago to attend the Boone and Crockett Club dinner at the Columbian Exposition, or World's Fair, of 1893. He had been elected the year before to membership in the club, founded in 1887 by Theodore Roosevelt and George Bird Grinnell to promote conservation, "manly sport with the rifle," and wildlife management. Its elite membership, limited to a hundred men, included Senators William A. Clark of Montana, Redfield Proctor of Vermont, and Henry Cabot Lodge of Massachusetts; lawyer and future Nobel laureate Elihu Root; the forester and politician Gifford Pinchot; and the sportsman Caspar Whitney. The attendees gathered for dinner in the evening of June 16 on the Wooded Island at the Exposition, and there Wister socialized with Roosevelt, Frank Edwards, the architect Daniel Burnham, and the artists Frank Millet and Augustus St. Gaudens. He finished a draft of the story early in the morning of June 18, a few hours after his return to Philadelphia.

Wister was slowly earning renown among editors for his western fiction. After rejecting "Balaam and Pedro" in the spring of '92, Scudder of the *Atlantic Monthly* had solicited a Wyoming story from Wister, who was "most anxious to send [him] one at once." But upon Wister's return from Chicago, he found a letter from Alden expressing the hope he "would not desert the Harpers for 'rivals.'" After Wister submitted the manuscript of "The Bear Creek Barbeque" to Alden on June 23, however, the editor declined it. He thought it "too much of a link to be published alone—He said it was 'admirable' to lead up to sequences and would do in the book" Wister planned, "but not alone." Alden said specifically that it "needed a sequel" or a stronger ending. He hoped Wister could deliver an acceptable replacement in time for it to appear in the magazine after "Em'ly" and before the Virginian died in "Balaam and Pedro." Meanwhile, Wister made plans to return to the Columbian Exposition in Chicago with his mother at the end of the month and then continue alone to Wyoming.

Western stories were too popular and Alden too experienced an editor to lose Wister as a contributor. The same day Wister carried the manuscript of "The Bear Creek Barbeque" to New York, Alden chatted with him about his literary prospects. Alden was interested in the long-unfinished story of Chalkeye and, Wister observed, "spoke of [it] as possible for the Weekly if, when it should be written, the Monthly was full." Wister also had in mind a magisterial history of the American West tentatively titled "The Course of Empire," and Alden

at once suggested [it] would do for the Monthly. May I live to do all this as it should be done—and much more! Alden was flatteringly jealous of my giving stories to other people—and when I delicately stood on my will as to this, he said, 'Well, don't give the Atlantic any Texas stories.' So I made him that promise. He said he was maturing a scheme he wished to propose to me, but he could not today. Asked if my journey west this summer was laid out.

Alden telegraphed Wister the next day that he had "an important proposition to make which would if accepted by you modify your whole summer campaign and so [I] ought to see you before you go west." Wister replied that he doubted his plans could be "materially changed. They can of course, if the proposition is important enough—and we shall see what we shall see."

Alden's offer certainly warranted changes in Wister's travel plans. The editor proposed that Wister write a series of eight western stories for *Harper's Monthly* in 1894, each of them about 7,500 words in length, for which Wister would be paid thirty to thirty-five dollars per thousand words, or two hundred-fifty dollars apiece, "the entire payment for the series not to exceed twenty-five hundred dollars." Alden had been paying him twenty dollars per thousand words, "which was an increase from $12" originally. Wister might select the topics he found "most suitable in each case," though Alden stipulated that they must be "thrilling, dramatic" pieces filled with the "adventure of the West" such as "Indian fighting and "train robbing" and based in each case on "a real incident." In all, the series ought "to portray certain features of Western Life which are now rapidly disappearing with the progress of civilization. Not the least striking of these is that of the appeal to Lynch law, which ought to give capital subject for one of your stories." Alden even proposed to send the western artist Frederic Remington "along with me if I desire it!" One of Wister's dreams—"to have Remington as an illustrator"—was "likely to be realized in a most substantial manner." Alden asked Wister to send the first story in manuscript to him by November 1, 1893, for publication in the April 1894 issue of the magazine, "after Balaam and Pedro," and to submit another story in manuscript by the first day of each of the next seven months. He expected Wister to "devote yourself to this work steadily and exclusively until its conclusion." Wister was to "do nothing else till [the series] was finished." After their publication in the magazine, Harper's would issue the collected stories in book form, paying the author the standard 10 percent royalty on all copies sold. "We attach more importance to [the proposed series] than to any of our undertakings for 1894," Alden assured Wister, "and shall make a great point of it in our Prospectus for that year, besides the widest announcement of it in other ways." In a miracle of understatement, Wister noted in his journal that "All this was certainly very encouraging to me." He was suddenly able to envision life after his law practice, and he agreed to "hunt material of adventure voraciously." He did not know (nor would it likely have made any difference) that Alden had recruited him to write the series of western stories only after Rudyard Kipling declined the assignment.

Wister departed Philadelphia on June 28 with his mother Sarah in tow. Before he could turn to writing the new stories, he first needed to fix the problem caused by Alden's rejection of "The Bear Creek Barbeque." "The chronological trap I have fallen into with my Western stories is rather a nuisance," Wister conceded on June 29, while riding in the Columbian Express en route to Chicago.

> If Alden wont wait until I can write a missing link in the Virginian's story, Balaam and Pedro will leave him apparently killed before he has fallen in love with the girl who subsequently is to marry him . . . ! This tangle will not hinder the links appearing in a book, orderly, but I want the double benefit of this [link] coming first in the magazine—and so my next week is now booked for scribbling at the Fair [a] . . . story that shall be in itself complete enough to be published alone.

On July 1, in the Hunter's Cabin on the Wooded Island at the fair, Wister began "The Winning of the Biscuit-Shooter" (working titles "At the Bar-Circle-Zee," "A Wyoming Pastoral," "Calamus Agonistes," "Lin McLean's Courtship," and "At the Goose-Egg Outfit"), set chronologically after the Swinton barbeque. The new story contrasts the Virginian's "elegant courtship" of the chaste Vermont schoolmarm—he "has quit spreein' with the boys"—with Lin's "tawdry affair" with Katie Lusk, a fleshy, slatternly waitress from Nebraska, "handsome in a large California-fruit style" and with "a somewhat vague past." The eastern narrator, resurrected from "Em'ly," remarks that Katie "appeared to me as what might be termed an expert in men" and adds, with deliberate double entendre, that she "might make a good helpmeet in spite of her horticultural appearance." Wister finished the 3,500-word manuscript on July 13. Alden accepted it for publication in late September and paid

him a hundred dollars for it—his old rate of payment—
and it appeared in the December 1893 issue of *Harper's
Monthly*, sandwiched between "Em'ly" in the November
issue and "Balaam and Pedro" in January. "The story I
wrote him in Chicago will go in the Christmas [issue],"
Wister gloated, "and this I like all the better, for it places
the three in chronological order."

Meanwhile, he reveled in the attractions of the fair. "Only
two or three times before in my life, and never to such an
extent, have I been moved and impressed as here," he wrote
in his journal. One day he crossed the street to attend a performance of Buffalo Bill's Wild West. On July 12, he read a
poem, "A Columbian Improvisation," on the fairgrounds at
the St. Paul's School dinner. The same day, only a few miles
away, Frederick Jackson Turner delivered his seminal paper
on "The Significance of the Frontier in American History"
at the annual meeting of the American Historical Association—a convergence of stars in the western firmament.
Like Turner, Wister believed the frontier a central source
of national renewal and transformation, though with a difference: Turner believed the frontier maintained equality of
opportunity, and Wister thought it revitalized aristocracy.
In Wister's ideal world, political and economic influence
would remain in the hands of an elite, the traditional custo-
dians of culture.

Two days later, after shipping west 450 pounds of bag-
gage including a tent, fishing equipment, ammunition, his
medicines, and a pillow, he left Chicago for his first extended
trip to Wyoming since the Johnson County War. As usual,
before crossing the Missouri River he bought virtually all
the food required for the trip, save for game he would hunt
and a few delicacies such as canned frankfurters. "When it
comes to evaporated vegetables, condensed soups, and pel-
lets that can expand into a meal," he remembered, "you
pause over each novelty, and with divided purpose wretch-

edly choose and unchoose until you are scarce more man-like than a woman."

His first days back in the territory were bittersweet. On the stagecoach from Rawlins to Fort Washakie on July 17, he sat beside the driver, who "entirely sympathized with the horse thieves and rustlers over in Johnson County and told me there were four men who ought to be killed," including Frank Wolcott and Frank Canton, the former sheriff of Johnson County and now a private detective in the employ of the Wyoming Stock Growers Association. On July 16, he was introduced to Ethelbert Talbot, the Episcopal Bishop of Wyoming, and he reconnected with his friend George West. "He would do anything to be of service to any man he liked—and to many he does not care for," Wister avowed. West had worked—"it was plain to see how hard"—to improve his ranch on Horse Creek, yet he was considering selling it "because the winters are too long." Habitually destitute, West "admitted [that] drink-ing had kept him from getting ahead—but said that he was changed." West spent the spring of 1893 working, as he put it, "like a d—m fool" to fence his land "so that I can cut my own hay this year," but he was eager to guide Wister on a hunting trip that summer. "God knows I would not go with any body else other than you & your friends for love or money," he insisted. Then again, West was unsure what would happen to him "if you don't come." He depended on the cash Wister paid him for his livelihood, and Wister routinely loaned him money and subsequently forgave the loans because "they did him no good beyond helping him to live until it was spent." Still, West had "almost the most lovable nature I have ever known," Wister wrote in his jour-nal in July 1893, and a year later he told an interviewer in San Francisco that "I think a good deal" of West, who "has been a cowboy and a little of everything, and he has been of great use to me." By 1902, West had become the managing partner of the West, Lovering Land & Live Stock Co. in Dubois, Wyoming, though he was eventually deposed and thirty years later, during the Great Depression, earned his living as a janitor in Seattle.

Within a week of his arrival in Wyoming in July 1893, Wister had begun to take notes for the tales of western adventure he had contracted to write for *Harper's Monthly*. "The material I want to draw from is Indian Fighting, Lynching, & Train Robberies," he advised Frank Edwards. He was told a tribal legend about "a strange sound of moaning" at Bull Lake that, according to the Indians, emanated from a herd of buffalo once drowned there. He never wrote the story. At Fort Washakie, Captain Patrick Henry Ray—a veteran of the Sioux and Apache wars who would later be promoted to brigadier general—obliged by relating to Wister an ostensibly true story about the nephew of Red Cloud: "Captain Ray told me his Fort Robinson experience where he and a brother lieutenant . . . took the law into their hands and shot a Sioux half breed who had escaped from jail under sentence of hanging for a double murder. It was certainly a striking story and I told him I should make it into fiction if he had no objection."

Over the next couple of weeks, Wister whipped into shape a tale he entitled "A Kinsman of Red Cloud" based on Ray's anecdote. The title character, Toussaint, is a "half breed," the son of Red Cloud's sister and a French trapper. That is, in Wister's racial hierarchy, which was no more progressive than Cooper's three-quarters of a century earlier, "his heart beat hot with the evil of two races, and none of their good." After cheating at cards, Toussaint kills two of the other cardplayers and is tried, convicted of murder, and sentenced to hang. Red Cloud initially demands his release on threat of war, but when the warrior visits his nephew he recognizes "the mongrel strain of blood" in his veins and disowns him: "Toussaint heap no good. No Injun, anyhow." The narrator insists on the historical accuracy of the tale: "These things happened in the early seventies; but there are Sioux still living" who remember them.

Wister finished "A Kinsman of Red Cloud" while camping in Wyoming on August 9. On the manuscript that survives among his papers in the Library of Congress, Wister scribbled this note: "The main facts were told me by the person [Ray] who figures as Lieutenant Baldwin. The Chief Characters are real people." More than thirty years later, he publicly reiterated the point: "I have taken hardly any liberties with the actual facts; the capture of Toussaint the 'breed' was told me by one of the officers who caught him, and who also witnessed his interview with Red Cloud."

Trouble is, the story is largely if not entirely apocryphal, a mishmash of historical inaccuracies. First, Red Cloud did not have a nephew named Toussaint; Wister apparently borrowed the name from Toussaint Charbonneau, the mixed-blood husband of Sacagawea, who also traveled with the Lewis and Clark expedition. Nor did Red Cloud have, strictly speaking, a nephew who resembled Toussaint; Wister apparently refers to Short Bull, the half-brother of He Dog, the son of the minor Oglala leader Black Rock and Red Cloud's sister Blue Day. A participant at the Battle of the Little Big Horn, Short Bull was the son of Black Rock and Scatter the Feather. That is, Short Bull was not a "half-breed" or mixed-blood, as Wister characterizes Toussaint, but simply the half-brother of Red Cloud's nephew. Finally, Short Bull does not die like Toussaint in Wister's tale; rather, he lived into his eighties on the Pine Ridge Reservation. Despite his claims for the truth of the tale, Wister conceded that he had taken poetic license in it: "The first part was hearsay—to the effect that the half breed had been seen by the scout to commit a double murder at a cabin near Fort Laramie, & that the scout subsequently identified him at the railroad and had him arrested & convicted. This had to be elaborated, as my friend knew none of the particulars." The narrative contains less truth than truthiness. Still,

Remington later pronounced "A Kinsman of Red Cloud" a "bully story—it's so subtle—dead true and so well thought out—it's just as good as Bret Harte and I can't say any more, except that I know your *range* is greater."

By late August, Wister had started another story, "The Promised Land," based on a personal experience related to him by Guy and Helen Waring in the Methow valley in the fall of 1892. In Wister's fictionalization, a family of emigrants modeled on the Warings "had driven twenty-one hundred miles" and crossed the Columbia River near the Colville Reservation in western Washington to reach their homestead. The cable ferry has been destroyed in a storm, however, so with the help of Wild Goose Jake, who operates an illegal saloon patronized by Indians, they build a raft. Jake is killed in a drunken melee as the tale ends. "There were only about a couple of drops of invention" in the story, Wister asserted; "everything happened, as there described; happened to intimate friends, who told it all to me." The real-life model for Wild Goose Jake, Samuel Wilbur Condon, actually owned a trading post on the Colville Reservation, for example, though he did not die until a couple of years after Wister wrote the story. Still, he "brought himself to an end identical" to the one Wister imagined for him—"a bloody and violent end" in a shootout. Condon "broke the laws of his country as naturally & as it were by instinct," Wister noted. "Nothing safer than to prophesy correctly about a lawbreaker who sold whiskey to Siwashes and was free with other men's women."

But on the whole he was not pleased with the story. He felt "greatly hampered" by the conditions Alden had specified in their contract, especially the "demand for excitement & exclusion of study of character." He was reluctant to sacrifice characterization to sensational plotting. "I think the appearance and talk of Wild Goose Jake will do as it is written," he rationalized as he was writing the story, and "the end would lose force if the man's personality was not given at some length." Still, in the actual composition of the story he "had more trouble than I can ever remember before—I wished to paint the hardships of emigrants a little, and the 'prairie schooner,' along with the criminal selling of whiskey to Indians." He was resigned to ending the tale with "shocking" events, but "the toil of leading up to them and making a situation that at all satisfied me was really a time disheartening. I think I must have been unwell somehow, for invention dribbled in muddy drops and I destroyed much paper." He "grubbed away" over the manuscript "so hard and so long, in camps, hotels, trains, and now at home, that I almost hated the sight of the paper."

Perhaps more than any of his other stories, "The Promised Land" exhibits a characteristic tick in Wister's style best described as his typological imagination. Like many other western writers, including Cooper and Steinbeck, he repeatedly evoked biblical types in his fiction and/or patterned his plots after biblical events. In the journal he kept on his first trip to Wyoming, for example, he compared the landscape of the West to something "like Genesis" or an unspoiled Eden, and he observed that "in the Old Testament Lot and Isaac and Uncle Laban and the rest had times not unlike this." He later compared "the Rocky Mountains before the wire fence" to "Paradise before the Fall." In "Balaam and Pedro" he evoked the Old Testament account of Balaam and his ass, and in "How Lin McLean Went East" he parodied the parable of the prodigal son. In "The Promised Land," an emigrant family, a new chosen people, must cross the Columbia River (the Red Sea), much as the Joads in *The Grapes of Wrath* must cross the Red River, to reach an ironic land of milk and honey. In his journal for May 29, 1894, he again implicitly compared the West to Israel when he learned that Apache mothers "now give their children condensed milk! Truly the glory of the frontier is departed." Wister humorously evoked here the solemnity of I Samuel 4:21 ("The Glory has departed from Israel, for the ark of God has been captured") and he continued to use this typological device occasionally—to reenact biblical history in his fiction, either literally or satirically—for the rest of his career.

On September 8, at lunch in the Norris Basin in Yellowstone Park, Wister by chance met Frederic Remington. He had long been a fan of Remington who, he said, "has made a page of American history his own." Remington had "caught alive" the "roped calf," "the troop cook sucking his comfortable corn-cob, the day-by-day facts of the wilderness," and "the eternal note also. . . . He has made them visible by his art, and set them down as a national treasure." The two men met soon after Remington had drawn an illustration for "Balaam and Pedro," and the more they talked the more Wister was beguiled. "Remington is an excellent American," he remarked. "That means, he thinks as I do about the disgrace of our politics and the present asphyxiation of all real love of country. He used almost the same words that have of late been in my head, that this continent does not hold a nation any longer but is merely a strip of land on which a crowd is struggling for riches." Wister and Remington became such fast friends that they traveled together to St. Paul, Minnesota, a day or two later, and while en route they "discussed our collaboration and many other things. He made a good criticism on the first two pages of 'The Promised Land,' which I accepted and profited by."

Soon after his return to Philadelphia on September 15, Wister carried the manuscripts of both "The Kinsman of Red Cloud" and "The Promised Land" to Alden in New York. The editor was troubled by the former story, which he again complained was "very bloody." Wister replied, "You're not going to get much American western adventure without blood," and his point again carried the day. Alden accepted both stories and paid Wister four hundred dollars for them. They appeared, with illustrations by

Remington, in the April and May 1894 issues of *Harper's Monthly*. But neither counted toward the stories Wister had contracted to contribute to the magazine because they were "not made from material gathered by special journey." He was reconciled to the exclusion because of the publisher's past generosity, but "had I known it, I should certainly not have spent so many days in a tent on the Rocky Mountains, holding a pencil instead of a rifle." While neither of the stories counted toward the eight he had agreed to write, it was as though the terms of the contract had been effectively extended: he would be paid well to write ten western stories for the magazine instead of eight.

2

1893–1895

Wister lit out on his tenth trip across the Missouri River, his initial official trip west to collect material for his series of stories in *Harper's Monthly*, on October 2, 1893. For the first time, he traveled to the Southwest—across New Mexico and Arizona to southern California. His train fare from Philadelphia to San Francisco and back, not including meals and Pullman accommodations, amounted to $133—the equivalent of about $3,000 in 2014 dollars, or what Alden paid him for nine thousand words of published fiction. He rolled through the Raton Pass on the Colorado-New Mexico border on October 5 and arrived at Fort Bowie, Arizona, on October 8. There he met Charles Skirdin of the Second Cavalry. "I rode many miles of desert and mountain" with Skirdin in Arizona that summer, he remembered, and their "views of life were precisely similar."

Gradually Skirdin told Wister the story of his "amazing" life. Born in Arizona, he had been abandoned by his family and left with "an old drunkard" in Tempe when he was only eight years old. When he "tired of being sent after stage relay horses before breakfast and being whipped if he failed to bring them in," Skirdin "stood off [the] old drunkard with a Spencer 50-bore" and ran away. He slept the first night in the Pinal range in the middle of Apache country, with no belongings except what he wore, a pony, a gun, and an extra pair of trousers. He earned his living by delivering supplies between mines and Tempe with a mule team. "His story, literally and faithful recorded," Wister noted in his journal, "would make a book as absorbing as Robinson Crusoe, and he's only 27." Though he was "uncouth, ugly, and knows only what he has taught himself," Skirdin's "talk is as simple and strong as nature, and he has a most beautiful eye. The officers place a high value on him." Wister always insisted that he modeled the character of the Virginian on nobody "in particular. . . . He has characteristics of half a dozen men." Wister had, after all, already written "Em'ly," "Balaam and Pedro," "The Winning of the Biscuit-Shooter," and a draft of "The Bear Creek Barbeque." Yet he also allowed that "more definitely than any frontier character I had met," Skirdin "continually realized and ratified my imaginary portrait" of his hero.

Wister spent the last two weeks of October in San Carlos and the first two weeks of November in Fort Grant, Arizona, in company with Frank Edwards. He was underwhelmed by the region—and he did not even suffer the summer heat. In "Specimen Jones" (1894), one of his characters describes San Carlos: "There ain't no streets. There ain't no houses. There ain't any land and water in the usual meaning of them words. . . . Mix up a barrel of sand and ashes and thorns, and jam scorpions and rattlesnakes along in, and dump the outfit on stones, and heat yer stones red-hot, and set the United States army loose over the place chasin' Apaches, and you've got San Carlos." Wister traveled by train from Yuma to Los Angeles on November 16, across the San Joaquin Valley the next day, and arrived in San Francisco on November 19. For more than six weeks he had been on vacation. "Bowie and Carlos and Grant were all so full of pleasant days and kind hospitality that October and November in Arizona seem to have passed in a minute and left me nothing but regret they should be gone," he wrote Edwards from the Palace Hotel. But his holiday ended as soon as he reached San Francisco, even though he had succeeded in postponing the deadline for the first story under his Harper's contract from November 1 to December 20. He began to write "Little Big Horn Medicine" (working title "Cheschapah," based on an anecdote Edwards told him) on November 19 and finished it in early December. "I wrote it painfully," he remembered, "but I find the more time I put in on a story the better it is received."

It was a thinly-disguised history, as Wister imperfectly understood it, of the Indian Ghost Dance religion and the events leading to the massacre at Wounded Knee in 1890, mostly from a naively native point of view. He "twisted history a little," as he explained to Edwards. In "Little Big Horn Medicine," Wister's protagonist Cheschapah is repeatedly called a "prophet" and he organizes a frenzied dance, much as the shaman Wovoka was the prophet of the Ghost Dance. The narrator describes it, albeit stereotypically: "The thudding drums were ceaseless" and "the dance went always faster. . . . The steady blows of sounds inflamed the dancers; their chests heaved, and their arms and bodies swung alike." As Wovoka reportedly could control the weather, Cheschapah claims credit for an electrical storm that kills six cattle that feed his people. Some of his followers live on the Pine Ridge Reservation. "Ambition and success had brought him to the weird enthusiasm of a fanatic," Wister writes. "He was still a charlatan, but a charlatan who believed utterly in his star. He moved among his people with growing mystery." Much as the Ghost Dancers wore Ghost Shirts they thought would repel the white man's bullets, Cheschapah promises to protect his people with his medicine, including garments of red flannel. In battle, he says, he will don such clothing "and let the white soldiers shoot at me until they all lie dead." In short, Wister exploited in the story the common misconceptions about Wovoka, who was a pacifist.

He also portrayed an unscrupulous white trader who tries to "nourish the sinews of war" between the whites and Indians because he supplies "grain and steers to Fort Custer"— that is, he incites mischief for profit. Wister voices the suspicions of many army officers he knew in the West that Indian wars were unnecessary but good business for civilians, especially politicians. As Lieutenant Stirling declares in Wister's story, "What a bungle! And how like the way we manage Indian affairs." ("I've made you a very decent person indeed, under the name of Stirling," Wister wrote Edwards after finishing the story. "You & Wainwright & Ayleshire are all there in disguise and you do exactly what you really did.") In his journal, he noted at about the same time: "There are, and always have been, and always will be, three ingredients of the Indian Question: the greed of the frontier settler, the folly of the peace party, and the time-serving of the politician." He elsewhere disparaged the white villainy that had occurred during the Nez Perce campaign of 1877, yet ever the ameliorist, he concluded that "forgetting [it] is best."

Despite his use of caricature, Wister exhibits sympathy for Indians in "Little Big Horn Medicine," for example by investing the character of Pounded Meat, Cheschapah's father, with dignity. Elsewhere in the story, Lieutenant Stirling asserts that, hardly a savage, "the Indian is of a subtlety more ancient than the Sphinx." Or as John Cobbs has argued, perhaps to the surprise of readers familiar only with *The Virginian*, "the red men in [Wister's] early stories have a considerable nobility."

While in San Francisco during these weeks, Wister made several new friends. Dining one evening at the University Club, he met the hydrologist Arthur De Wint Foote, the "very agreeable" husband of the western writer and illustrator Mary Hallock Foote. He also was introduced to James O. Bradford, the archivist for Wells, Fargo & Co., who urged him to consider another project: a history of the company, whose corporate offices were in the city. Wister was permitted to examine the archives and relics in an "old building in Montgomery Street," and "I went across to it from the Palace Hotel quite often to chat with officers of Wells Fargo; and retain to this day a vivid remembrance of their courtesy and their interest in my project." In fact, he proposed such a book both to the corporate officers who "have been most cordial" and to Harper's, and it "appealed to them all." As it was, he "did not have time to touch" all the "mines of wealth waiting" for him and it seemed "a pity to leave them so." But he realized that to chronicle the history of Wells Fargo from its beginning in 1852 would require

> a long book. . . . To tell their growth and experiences would be to tell of the mines, the mails, the pony express, the stage coaches, and a world of courage and skill not much like anything else in the world. Such a book might be called The Romance of a Corporation. It would need a long study and the meeting and knowing well many people—'old timers' who don't as a rule talk to order, and however friendly in intention, must be lured into unconsciousness over a cigar late at night. I should like to write such a book—It would be a real contribution to our literature, and a new thing, too, I think. No one has yet made a Corporation his hero.

He made plans to return to San Francisco the following year "and devote as many weeks to this as needed."

Wister spent the next week in Portland, Oregon, and Vancouver Barracks, Washington, across the Columbia River, with a pair of army officers to whom Edwards had introduced him by mail. Major James A. Jackson and Captain Frazier Boutelle were both veterans of the Modoc War of 1872–73 in northern California and southern Oregon, and Wister was thinking about writing a story for his series set during the conflict. Boutelle "is full of recollections, both as a soldier and an officer," he wrote Edwards. Wister interviewed Jackson one morning "in his office, and he showed me maps of Tule Lake and the Lava beds—also many photographs taken during the Modoc campaign." As late as July 1894 he was contemplating a tale based on "an episode of actual life" on the border, "a war of extermination which occurred a few years ago in the West." He wrote Edwards in December 1893 that "if there are things of the Modoc Campaign I don't know, it's my own stupid fault." He told an interviewer the following July that he had "nearly all the details collected" for the story, but he never wrote it, and for a good reason.

> I completed my facts about the Modoc War and Captain Jack and the massacre of General Canby, which had taken me from Arizona to Portland in distance, and two years in time. When participators and witnesses found I had struck the real trail, they became frank. I talked with every accessible army officer surviving, and was ready to begin a tale based upon that war and the Battle of the Lava Beds, when I suddenly discovered that the villain of the piece had been the father of a lady who had shown me every hospitality. That ended it. To change my villain was utterly impossible, owing to the facts of the case. So that book was never written; and I doubt if the true story of the Modoc War will ever be told, which is a pity; it would make a dark and thrilling page of our frontier history.

His time was not entirely wasted, however. He was impressed by the scenery around Vancouver, "among green levels and huge fir trees—with snowy Mt. [St.] Helens shining over purple hills to the East, up the wide river—a very beautiful post." He left Portland on December 18 and arrived back in Philadelphia on the 23rd. He soon reflected that all of his trips west to date had been "holidays from the law [practice] and my perfunctory days at the office—the forgetting for a moment a detested occupation. This made them delicious."

The last two weeks of January 1894 he escaped to a house in Tuxedo, north of New York City. He also visited Remington at his home in New Rochelle, in Westchester County, New York, and read "Little Big Horn Medicine" aloud to the artist. Remington had agreed to illustrate the story for *Harper's Monthly* and needed to choose the most picturesque scenes. "Put every person on horseback and let the blood be half a foot deep," he wrote Wister. "Be very profane and have plenty of shooting. No episodes must occur in the dark." Wister also solicited comments about the story from Frank Edwards, who offered some suggestions. Wister thanked him for his "points" and admitted he had been "reserved" in his description of the Dakota landscape, a region he had hardly toured, and "dealt only in safe allusions to hills & valleys & water, with cottonwoods gingerly thrown in once or twice." Alden printed the tale in the June 1894 issue of the magazine and paid Wister $334 for it.

It was the first of his stories to attract widespread praise. The *Chicago Standard*, for example, suggested that it exemplified "the well known fact that in dealing with the Indians our government has not only acted unjustly but stupidly." The *New York Tribune* also selected it for special mention: The author, it said,

> has fairly won his spurs. Mr. Owen Wister has done enough good work to prove his right to a place high in the list of our original writers. He has the happy art of portraying character by indication rather than description; he has humor and sympathy; and his masculine style shows the finish of culture as well as the strength of nature's gift. If Mr. Wister is not spoiled by undue literary petting he will probably be a notable accession to the group of American authors who are really "worthwhile."

It was, as Wister remarked, "the most flattering notice yet conferred upon me. They say I've already 'won my spurs' and if not 'spoiled by under literary petting' I shall probably etc. etc. I don't think I've won my spurs, though I propose to. . . . As for the spoiling, there's less and less chance of it. My success has but one inward effect, to increase the desire to do better." For the first time, Wister began to be compared to Rudyard Kipling by reviewers. His friend E. S. Martin added to the encomiums in *Harper's Weekly*: "No one since Bret Harte has made the wild West contribute so much to the entertainment of readers." Roosevelt commended the story from Washington, D.C., where he was serving on the U.S. Civil Service Commission: "I greedily read all your western articles" and "I can quite sincerely say that they rank with Bret Harte's and Kipling's pieces. I have long been praying to have somebody arise and write articles of that kind, and I am delighted that it should be a friend of mine who has arisen."

While in Tuxedo, Wister also wrote a new story, "Specimen Jones," to "give a true picture" of Arizona. It was not the type of tale that attracted tourists to the Southwest or endeared the author to the local chamber of commerce. On the contrary, Wister's fictional town of Twenty Mile—modeled on San Carlos, Arizona, and named for its distance to the next water hole—"was chronically hilarious after sundown—a dot of riot in the dumb Arizona night." The "cruel, assassinating, cowardly Southwest" was little more than a wasteland, according to Wister, "where prospered those jail-birds whom the vigilantes had driven from California." Years after his first visit, he wrote "Arizona and New Mexico have a special inheritance—the scum from California, Texas, and old Mexico." While traveling by train through New Mexico the previous October, Wister had heard a saloon story from a fellow passenger about a young lieutenant whose army uniform "antagonized a bully who fired at his heels and made him dance, and then took him up to the bar for a drink. He then asked the bully to drink in turn, as the man was occupied in lifting his glass, the officer reached and pulled out the man's own six shooter and made him dance."

Wister used the anecdote to open "Specimen Jones." The title character—a laconic cowhand so named because he "always carried pieces of stone in his pockets, discoursing upon their mineral-bearing capacity, which was apt to be very slight"—watches as a bully shoots at the feet of a tenderfoot. Finally, the tenderfoot offers to buy his tormentor a drink. As the bully lifts his glass, "exposing his waist, the boy reached down a lightning hand, caught the old gentleman's own pistol, and jammed it in his face. 'Now you'll dance,' said he." The story ends as Jones and the tenderfoot impersonate lunatics when they are threatened by Indians because "Injuns'll never touch lunatics." Like Chalkeye and Lin McLean, Jones was another fumbling attempt at a Western hero in an arc that eventually culminated in the Virginian. As G. Edward White explains, Jones "achieves certain small successes but primarily serves as a humorous foil to more respectable figures. Actually, the Specimen Jones stories are whimsical salutes to the frivolity of a nomad." Still, Wister was uncommonly pleased with this tale. He wrote Edwards that he thought it "the first entirely satisfactory piece of work [he had written] since Balaam & Pedro, for I have succeeded, I think, in telling a fairly good story but better than that, in touching the human chord." Remington read it in manuscript, wrote Wister that "it's a hypnotizer from Hypville," and agreed to illustrate it. Alden printed it in *Harper's Monthly* for July 1894 and paid the author $280. Mary Hallock Foote thought its opening sentences "simply perfect."

By early 1894 Wister was producing a manuscript per month for Harper's. On February 12, he started another story entitled "The General's Bluff" about a frontier campaign by General George Crook based "on a very pretty thing [Frazier] Boutelle told me" in Vancouver the previous December. "I'm going to take you and E-eganti [a Paiute Indian chief] and boil up something," he reported to Edwards, "chucking in the Umatilla Agency, & Ume Pike & carrots and onions & the dear knows what." In December 1866, Crook had assumed command of the 23rd Infantry in Boise. He "had come to hunt Indians in the district of the Owyhee" and was well known in the army for attacking in winter. In Wister's story, Crook stalks E-egante for a day, then bluffs the Paiute chief into believing that he has a larger force at his command than he does. With only forty soldiers, one of them Specimen Jones, Crook captures three hundred Indians without firing a shot and reports his success to "the superannuated cattle of the War Department." Alden printed the story, illustrated by Remington, in *Harper's Monthly* for September 1894. Years later, in reply to an inquiry, Wister allowed that he "never saw General Crook; and the slight sketch I attributed of him in The General's Bluff was merely a guess at him, so to speak. Founded on army talk here and there."

The next month, he finished two more manuscripts. "The Serenade at Siskiyou" was based on a true story that James Bradford had told Wister in San Francisco the previous autumn. After robbing a stage on May 14, 1892, and killing the Wells Fargo messenger at Redding, California, (which Wister renames Siskiyou), the handsome brothers John and Charles Ruggles were arrested for the crimes and imprisoned. But "prison time was made pleasant for them by the women of the place, who filled their cell with flowers and feasted them on dainties," as the *Chicago Tribune* and other papers reported. "Public indignation was slow and might never have risen to the lynching point but for the sickly sentimentality of the women." The germ of the story appears in Wister's journal: "Robbers in jail would have had a fair trial, but women in town kept sending them things—*Pound cake!* and praying for them." Rather than await a trial, several dozen men peremptorily hanged the brothers early in the morning of July 24. Their lynching, the *Los Angeles Times* editorialized on July 27, "was not at all in accordance with law and order, but that it will have a discouraging effort on the 'hold-up' industry, there is little question." The *Nation* regarded it as "a timely satire on the mushy sentimentalism which sympathizes with riotous strikers."

Wister's version of events was almost identical to the news accounts. He changed the name of the criminals to the Healy boys but altered little else—not even the name of the murdered messenger. The local Ladies' Reform and Literary Lyceum take the poor murderers under wing, like the "sappy women" with bleeding hearts who petition the governor to pardon Injun Joe at the close of *The Adventures of Tom Sawyer*. They send bouquets of flowers and cakes to the jail and pay a band to entertain the prisoners. They blame the victim for his own death during the holdup; after all, the "boys had no employment, and they only wanted money." The men in the town are so incensed by the misguided charity of the women that, rather than wait for the trial, they lynch the culprits—"an irregular but highly wholesome dealing with crime," in Wister's opinion. "If it happened oftener, it might clear the air of some sentimentalism" and deter murders. "The Serenade at Siskiyou" was the first story he had ever written in which, Wister claimed, he introduced a moral. In it, he illustrated "the typical American outbreak of female sympathy for murderers, female indifference to the victim, female inability to comprehend that the swift punishment of crime by law is one of the cornerstones upon which civilization rests." Alden printed it in *Harper's Monthly* for August 1894 and paid Wister five hundred dollars for it and "The General's Bluff."

Of all Wister's tales, "Salvation Gap"—named for the mining camp where it is set—is the most reminiscent of the western fiction of Bret Harte. A hapless miner kills his mistress, the putative proprietor of the dance-hall—in fact the madam of a brothel—because she has taken another lover. The miner frames his rival for her murder, and the rival is hanged, but then the miner in a spasm of conscience kills himself. Wister thus betrays his own ambivalence about lynch law. On April 16, not surprisingly, Alden asked for revisions to the conclusion, and Wister was able to make the necessary changes so quickly that five days later he received a check for $156. He fell back on a hackneyed way to address Alden's reservations: by emphasizing the miner's remorse for his crimes and by echoing the final lines of "Tennessee's Partner." In the Harte story, in the delirium of Partner's last moments he sees the dead Tennessee, whom he helped send to the gallows: "'thar he is,—coming this way, too,—all by himself, sober, and his face a-shining. Tennessee! Partner!' And so they met." In Wister's story, in the delirium of his last moments the miner sees the dead man he framed for murder: "'I'm overtakin' him!' he said. 'He's going to know now. Lay me alongside—' And so they did." Apparently mollified despite the crude emendation, Alden printed the story, illustrated by Remington, in the magazine for October 1894.

By April 1894, Wister had completed five of the eight manuscripts he had contracted to write for *Harper's Monthly*, but he feared the quality of the stories he had furnished had declined. He explained to Alden that "I could do better work if I had more leisure, & was told there would be no harm in running the 3 remaining stories over into the year '95." He already knew what the three stories were going to be. All he needed was "to gather more of the original facts." He started to write "Lin McLean's Honeymoon" (working title "The Rain Maker of Cheyenne"), in which Lin and his new bride Katie, a waitress or "biscuit-shooter," take a wedding journey to Cheyenne. It would not count toward the remaining three stories he owed Harper's, however, because it belonged to the book he was writing about Lin and the Virginian. In Wister's story, while Lin and Katie holiday in Cheyenne the town fathers there hire a rainmaker from Kansas in hope of ending a drought. In real life, Frank Melbourne, aka "the barnyard Barnum," one of the best-known "pluviculturists" (rainmakers) at the time, had in fact arrived in Cheyenne on August 27, 1891, accompanied by his brother Will. He set up shop in a barn on Twenty-Fifth street and began to vent ostensibly secret chemical gases into the atmosphere on August 30. The next day, a cloudburst struck the area that was so intense it killed two cows. Melbourne's success in Cheyenne attracted national news coverage, but Wister could have read about it in a local paper. He was at the time virtually on the scene, camping out in Yellowstone National Park.

The following year, while in Cheyenne, Wister "saw the famous barn where Melbourne produced the rain." In Wister's retelling of these events, Melbourne's brother Will is replaced by Katie Lusk's legal husband. As it happens, that is, Katie is a "sage-brush bigamist." She leaves Lin and reconciles with Jim Lusk. Wister finished the story in May; Alden would print it in *Harper's Monthly* for January 1895 and would pay Wister $272 for it.

On April 28, 1894, shortly before he had completed the manuscript of "Lin McLean's Honeymoon," Wister left for his first trip west in sixteen months. At Columbus, Ohio, he "passed a division of Coxey's Army," a group of unemployed workers who were marching to Washington to protest depressed economic conditions in the nation after the financial Panic of 1893. Heading southwest, by mid-May Wister arrived in the boot-heel district of southern New Mexico near Deming, Silver City, and Fort Bayard, where he met Zenas Bliss, the commander of the Twenty-Fourth Infantry stationed there. From late May until late June he stayed at Fort Bowie, where he reunited with Charles Skirdin, and then at Fort Grant, Arizona, with day trips to Bonita Canyon, the Copper Queen mine near Bisbee, Tucson, and the Mission San Xavier del Bac. He was struck by the number of cattle that had died of thirst in this drought-stricken part of the country. The "cows leave their calves to hunt for water, find none, fall from weakness, and both cow and calf die and dry on the naked plain," he observed. "I have never got such an impression of distress and suffering before. The country is littered and strewn with carcasses from 1 day to months old. It is like a plague in the Old Testament"— another example of his use of biblical typology.

While in Tombstone for three days, he researched a story about the Earps and Clantons—"the whole history in its main points"—that he hoped to contribute to *Harper's Monthly* (working title "Tombstone Corral"), though he quickly realized there was "too much of it to be told in a single number. I think it will require at least two." He was unsure whether to give the principal actors in the drama "fictitious names or not. One or two are still alive." In the end, he never wrote this story, either. But he was left with an indelible impression of Tombstone. It was "quite the most depressing town I have ever seen," he wrote. "'The glory is departed' is written on every street and building"— still another biblical allusion. A decade earlier, the town had boasted a population of eight thousand, but "now there are 600 people, and the idle mines loom in all directions on the miserable barren hillsides." Wister's disaffection with Tombstone was symptomatic of his distaste for the entire "southwest corner of our country." It was such a "forlorn wretched place," he believed the United States would have been "better off if we had never got it from Mexico" in the Treaty of Guadalupe Hidalgo. "It's all right to write fire-and-smoke romances about, but there it ends."

He left Tucson on June 27 but, as he wrote with uncharacteristic understatement upon his arrival in Los Angeles two days later, "My journey has become somewhat chequered." More specifically, his travel plans were snarled by the Pullman Strike of 1894, led by Eugene V. Debs, which virtually shut down all rail travel and transport in the West. In an effort to redress falling wages in the Pullman factory and exorbitant rents in the company town of Pullman, Illinois, among other grievances, the American Railway Union (ARU), headed by Debs, had authorized a boycott and strike against the Pullman Company on June 26. The strike quickly spread among railroad employees throughout the West. The U.S. Attorney General obtained an injunction forbidding the strike in federal court in Chicago on July 2. Debs and the other ARU leaders defied the injunction, whereupon President Grover Cleveland, citing the threat to railroad property, sent federal troops to Chicago on July 4 and soon to other western cities. Although some pockets of rail workers held out until September, the strike was largely crushed by August. Debs was arrested and charged with conspiracy to obstruct a mail train and contempt of court for ignoring the injunction. He was sentenced to six months in the federal prison in Woodstock, Illinois. That is, the strike ended disastrously for the union, which was effectively broken.

While traveling in the Southwest in late July 1894, Wister witnessed the strike at firsthand. As he later remembered, "Vaguely I had heard something about a strike at the town of Pullman, where the company had its works; vaguely I had noticed here and there the name of Eugene Debs. One day I got on the Sunset Express at a junction called Benson, [Arizona,] and I expected to get out of that train at Oakland in two days, and cross in the ferry to San Francisco." Instead, the next day in Los Angeles the passengers "were informed that our Pullman would go no farther, because it was a strike against the Pullman company; and we were advised to get into the day coaches. We crowded into the day coaches and sat in them till it grew dark. Nobody told us anything." At least, as he conceded, he had been marooned in Los Angeles and not at some woe-begotten "siding with a water tank and coal-chute."

Given the plight of the working class during the economic depression in the country, Wister was initially sympathetic to the strikers. He noted in his journal that several "rioters" had been shot and millions of dollars' worth of "property burned or otherwise destroyed. . . . Yet still I am glad" because "the cause and root of this present evil is that money has grown too powerful in our republic." The strikers' "protest and grievance is against the Jay Goulds, the Carnegies, the Huntingtons, the Sugar Trust, and they'll go on protesting till they've reduced those abuses to unrecognizable powder—if the thing is not corrected. So far as that, I'm on their side."

Then he was personally inconvenienced.

After an idle (not idyllic) day, he booked passage aboard the steamer *San Pedro* for San Francisco and "found my first-class ticket gave me the privilege of sleeping on any portion of the vessel that I could find unoccupied." For two nights he shared the floor "with 55 other cabinless wretches" who "seemed bent on plunging" their feet "into my hair" and "reached San Francisco with a bad cold and greatly disgusted." He checked into the Palace Hotel, where he "could sleep clean and comfortable in a bed," but "if I had wished to leave San Francisco, I could not have done so, except again in some boat" because "by land, the town was in a state of blockade" as if by the army of "a foreign country."

He dallied around the bay for most of July. He spent much of his time reading in his hotel room; he thought Arthur Conan Doyle's *A Study in Scarlet* was "dull trash," and he "tried Jane Austen twice and cannot go her," much as the Virginian in "Grandmother Stark" cannot abide *Emma* and *Pride and Prejudice*. On the other hand, he read Rudyard Kipling's "Kaa's Hunting" and "Mowgli's Brothers" and Henry James's "The Real Thing" with "great great delight." He visited Angel Island and the Sequoias in Calaveras county east of the city, and on July 18 the California Midwinter International Exposition in Golden Gate Park, but he wrote little fiction during his month of enforced idleness. He told an interviewer for the *San Francisco Examiner*, which had gotten wind of his presence in the city, that he had started a story that "will, I think, be called 'The Second

Missouri Compromise,'" though he was so depressed by the strike that he said he could not focus his mind on it. He confided to his journal that he had "tried to begin a story here, but the national crisis makes humorous fiction come hard, and humorous it must be this time, to contrast with the gloomy 'Salvation Gap.'" He laid the manuscript aside until his mood improved.

On July 26, as soon as "travel became reasonably reliable" again—that is, after federal troops were deployed in Sacramento, a labor stronghold and the hub of the strike—Wister hurried east. In the Sacramento depot, "I never saw so strange a sight," he noted in his journal. "The platform was covered with sleeping soldiers. . . . It was in fact a camp ready for action on short notice," and a Gatling gun "commanded the approach from the street." Three days later he stopped in Cheyenne for "a much shorter time than had been my original plan" to dine at the Cheyenne Club with Amos W. Barber and W. C. Irvine, the manager of the Ogalalla Cattle Company and, according to John W. Davis, "a man with malice in his heart toward Johnson County small cattlemen." After the range war, more than ever, according to Christine Bold, the club was "the velvet glove over the iron fist of the Wyoming Stock Growers Association, the organization through which the cattle kings controlled open-range ranching and policed the activities of small farmers." Over dinner on July 29, Wister wrote in his journal, Irvine "branched onto his experiences during the 'invasion' of Johnson County. The story was thrilling and picturesque. . . . I made bold to request him some day when I should ask for it, for a written account of all these things." On August 2, Wister and Barber lunched at the club, and the former Wyoming governor reminisced about his "extraordinary experiences" as an army surgeon at Fort Fetterman, Wyoming, in the mid-1880s. "The memoirs of that sink of crime should be written," Wister insisted. "If Barber merely wrote what he has seen, no western book could touch him. Most of the things are too violent or gross for fiction, but as history they would be perfectly permissible." A day or two later Wister left Cheyenne to return to Philadelphia.

Wister normally regarded the railroad as a progressive force in modern civilization. His daughter Marina remembered after her father's death that "his lifelong hobby was railroads. He knew every line, branch and junction in the country, almost every bridge and grade; the spanning of the Continent was to him epic. Railway men remained his friends, and he read himself to sleep with timetables from all over the world." But the 1894 Pullman Strike crystallized his class prejudice and opposition to foreign immigration. On the train in Nebraska en route east, he fumed, "Uncle Sam has cast the pearl of suffrage to swine. Hitherto they have tried their rending by bullets, but presently it will be by ballots, I suspect, and we shall have a crew of tramps and anarchists for our legislators. . . . It is our destiny to demonstrate the eternal lie of equality. Dogs and horses are not equal. Why shall men be?"

His frustration over the rail strike boiled over in an essay laced with ethnic hatred, "The National Guard of Pennsylvania," which he sent *Harper's Weekly* soon after his return. Long a champion of class privilege, Wister feared the consequences of "foreign" influence, and the economic depression only exacerbated his prejudices. "The deluge of immigrants is diluting our Anglo-Saxon race pretty fast— poisoning us, in fact," he had jotted in his journal the year before. In the *Harper's Weekly* essay, he expressed his class anxieties without reservation. During the last major U.S. rail strike in 1877, he declared, "we saw how a horde of vermin"—Wister's code word for immigrants—"swarmed over our body social." During the Homestead steel strike near Pittsburgh in July 1892, "the rats came out of their holes again" and the state militia was needed to quell the violence of the "mutineers." Now, "I have had a recent

experience in California—not relevant here, save for comparison," he fumed, "and Sacramento in '94 was worse than
Pittsburgh in '77." In the nativist subtext of the essay, that
is, Wister blamed unchecked immigration and the foreign
hordes for the strike. Wister invariably identified labor "agi-
tators" as immigrants and believed a crackdown on immigration would help solve the problem of unemployment
during the depression of the 1890s. His animus against
immigrants also helps explain, by contrast, his respect for
cowboys, at least the Anglo-Saxon variety: they "are of the
manly, simple, humorous, American type which I hold to be
the best and bravest we possess and our hope in the future.
They work hard, they play hard, and *they don't go on strikes*"
(emphasis added).

At home he turned again to the manuscript of "The Second Missouri Compromise." The first Missouri Compromise
had occurred in 1820 between pro- and anti-slavery factions
in Congress. Wister's tale chronicles ostensibly true events
that transpired in Boise, the capital of Idaho Territory, soon
after the Civil War, when some of the fugitives from General
Sterling Price's Confederate army brigade settled in Idaho
and were elected to the legislature. Unreconstructed rebels,
they refused to take the oath of office to respect and defend
the U.S. Constitution, a move that the governor, David W.
Ballard, a presidential appointee, checkmated by refusing to
authorize payment of their six-dollar a day stipend for their
service during the forty-day legislative session. In Wister's
account, Corporal Specimen Jones of the U.S. Army helps
resolve the impasse by a timely intervention. He arrests the
governor and the territorial treasurer, saving them from
assault by the legislators, who in turn eventually swear allegiance to the Union and receive their money.

Wister was pleased with the story. He thought it came
"much closer [to] my notions [than other tales in the series
for *Harper's Monthly*], and as a matter of fact was the most
difficult of the lot, owing to the utterly particular and (to

the reader) unknown historical atmosphere that I had to crack & dissolve as the medium of presentation." Roosevelt wrote Brander Matthews that he considered it "capital" and he advised Wister that he thought it "one of the best things you have written yet." The *Nation* agreed that, but for "a slight defect in construction (a superfluous scene between the captain, his wife, and the surgeon), 'The Second Missouri Compromise' is as good a frontier tale as has ever been written." This objection ignores the larger point of the story, however. As Forrest Robinson has explained, Wister dramatizes in it "the rectitude of federal military intervention in state and local affairs," as in the Johnson County War in 1892 and the Pullman Strike in 1894, when federal troops were mobilized to suppress rebellion. As the captain in Wister's story explains, Governor Ballard "represents the Federal government in this Territory, and Uncle Sam's army is here to protect the Federal government. If Ballard calls on the army it's our business to obey, and if there's any mistake in judgment it's Ballard's, not mine." Wister adds in his own voice that the captain expressed both "sound soldier common-sense" and "equally good law." In context, that is, "The Second Missouri Compromise" indicts sectionalism and defends federalism.

Wister finished the manuscript in September 1894. Alden published the story in *Harper's Monthly* the following March with illustrations by Remington and paid the author $262 for it. Even more happily, Alden released Wister from the constraints of a deadline in which to finish the other two stories promised under the contract. "We leave dates to you and what we are chiefly desirous about is that you have your own way with your stories," he wrote. Or as Wister put it, "The favor I had found with the public by this time gave the Messrs. Harper confidence in me & nothing more satisfactory or encouraging has happened throughout."

The penultimate story Wister contributed under the terms of his Harper's contract was inspired by the dead cows he had seen while traveling through the Southwest the previous spring. He had also witnessed two soldiers rescue a man crazed by thirst as he was about to plunge into a trough "and kill himself drinking water" (or, more correctly, drinking too much water too quickly). He composed "La Tinaja Bonita" (or "the pretty water hole") in November to represent, he insisted, "the lonely horror of this sunshine desert, but the real thing outdoes anything my words can convey." Wister set the story in southern Arizona Territory, a dry landscape with which he was familiar: "From Tucson to Gunsight is 110 miles, and you find water 3 times on the way," he had noted. "From Maricopa to Gunsight there is water once in the 200 miles." Or as he joked in his journal, "In New Mexico and Arizona the rivers die in their beds—indeed they're about the only things that do." The tale features a young, sexually precocious Mexican girl named Lolita who "was a woman," and her erstwhile lover "as yet merely a boy; he was only twenty-two; she was almost sixteen." (Might Vladimir Nabokov have discovered the name of his nymphet in this story? Nabokov was, after all, fond of westerns.) At the close of the tale, Lolita and her gringo admirer Genesmere die at the spring—she from the knife wound he inflicts in his wild thirst, he from drinking too much water too quickly. Alden published "La Tinaja Bonita" in the May 1895 issue of *Harper's Monthly* and paid Wister five hundred dollars. On the whole, Wister was also satisfied with it. "From the beginning of Genesmere's ride across the desert," he wrote his friend Langdon Mitchell, "I have done what I intended." Remington was impressed, too, after reading it in manuscript and agreeing to illustrate it. Wister had depicted Arizona, Remington told him, "just the way [it] is but after its published you can't go down there any more or the real estate fellows will hang you. . . . You have an air tight cinch on the West—others may monkey but you arrive with a horrible crash every pop."

In January 1895, at Remington's behest, Wister dashed off a rump version of "The Course of Empire," the history of the West he had once thought of writing. "The Evolution of the Cow-puncher" may be both the most original and yet most fatuous article he ever published. In it, he theorized that the modern-day cowboy was the evolutionary heir of the Anglo-Saxon knight and nobleman. Both thrived on adventure, "the cardinal surviving fittest instinct." Transplanted to the West, the English nobleman with his superior capacity to adapt to a new environment "quickly learned how to rope a steer. The card habit ran in his noble blood as it did in the cowboy's. He could sleep on the ground and rough it with the best of them, and with the best of them he could drink and help make a town clamorous." In "personal daring and in skill as to the horse, the knight and the cowboy are nothing but the same Saxon of different environments," Wister insisted. The horse was "his foster-brother, his ally, his playfellow, from the tournament at Camelot to the round-up at Abilene." The cowboy's chaps or leather breeches are "next door to armor," the gunfight the modern equivalent of the joust, and the ranch owner was to his hired hands as the feudal baron was to his serfs. As the title and substance of the essay make clear, Wister was an unequivocal proponent of social Darwinism. Implicit in his argument is the notion that stages of evolution exist in parallel waves or gradations east to west across North America or that degrees of longitude might be correlated to degrees of culture and civilization. As he asserted in his journal, "Speaking broadly, you can divide this country . . . into 3 strips—Atlantic to the Appalachian system, civilized and decent[.] Appalachian system to Continental Divide range, half civilized filth. Continental Divide to Pacific, wild but decent."

Unfortunately, he developed two corollaries to his thesis. First, "the cow-puncher, the American descendant of

Saxon ancestors," was "not compatible with Progress" and "is now departed, never to return," except in New Mexico, his "last domain." He has been superseded in the "next stage of Western progress—that unparalleled compound of new hotels, electric lights, and invincible ignorance"—by the populist and advocate of free silver. A sound-money Republican, Wister prayed such a detour from sound monetary policy was only temporary. As he wrote at about the same time but in another context, the West "is like an able but *untrained* man—and therefore continually committing huge follies. Silverism & Populism, for instance. For there were many sincere silverites & populists. And no *books* will ever train the West. No talk or theories. It must burn its own fingers every time"—as when Davis H. Waite, a free silver Democrat, was elected governor of Colorado in 1892. Wister made the same point more succinctly in his journal entry for July 6, 1895: "the bimetallist reasons with almost the precision of the mad dog."

The second corollary to Wister's thesis was even more problematic because it demeaned all non-Anglo-Saxons. The United States was, from his perspective, increasingly "debased and mongrel with its hordes of encroaching alien vermin, that turn our cities to Babels and our citizenship to a hybrid farce, who degrade our commonwealth from a nation into something half pawn-shop, half broker's office." But to "succeed in the clean cattle country requires spirit of adventure, courage, and self-sufficiency." Hence "you will not find many Poles or Huns or Russian Jews" in the West. Wister's ideal cowboy was, as Jane Kuenz observes, "quite explicitly, a pure racial type." Or, according to Mody Boatright, "Wister subscribed wholeheartedly to the myth of Anglo-Saxon racial superiority." No Irish, Jewish, Slavic, Asian American, Latino, African American, or Native American need apply. As if suffering from tunnel vision, Wister almost entirely ignored the pluralism of the region—or to the extent he acknowledged it, he deplored it. Louis Tanner concludes that Wister in this essay "set aside his genuine concern for Western history, choosing instead popular fantasy and political posturing." Still, Alden paid him $150 for it and printed it in the September 1895 issue of *Harper's Monthly*.

It was also illustrated by Remington. When Wister received his copy of the magazine in late August, he was fascinated by one of the drawings—of a cowboy on horseback surrounded by men in medieval dress, some carrying lances. "The Last Cavalier comes home hardest, and I love it & look at it—It's so very sad and so very near my private heart. . . . The Last Cavalier will haunt me forever. He inhabits a Past into which I withdraw and mourn." As his comment suggests, Wister always viewed the West with an imperial gaze and wrote about it in a tone of colonial nostalgia. Remington made Wister a gift of the original drawing of "The Last Cavalier," and to square accounts Wister bought for $255 a Remington painting: "What an Unbranded Cow Has Cost," depicting a pasture scattered with dead and dying men and horses, the aftermath of a gunfight.

In "La Tinaja Bonita," Wister alluded in passing to "the trial of several Mormons for robbing a paymaster." The reference served to advertise the last of the eight stories he had promised to *Harper's Monthly*. "A Pilgrim on the Gila" (working title "A Boom in Tucson"), written in February and March 1895, was based on the Wham payroll robbery. On May 11, 1889, army paymaster Joseph W. Wham and his escort of eleven African American soldiers, known as buffalo soldiers, were ambushed near Pima, Arizona, between Fort Grant and Fort Thomas, and were robbed of more than $28,000 in gold coins after a two-hour gunfight. Several men implicated in the theft were arrested by June 5, but they were acquitted on December 14 after a trial in Tucson, despite overwhelming evidence of their guilt. Much to Wister's chagrin, their lead defense attorney was Marcus A. Smith, the Arizona territorial delegate to Congress.

Frederic Remington, "The Last Cavalier," *Harper's Monthly*, 91 (September 1895).

While visiting Arizona in autumn 1893 and spring 1894 Wister had

> slowly and carefully gathered and jotted down detail after detail, from the lips of commissioned officers, and enlisted men, and civilian dwellers in the vicinity of the robbery; I rode over from Fort Grant to the spot where it occurred, and passed the night in Cedar Springs in order to get the version of the incident which the entertaining master of that road ranch [Barney Norton] had to give.

That is, as he said, his fictionalization of events rested "upon a foundation of concrete fact more extensive than usual." In fact, "my Wham robbery story" is "scarcely a story at all—much more like a narrative of travel. . . . I think the picture it gives of Arizona is faithful." He later asserted that almost every one of the eight stories for *Harper's Monthly* "might be called 'a foot-note to history.'" Roosevelt, a historian by avocation, also judged "Pilgrim on the Gila," Specimen Jones," and "The Second Missouri Compromise" among Wister's "very best" stories and asserted that, in his opinion, "they have a really very high value as historical documents."

Unfortunately, not true. As in several of the tales, Wister skewed the facts in the retelling. He wrote "A Pilgrim on the Gila" with an agenda. He had just read Roosevelt's essay "True American Ideals" in *Forum* for February 1895 when he began the story. There, TR excoriates the "reckless labor agitator" like Debs "who arouses the mob to riot and bloodshed," commends "the admirable action of the Federal Government" in ending the rail strike, and warns of "the lawlessness of the disorderly classes," especially when "they are able to elect their own chiefs to power." Ironically, TR acknowledged to Wister later that he had written the essay "at a white-heat of indignation after the [railway] strike. Funnily enough, the immediate suggestion as to writing it came from a paper by you on the Pennsylvania National Guard in Harper's Weekly." That is, Wister composed "A Pilgrim on the Gila," his own indictment of political corruption, in a kind of echo chamber. It was historical romance, not history, with embellishments and an ideological point of view. Wister also omitted or distorted a couple of significant details. He failed to mention—more evidence of his tunnel vision—that, of the eleven buffalo soldiers in the military escort, two were awarded the Medal of Honor the next year for their bravery in the shootout. He also insinuates that the verdict was the result of a conspiracy among Mormons to acquit Mormon criminals, much as Mark Twain expressed distrust of Mormon juries in *Roughing It*. Wister asserted in his journal that "of the thieves there were only two not Mormons." In fact, none of the defendants was a member of the Church of Jesus Christ of Latter-day Saints.

"A Pilgrim on the Gila" begins as the narrator, pausing in Washington, D.C., en route to the Southwest, visits the U.S. Capitol and hears a debate over Arizona statehood. He listens as the so-called "Boy Orator of the Rio

Grande"—an obvious swipe at William Jennings Bryan, the Nebraskan nicknamed the "Boy Orator of the Platte"—earnestly appeals on behalf of admission. Wister considered Bryan—a leading Democratic politician for decades who was first elected to Congress in 1890—a blowhard if not a demagogue. "As far back as the early nineties," Wister later explained, "I had formed the same opinion of William Jennings Bryan . . . which the ensuing years steadily confirmed." Wister thought the admission of Arizona to the Union nothing more than a ploy by the Democrats to foist "one more silver State upon our Senate."

Upon his arrival in the Southwest, the narrator is assailed by more scoundrels, rapscallions, and ne'er-do-wells than Huck and Jim encounter on the Mississippi River. He is repeatedly offered worthless silver mines for sale. A polygamous Mormon bishop "fixes the county elections and the price of tomatoes," even though he is illiterate—like the real Arizona bishop, according to Wister's narrator, who reportedly had nine wives and dozens of children, "cannot read or write" but "signs government contracts with his mark," and rules the Gila Valley "absolutely and with much commercial wisdom, not allowing his fruit raisers to peddle too often or in competition . . . lest prices should fall." The narrator also meets the corrupt territorial delegate to Congress, Luke Jenks—modeled on the real congressional delegate, Marcus Smith, the defense attorney for the defendants in the Wham trial. Jenks brags about the ease with which he buys votes every election day: "This Territory's so poor they come cheap. Seventy-five cents a head for all the votes I wanted in Bisbee, Nogales, and Yuma."

No wonder, as Wister depicts Arizona, that the Wham robbers were acquitted at trial. Much as Jenks buys votes, the Mormon bishop bribes the jurors with part of the stolen loot. Wister connected the bishop "with the affair entirely from my own imagining," he noted, "really thinking he had nothing to do with it—and I find he played a part not wholly unlike the one I've invented for him." In short, Wister attributed the not guilty verdict to the barbarism of an isolated town on the outskirts of American civilization. "If you would see the 'bad' man to-day," he once advised his readers, "go to the Southwest. It is there he has most flourished, and most survived." Or as he added elsewhere, "The territory of Arizona and New Mexico will always be a desert, except small strips" with much "the same proportion a postage stamp bears to a 10 acre lot." "For the ordinary traveler Tucson is not worth a visit," he wrote in his journal; and in "A Pilgrim on the Gila" he reiterated the point: it "is more than half a Mexican town, and in its crowd upon the platform I saw the gaudy shawls, the ear-rings, the steeple straw hats, the old shriveled cigarette-rolling apes, and the dark-eyed girls." Popular sentiment among the townspeople during the trial "was not only quite against the United States, but a sentiment amounting to hatred was shown against all soldiers. . . . The mildest opinion was that Uncle Sam could afford to lose money better than poor people, and the strongest was that it was a pity the soldiers had not been killed. This seemed inappropriate in a Territory desiring admission to our Union." So much, too, for Frederick Jackson Turner's notions about the democratizing influence of the frontier.

Wister also attacked Smith, the "Delegate to Washington [who] defends these thieves who robbed the United States," in return for the legal fees allegedly paid him in stolen gold. Wister was particularly outraged that, after the verdict was announced, Smith and the defendants

were photographed in a group! I don't think I ever have heard [about] any performance so discreditable through to all concerned as was this robbery. I saw the photograph, a set of average Western unscrupulous faces. The face of Mark Smith, member for Congress

Defendants and counsel in the Wham robbery case (1889). Marcus A. Smith seated, third from left. From James H. McClintock, *Arizona*, vol. 2 (Chicago: Clarke, 1916).

(territorial representative) and defender of thieves against the government he was elected to serve, being not distinguishable in quality from those of the . . . robbers.

Ironically, Wister had not objected at all to the photo of the "Invaders" in the Johnson County War taken shortly after their arrest in 1892. In "A Pilgrim on the Gila," too, Jenks brazenly poses for a group photograph "with his acquitted thieves." In Wister's telling of events, however, Jenks pays a political price for his poltroonery: "A pamphlet appeared with the title, 'What Luke Jenks Has Done for Arizona.' Inside were twenty blank pages, and he failed of re-election." In fact, Marcus Smith was elected to the U.S. House of Representatives eight times, and in 1912 he was elected one of the two original U.S. Senators from new state of Arizona. He remained a fixture in Congress until 1921, three years before his death at the age of seventy-three.

The story appeared with illustrations by Remington in the November 1895 issue of *Harper's Monthly*, and Alden paid Wister $665 for it. The critical response was decidedly mixed, however, depending on the reader's political perspective. Roosevelt wrote Wister, as usual, that he thought the story "A1." The *Brooklyn Eagle* declared that it was "one of the finest arguments that could be advanced against the admission of Arizona as a state," and the *St. Louis Globe-Democrat* affirmed that "it appears quite true to life" to "anybody familiar with methods of justice in Arizona." The Republican Territorial Committee in Arizona even asked permission to reprint it as an anti-Democrat campaign document. On the other hand, the Pima County treasurer wrote Harper's that he considered it "the most outrageously slanderous libel ever uttered against a law abiding people" and implied Wister would not be safe if he returned to the state (so, ironically, reinforcing Wister's portrayal of it). When the November 1895 issue of *Harper's Monthly* reached Arizona, according to the *Boston Times*, "the country was aroused and the brilliant career of Mr. Owen Wister would have been closely nipped, and he would in all probability have dangled at the end of a rope, had he ventured into that land of sunshine." The *Cincinnati Tribune* remarked that, as the result of "A Pilgrim on the Gila," Wister was "about as cordially hated a man as this country fosters." Fifteen years later, the story still so rankled an editor in Arizona that he referred to Wister as an "assassin."

3

1895–1897

On May 9, 1895, a month after completing the manuscript of "A Pilgrim on the Gila" but six months prior to its publication, Wister returned to the Southwest via New Orleans. He had been invited to visit Apache Tejo, a ranch a few miles southeast of Silver City and Fort Bayard, New Mexico, by the young ranch superintendent, Dean Duke. Wister and Duke had been introduced via mail by a mutual friend, Lansing Kellogg, a San Francisco businessman. "We have the largest herd and ranges of any outfit in this Territory & Arizona," Duke assured Wister, "and I have the jolliest and best working lot of cowboys in the West." He urged Wister to "come out and share bed and beans with me." On May 13, Wister rendezvoused with Duke in El Paso and discovered that the superintendent, despite his youth, was "a man of superlative humor. . . . When we were in the train again he kept the smoking compartment in a steady roar of laughter with his reminiscences of his not yet very long life." One night while camping and sightseeing in the region, Wister and Duke heard gunfire in the hills nearby, and both of them grabbed their rifles. "I have never been so frightened as that before, and am glad to know the sensation, though I hope it will not be repeated," Wister reported. (Years later, he admitted that he had "met no dangers worthy of the name" during his many travels in the

West. It was hardly the Wild West.) On May 31, he joined Duke at Apache Tejo. Though isolated, it was "a little oasis of hay field, cottonwoods, a spring, and some flowers and grass in front of the adobe house."

During Wister's twelve days there, his first extended stay at a ranch since his visit to the VR in 1885, he seems to have remained indoors most of the time, probably because he was ill. Nearly sixty years later, in April 1953, foreman Henry Brock reminisced into an open microphone with an oral historian about Wister's visit. His memories were remarkably accurate, if not in all details: "He [Wister] was small, brown-eyed, right small and really when he was here he was delicate. He had a Boston accent, you know, something like an Englishman. . . . And he wasn't active and lively, you know, he was kinda quiet, a studious like fella." During target practice with clay pigeons, Wister "seldom ever hit one but he kept shootin' at 'em. . . . He just didn't leave the house. He wasn't one of them to get out and prowl around. He didn't leave the place and mix up any at all," though Wister and Duke spent time in Cow Springs, Fort Bayard, Silver City, Separ, and Deming. Brock noted that Wister missed an opportunity to learn more about ranching during his visit. Though "a thousand or two head watered there at Apache," Wister never wrote "much about the cattle business" because "he doesn't know about it."

In his journal, Wister recorded the results of some of his shooting matches with Duke. The superintendent was "truly an admirable shot—hitting clay pigeons with a rifle bullet 4 in 5—and with shotgun 28 in 30." On the other hand, Duke paid Wister a faint compliment, telling him that "I could be a good shot in two months. . . . This remark after seeing me and my hits and misses for a week." Later, he conceded that he was "dreadful with a shotgun. Must correct this. No excuse except I've never gone at it. I shot pretty well (considering) at Duke's down in New Mexico."

As in the case of Charles Skirdin, moreover, Duke "did and said things which reminded me of the Virginian," Wister recounted in his journal. Wister had "never met any man so young—he's but 27—who has passed through so many desperate chances." At fifteen Duke had left home; at eighteen, he was "a riding-boss on the Owyee, and the boys began referring to me as 'the old man' and I've been a boss and referred to as 'the old man' ever since." Duke also forbade liquor on the ranches he managed and "lived up to all the rules I made for the men." Duke mentioned another incident when he risked his life to keep order. Whereas his predecessor at Apache Tejo paid the cowboys in cash that they splurged on binges in town, Duke began to pay his employees by checks they deposited in a bank. As a result, they "spent money no longer in town in saloons—but bought things" from mail-order catalogues. The saloon owners in Deming, losing business, conspired to hire a gunman to kill Duke. The gunman got a job at Apache Tejo—"ugly eye, Duke noticed"—and suspecting "something was wrong" Duke asked him about his riding skills. Duke "traps him" into

> bragging in a manner that antagonizes the cowboys who gather round to listen. Next morning Duke puts him on a bad horse which bucks him off—He complains. Cowboys derisive—He says nothing and nobody could ride that horse. Duke calls Henry Brock. Brock rides horse—whips him all round—Cowboys down on this braggart—his quarrel is with *them* now and not with Duke and they practically run him out of camp.

On June 11 Wister left Apache Tejo to continue his journey. The visit had been "a delightful success—I have enjoyed every minute, almost, and gather much valuable and original matter. Duke as a host is the rival of an army officer—and I can't say anything stronger."

He had finished his research in the Southwest and did not return there for more than fifteen years. "My journeys in search of material will never take me here again," as he noted in his journal. After the publication of "A Pilgrim on the Gila," he also became *persona non grata* in the region. Nor would he ever again keep such detailed journals of his trips west as he had to this date. "I have gathered enough from the Sulphur Spring and Gila Valleys, and I prefer to let Grant be a closed chapter, a pleasant memory." He traveled by train from Deming through Tucson to Los Angeles and San Francisco, a stretch of rail he knew well. "It's truly comical," he noted, "how familiar this piece of the Southern Pacific between Willcox and Deming, 3000 miles from home, has become to me."

He planned to devote as much time as necessary to researching the history of Wells Fargo, the project he had deferred for a year. But when he returned to San Francisco "something had happened! New powers sat in command, the archives were no longer at my disposal. I was assured indirectly that this change was due to nothing personal." Like "Chalkeye" and "The Course of Empire," "The Romance of a Corporation" died aborning, and he suddenly had no new project to replace it. As he explained to a stringer for the *New York Tribune* in his room at the Palace Hotel a few days later, he often feared

that my stories of Western life may grow dull and unalluring, that is, that the public may get tired of that kind of matter. But I can't write anything else. I have become permeated with it, and it is a part of me. In many stories I invent very little. There is no need of it. I have long held that there was so much of the strange, even the marvelous, in the real life of the far West, that there is no need of using much fiction. Some change of setting, perhaps, with details altered to serve the leading idea in the story is all that is required.

But then a revelation: Wister was contemplating a serialized novel about the Bannock Indian War of 1878 in Idaho and Oregon. "There is a great fund of fact, romance and detail of various sorts in the subject," he said. "To me the

Bannocks seem very interesting." He was contemplating a sequel to "The General's Bluff," in which E-egante saves Specimen Jones's life "when the hostile Bannocks were planning his immediate death as a spy." At first planned as a short story, the idea had grown over time into the germ of a novel. "This history of E-egante bothers me," he explained to Edwards. He wanted "to do that [subject] all the justice that's in my power, and I find licking it into shape will need a lot of consideration."

The remainder of the trip was devoted to recreation, not research. The last week of June he camped in Yosemite National Park. He spent the last three weeks of July in Colorado, mostly in the area around Boulder, Fort Logan, Long's Peak, and Estes Park, though he thought the park, while "beautiful," so easily accessible from Denver that it was more playground than wilderness. It was overrun "with tourists, campers, fishermen, and bicyclists. Twenty years ago, bear, elk, sheep, and deer were all that knew this spot familiarly. Now it is a resort." In early August, he arrived in Cheyenne "for a day or two to see Barber and my other friends there." On the one hand, he admitted, "I miss Wind River more keenly than ever. I found myself gazing like a fool down the track of the Union Pacific stretching westward towards Rawlins." On the other, he was struck by the poverty in Cheyenne, "a town over which the sadness of glory departed [Wister again invokes biblical metaphor] hangs more thickly each time that I revisit it. It is depressing to see a place that began so prosperously & to talk with the quiet disillusioned remnant of dwellers who recall the better days—days only 10 years ago, and yet of an era as absolutely gone forever as the Revolution." Wister wanted to end his novel about Lin McLean and the Virginian in Cheyenne but was uncertain how to do it: "It certainly is my mission to record Cheyenne at length—But how end a novel *decrescendo*? All the first part would have to be vitality and riot and youth and promise—how can a chilly end come after that? Must somehow leave my people happily married & settled and if chastened & regretful, still *content*." He never solved the problem; instead, he abandoned it. Neither *Lin McLean* nor *The Virginian* concludes in Cheyenne.

By early October, back in Philadelphia, Wister was behind in his promised writing due to illness. Albert Bigelow Paine contacted him to solicit a story for the Bacheller newspaper syndicate but Wister demurred. "My present hope," he replied, "is to be able sometime during the Winter" to send him a manuscript, but under the circumstances he expected it "to be rather a short one—5000 words; and it seems more distant now than it did." In any event, "I have some things to complete for Harper's Magazine which take precedence over all else." While he was no longer contractually obligated to write exclusively for Harpers, he continued to do so under the terms of an unwritten understanding.

First on the list was a story featuring Lin McLean written in the Dickensian mode. The editor of *Harper's Weekly*, Henry Loomis Nelson, had solicited a tale from him for the special Christmas issue of the magazine. "Didn't think I could. Was afraid," Wister admitted. "It's been done so well by so many great ones—and I did not want to be cheap and imitative. So I've tried to play my own original little tune on the C major Christmas chord. We shall see what they say." He was pleased with the result. "I think myself it's a proper Christmas story," he noted on October 16. "It was written with conviction & at times I believed in it so much that I was almost tearful myself over the pathos! The risk one runs is of slopping on these occasions of sentiment." Still, his sleight-of-hand was rarely more clumsy than in "A Journey in Search of Christmas" (working title "His Own Family"), a contrived and sentimental tale in which Lin McLean travels alone to Denver for the holidays and by accident encounters Tommy Lusk, a "street Arab" and son of Katie and Jim Lusk, who has run away from home to escape the beatings of his "debauched and shiftless parents." It was one of the few stories of the West that Wister did not base on a historical source. By its conclusion Lin has predictably adopted li'l Tommy and brought him to board at Sunk Creek. Despite its rough edges, Nelson ran it in the Christmas issue of *Harper's Weekly* and paid Wister $420 or thirty-five dollars per thousand words for it.

Before writing any additional western stories for the *Monthly*, Wister polished the prose in the eight he had already published under contract, to prepare for their collection in a book. He asked his friend Harry Mercer for advice, and Mercer "helped me more than anyone by adverse criticism." Still, all the stories were written "with joyous faith," Wister assured Langdon Mitchell, "& in a period that is sealed like a vault; and to me today it no longer represents Art bad or good, but autobiography, a story of expeditions into the unknown & home comings with trophies brought to people who are no more." In retrospect, to be sure, he suffered a few reservations. "Little Big Horn Medicine," through "inexperience, is not done worthy of the material, & to me now seems a pulpy & blurred piece of work with patches of better here & there." "Specimen Jones" he would "not change, though if written now it would be closer & better cadenced." "The General's Bluff" was "first class material," though "not enough distilled into fiction." "Salvation Gap" and "The Serenade at Siskiyou" were "scarcely done at all & were compelled to be hastily written; the Serenade is thin even to burlesque in places." But he was generally pleased with "The Second Missouri Compromise," "La Tinaja Bonita," and especially "A Pilgrim on the Gila," particularly "up to the trial; from that to the end" it fell below his expectations. "I was probably too much swamped by actuality, & in the contemplation of fact forgot truth."

Illustrated by Remington and dedicated to Mercer, the collection *Red Men and White* was issued by Harper &

Brothers on November 8, almost simultaneously with Bret Harte's *In a Hollow of the Hills* and in time for the holiday season. The critics almost unanimously hailed Wister as a disciple of the W. D. Howells school of realists. The *Review of Reviews*, for example, commended the "intense realism" of the stories; the *Buffalo Express* similarly declared them "intensely realistic, yet as romantic as Dumas"; the *Philadelphia Bulletin* claimed they were "faithfully photographic"; the *Boston Herald* asserted that they were written "with all the characteristic color of reality"; and the *St. Paul Daily Globe* pronounced them "reliable sketches of the Western frontier." Wister's "cowboys, soldiers and Indians are real," averred the *New York World*, "and one cannot but recognize the fact that they are drawn from [his] personal observations and experiences." Robert Bridges (aka "Droch") declared in *Life* that Wister "succeeded in making his scenes very real and very picturesque. Those who have lived the life say that his local color is correct." Nancy Huston Banks averred in *Bookman* that Wister might be "the first [author] to bring the real red man into fiction," and the *Chicago Inter-Ocean* asserted that he had "skillfully reproduced" the "peculiar Western dialect." (Ironically, Wister spurned the suggestion that he faithfully recorded the western idiom. "I do not believe much in dialect," he once told David Graham Phillips. "It should be indicated—a word here and there" such as "seh" for "sir" or "Yawk" for "York." He was hardly as systematic in the reproduction of regional speech as Mark Twain in *Adventures of Huckleberry Finn*.) Wister seems to have taken umbrage at only one critic, the reviewer for the *New York Express*, who lumped him together with "some other wretches" who allegedly imitated Howells "without his subtlety and with his defects."

The collection of tales also earned praise from several of Wister's friends. As each of the stories appeared in *Harper's Monthly*, Wister remembered, Theodore Roosevelt "used to say when we met, or write when we did not, Keep on."

Upon the publication of the collection, TR congratulated the author and hoped that he would "have the chance to review it. I feel that Remington and myself are almost the only men who can review your work as it should be reviewed." At the time superintendent of the New York City Police Department, Roosevelt was soon granted his wish. He opined in *Harper's Weekly* that Wister "may almost be said to have turned a new page in that form of contemporary historical writing which consists in the vivid portrayal, once for all, of types that should be commemorated. No better work of the kind has ever been done than that which Mr. Wister is now doing." Rudyard Kipling, whom Wister had met over dinner at Roosevelt's home in Washington, D.C., on April 5, 1895, privately congratulated Wister: "Your red men have come in and it is in my mind that they will go very far." The tales "are all good—really, honestly, truly." While in London early in 1896, Wister visited his mother's friend Henry James, whom he had known since the age of twelve and who discussed the stories with Wister in "minute" detail. James informed Sarah Wister that the collection had "in its vivid erudition great merit of form and . . . a wealth of adventurous observation and experience that I can only wistfully envy."

For his part, however, Howells was but slightly impressed. He was troubled by the tone of some of the tales, which smacked of melodrama. He lamented the "blue-fire" theatrics that "this most promising writer" was "fond of burning" and the "lingering traits of romanticism" in his style. Wister was utterly unconcerned whether or not he passed Howells's litmus test. As he wrote Langdon Mitchell, "It seems of moment to some people what of all this is 'true' & what 'invented.' I cannot talk very intelligently to such people, & certainly you are remote from that breed. Salvation Gap was pure invention, The Serenade of Siskiyou almost pure fact: where is the difference?" Unfortunately, the collection did not enjoy commercial success. During its first eight months in print it sold only about three thousand copies, and Harpers paid Wister only $366 in royalties. Sales had so decreased by the first six months of 1897 that Harpers owed Wister only $25. Obviously, he could not yet afford to abandon the law for a full-time literary career.

But *Red Men and White* won Wister at least one new enthusiastic fan. The popular western author Hamlin Garland wrote soon after its publication to ask if Wister planned to visit "New York within a few days—if you are I should like to see you. Your stories interest me very much and I'd like a chat concerning them." He offered to exchange an autographed copy of his recent book, *Prairie Songs*, for an inscribed copy of *Red Men and White*. Though Wister had read Garland's *Main-Travelled Roads* (1891) with pleasure, he refused at the time to meet the author. On January 4, 1896, Garland wrote him again.

> I am sorry I am not to see you. I wanted to get at your point of view. I became tremendously interested in the Pueblo peoples this summer and my childhood was spent near the Chippewas and Sioux. I have always taken a deep interest in these mysterious people but now that I comprehend them to some degree they take on great interest. I hope you'll be just to them always and without sentiment. . . . Do you ever come through Chicago[?] If you do let me know.

Before the end of the month, Garland wrote him a third letter—this one still more patronizing:

> I have finished your book which has confirmed me in my original impression of your power and definiteness of statement. I like it all exceedingly though there are points which touch me unpleasantly. "Medicine" and "E-egante" I knew before, "Specimen Jones" I did not know. He is a "corker" surely. Of course I can't afford to take on any airs of chief adviser but I would like to see you get in

a little near the heart of things—and I believe you will. There is
power of an unusual sort in these yarns and they all come close to
me. I have been on the ground of some of them.

Wister must have bit his tongue in composing his reply.
"I beg to thank you for your letter," he wrote. "Beside and
beyond the tempered approval of one's acquaintance, it
remains always a surprise to receive this from strangers as
well." But to judge from a comment he scribbled in the
margin of Garland's letter it is clear their admiration was
not mutual.

> I am a little ashamed of this treatment of a friendly intentioned
> person. But in spite of his unusual talent, his writings have been
> my bane since long before I ever thought of writing, and the igno-
> rance and bad taste which offended me in them upset me discredit-
> ably when he began his fond and didactic intrusions. I sent him a
> volume and was polite for twice & then . . . ! I had asked him for
> his opinions and should never have ventured to comment on the
> volume he sent me.

Wister mailed a copy of his correspondence with Garland to Kipling and asked for his impressions, and Kipling
responded in high dudgeon. Garland

> is I fear, my brother, a plain's plain common *ass* and for such there
> is no hope. . . . God has deprived him of Humour: he has put aside
> the one gift of the Devil which is style: he can't see things except
> according to the borrowed lights of his stale three-cent provincial
> reading. . . . He will die, fat and prosperous, beloved from Osh-
> kosh to Centralia for his "acute mentality," and his "truly national
> type of true-souled, hard minded outlook." Then I will dance on
> his grave. Truly, for a man who never did me harm he can make me
> almost rather annoyed.

In his defense, Garland was congenial when he finally met
Wister personally in New York the next year. "I found him
a self-contained young man," Garland remembered, "not

unlike Roosevelt in physical bulk, a sturdy, broad-shouldered individual with a peculiarly firm clip of mouth. I took satisfaction in his manly vigor and his genial personality."

As part of the promotion of *Red Men and White*, Wister agreed to be interviewed for the Bacheller Syndicate by Arthur Stedman, son of the poet E. C. Stedman. It was one of the longest interviews ever granted by Wister and it was printed in newspapers across the country, including the New York *Commercial Advertiser*, Philadelphia *Press*, *Dallas Morning News*, Denver *Rocky Mountain News*, and the *San Francisco Examiner*. In it, Wister praised westerners for their kindness and interest in national issues—in contrast to easterners.

> If you go to Chicago or San Francisco, or wherever the centers of population are, you will find that most people you talk with are familiar with things in New York and the east, and are interested to know what New York and other large eastern cities are doing, while, on the other hand, when you return from western regions to New York and Philadelphia, people in those cities seem very much less concerned with other parts of the country and are most concerned with their own immediate surroundings and life.

He acknowledged that he had hunted and "killed every species of big game in the Rocky mountains except the mountain lion," though he had "also missed every species of big game in the Rocky mountains, including the lion." As for his favorite western locale: "I have been out west fifteen different times now, and for the purpose of pleasure I find the country of Wyoming and the Wind river mountains more beautiful and more full of fish and game than anywhere else I have been." If possible, he planned to "return next summer to hunt, just as I have done in the past."

With the novel featuring both Lin and the Virginian still in mind, Wister finally returned to the manuscript of "The Bear Creek Barbeque" in November 1895 when, as he put it, he wholly revised the "shapeless bungle." He scribbled on the draft of his revision, "Owing to the added experience of two years and a half, scarce a phrase of the original [manuscript] stands in the new" version, which he titled "Children All" or "Concerning Children." The only snippet of dialogue from the first draft that survives in the second is Miss Wood's demand that the Southern cavalier be formally introduced to her before she will waltz with him. In the revision, Lin's suit is squelched before it begins. "I tried to kiss" the schoolmarm, Lin tells the Virginian, but she stopped him in his tracks. Wister again refers to the threat of fencing the range: "What with women and children and wire fences, this country would not long be a country for men." The baby-swap recurs, but in general the changes in the story are more significant than the similarities between the drafts. Miss Wood is given the same nickname as Wister's distant cousin Mary (Molly) Channing Wister, a member of his piano quartet whom he had begun to court. As Christine Bold observes, "the more involved [he] became with Molly Wister . . . the more closely he aligned the two Mollys." Wister was quick to give Molly Wood a backstory and pedigree as distinguished as Molly Wister's. Molly Wister was descended from William Ellery, a signer of the Declaration of Independence; the fictional Miss Wood is the great-granddaughter of Molly Stark, the wife of John Stark, a hero of the American Revolution. Wister in fact was acquainted with a granddaughter of John Stark who lived in the old family mansion in Dunbarton, Vermont. He also added a prelude to the story, eventually printed in *The Virginian* under the chapter title "The Spinster Meets the Unknown," in which Molly Stark, with "Independence and Grandmother Stark shining in her eye" departs Vermont for the West. The hero saves her from a dunking when her stage overturns at South Fork Crossing while en route to Bear Creek, so when she arrives at the barbeque half a year later she recognizes him. "He had pulled her out of the water once, and he had been her unrewarded knight," as Wister noted in the manuscript. The characterization was consistent with Wister's comparison of the cowboy and the English gentry in "The Evolution of the Cow-puncher." In a snippet of dialogue that survives in Wister's notebook but was omitted from the revision, moreover, Molly brags that she has traveled from New Hampshire "unescorted two thousand miles. . . . And never as much as twenty from home before. And you'll have to be scandalized, but I'd do it right over again tomorrow!"

To this mix of characters Wister adds "a man called Trampas" (Spanish for "treason" or "deceit"). Wister had mentioned a card shark with a suspicious past named Link Trampas in his aborted novel "Chalkeye" (1891), and he had referred to a cattle thief named Sorgy Trampas in the original "Balaam and Pedro," but a character named Trampas did not appear on stage until "Concerning Children." Wister modeled him on a Wyoming saddle tramp named Black Henry Smith, whom he had met in 1891 and who was, he avowed in his journal, "the only unabridged 'bad man' I have ever had a chance to know." Smith would soon be arrested twice for separate crimes, according to Darwin Payne: trying to burn down the Fort McKinney barracks with kerosene and murdering from ambush a special United States marshal. In both cases he was freed for lack of evidence. He was originally from Texas, Wister noted,

and pronounces Spanish very prettily. He has been 'run out' of every country he has resided in. His last coup was some eighteen months ago to persuade his friend Russell to borrow money from every man he knew and take him traveling to foreign parts on the proceeds. They disappeared suddenly. When Smith returned here this Spring he had been to South America and all over Europe. He could come back because it was not he who borrowed the money. Russell's whereabout is not known. Smith is at present stealing cattle, or, more politely, mavericking. . . . A tall, long-nosed dark fellow, with a shock of straight black hair on end, all over his head. Blue overalls tucked into boots of the usual high-heeled pattern, and a slouchy waistcoat. He is so tall he bends down over almost everyone as he talks, and he has a catching but sardonic smile. His voice is unpleasant, very rasping, though not overloud. The great thing is his eyes. They are of a mottled yellow, like agate or half-clear amber, large and piercing, at times burning with light. They are the very worst eyes I have ever looked at. Perfectly fearless and shrewd, and treacherous. . . . He is just bad through and through, without a scruple and without an affectation. His face is entirely cruel, and you hear cruelty in his voice. How do I know all this? Because I know something of his past & present, and I have heard him speak for himself. He has attended to scores of men and woman in his talk and never to one without a corrosive sneer. When I come to . . . my book about Wyoming—I shall strain my muscles to catch Smith.

When Trampas speaks disrespectfully of Molly at the Swinton barbeque, the Virginian calls him out: "Get on your lags, you pole-cat, and say you're a liar." Thus the dual plots of Wister's 1902 novel begin to merge: the love story of the Virginian and Molly and the hate story of the Virginian and the villain.

As Alden had recommended, Wister also inserted a follow-up to the events at the barbeque when, the next day, a Sunday, the Virginian calls on Molly at her cabin on Sunk Creek. As they verbally spar, Wister hints at Molly's atavism: "Grandmother Stark flashed awake immediately" in her soul. The quarrel ends when the Virginian tells Molly, "You're going to love me before we get through." This more elaborate version of "The Bear Creek Barbeque" satisfied Alden, who paid Wister three hundred dollars for it and printed it in the March 1896 issue of *Harper's Monthly*. He insisted on changing the title, however, to "Where Fancy Was Bred," from a riddle in Shakespeare's *The Merchant of*

Venice: "Tell me where fancy is bred, / Or in the heart or in the head?"

Wister began "Separ's Vigilante" (working titles "Lin's Second Venture" and "The Sister of Pennewell"), in which Lin woos a working-class Southern belle, in February 1896, shortly before his father's death on February 24. Owen Jones Wister left his wife an estate estimated at $80,000 and an annual income of about $4,550, adequate for her needs but not quite sufficient to maintain her in the style to which she had become accustomed. On doctor's orders, moreover, his grieving son laid aside the manuscript of his newest story. On July 18, apparently for medical reasons, the younger Wister left Philadelphia four days after his thirty-sixth birthday for his thirteenth trip to the mountain West. He was joined by the architect Grant La Farge and the physician Jack Mitchell, son of Weir and brother of Langdon. They arrived in Wyoming on July 20 and dined that evening at the Cheyenne Club with U.S. Senator Francis E. Warren, former chief counsel for the Wyoming Stock Growers' Association. A few days later they met George West at Dubois for a hunt in the Wind River country. Little more is known about the trip—Wister did not keep a full diary—except that in September, while in camp at Jackson's Hole, Wister wrote "The Passing of Ute Jack," subsequently reprinted under the better-known title "Napoleon Shave-Tail." Joseph H. Sears, editor of *Harper's Round Table*, had been pestering Wister "to write adventures and Indians" for the weekly juvenile magazine for the past year, but Wister had hitherto begged off because he didn't think he had the time. With comic irony, Wister tells of a callow and arrogant officer, a recent graduate of West Point, who, when he is appointed quartermaster, obsessively counts the horseshoes and belt buckles in the fort inventory. "As far as war is to be mastered on paper, his equipment was full," as the narrator observes, and the officer is variously nicknamed "Baby Bismarck," "Colonel Safetypin," and "Napoleon Shave-Tail" by the other soldiers. In the dénouement, he has a howitzer hauled a mile from the fort to the Indian agency to blast a single Indian out of a teepee, only to discover that the Indian is already dead. The story appeared in the *Round Table* for December 29, 1896, and Wister was paid a hundred dollars for it.

Wister, La Farge, Mitchell, and West visited Yellowstone National Park in September, and Wister afterwards left from Cinnabar for the return east. He resumed work on "Separ's Vigilante" in October and finished it in November. At about eighteen thousand words, the tale is some five times the length of "The Winning of the Biscuit-Shooter." In the story, the Virginian—whose courtship of the gentle Miss Wood is contrasted with Lin's love for the pleasant Jessamine Buckner—again appears in passing. Wister based the tale on events in the Southwest that he had recorded in his journal the previous year. In the story, the town of Separ is vaguely located in Wyoming. Lin might pass through it on his way to Riverside. In fact, Separ is in the Playas Valley of New Mexico about an hour west of Deming. A rail town, it was, as Wister described it, a "forlorn spot like all the others. Some sidings, off the long straight endless main line that merely goes out of sight over a hill." Dean Duke's "cowboys used to shoot playfully about the station and express office at Separ. So the Co[mpany] removed the agent and replaced him by a competent young woman. There was no more shooting," exactly as in the story. Like Molly Stark Wood and most other women in Wister's fiction, Jessamine is a civilizing influence. On May 17, Wister and Duke "visited the young lady express agent at Separ" who maintained order without formal legal authority and who became the model for Lin's *femme ideal*.

Like the Virginian in the original version of "Em'ly," Lin complains in "Separ's Vigilante" that wire fencing was threatening the cowboys' livelihood, just as fishing nets on the Columbia River later destroyed salmon runs. That is, the dispute between cattle ranchers and homesteaders simmers just below the surface. Wister revises the arc of his narrative in a nominal way: he changes the name of Judge Henny (who owned the deranged hen Em'ly) to Judge Henry, apparently in honor of Patrick Henry, a herald of the American Revolution. Like Miss Wood, that is, Judge Henry is a throwback to the generation of the Founders. The story also ends with a complication: Jessamine learns by accident that Lin "has a wife livin,'" the trollop Katie Lusk, and so cannot marry her. Alden paid Wister six hundred dollars for the tale and it appeared in the March 1897 issue of *Harper's Monthly.*

Almost immediately, during the last two weeks of November, Wister wrote another installment in the saga of the Virginian and Molly Wood. In "Grandmother Stark" (working titles "The Virginian's Romance" and "Love Among the Alkali") he repaired a loose end that had been dangling for nearly three years by having Molly rescue her lover from the Indians who shoot him in "Balaam and Pedro." The story takes its title from the miniature portrait of her grandmother that Molly hangs on the wall of her cabin at Sunk Creek and to which she occasionally appeals "for support across the hundred years between them." As the tale opens, the Virginian takes his leave from her. In a line later deleted, he explains that he has "branding and a heap o' things to see to oveh in our country." (As many critics have noted, *The Virginian* is a cowboy novel without any cows. Wister might have included cattle-driving scenes, as in this chapter, so the omission seems deliberate.) On her part, Molly has planned to escape from Sunk Creek and return to Vermont rather than marry below her station. Before she leaves, however, she discovers the hero's near-lifeless body, helps him to her cabin, and in the spirit of her grandmother nurses him back to health. She remembers, from "The Winning of the Biscuit-Shooter," that he once told her that "cow-punchers don't live long enough to get old." Molly's ata-vism, like Judge Henry's, illustrates the renewed spirit of the Founders on the frontier. In the course of the romance she becomes a virtual reincarnation of her grandmother. As John Cawelti concludes, "Wister suggests that the West is not entirely a new cultural experience, but a rebirth of the revolutionary generation's vigor." The tale ends with the Virginian and Molly professing their love. Much as Lin meets his soul mate in "Separ's Vigilante," the Virginian and Molly "plight their troth" in "Grandmother Stark," published in *Harper's Monthly* in June 1897 and for which he was paid $350.

During the second two weeks of December 1896, Wis-ter finally wrote a piece about Deming, New Mexico, and its "whimsical history." The previous May, he had jotted this note in his journal: "What a familiar spot on this broad surface of the Earth Deming is growing to be to me! At best 3000 miles from home, and a forlorn wind parched hole." The next month, he wrote his mother: "I wish I were like Charles Dickens. For then I should write a whole long book about Deming." Founded in 1881 by Charles Crocker of the Southern Pacific Railroad, Deming was ini-tially promoted by real estate developers as the next great rail center in the country and, in fact, it was briefly a minor rail hub, the junction of the Southern Pacific and the Atchi-son, Topeka & Santa Fe. Wister passed through the town, renamed Sharon in the story, repeatedly between 1893 and 1895. By then it was in fast decay; as he observed, "Sharon has an immense future behind it." The two rail companies refused to coordinate their schedules, and as a result

eastern consumptives bound for southern California get left here. . . . Symptoms of neighboring Mexico basked on the sand heaps along Sharon's spacious avenues—little torpid, indecent gnomes in sashes and open rags, with crowning-steeple straw hats, and murder dozing in their small black eyes. They might have crawled from holes in the sand, or hatched out of brown cracked pods on some weeds that trailed through the broken bottles, the old shoes, and the wire fences.

Wister based "Sharon's Choice" (working titles "Vox Populi" and "Deming's Choice") on a true story told him by a pair of former members of the local School Committee. Though the official judges of the annual school declamation contest name a young girl the winner, the citizens of Sharon prefer to award the prize

> to a small boy in spite of his speaking like nothing at all—voted it tumultuously over the heads of the appointed judges, upsetting their decision, because the small boy's father had recently left town with a voluptuous Mexican and the family cash; still more recently his mother had turned out to be a dope fiend; his aunt, who had taken him to raise, had the personality of a decayed tooth; and only two days before the prize speaking the boy had experimented with the couplings of a freight train and parted with three of his fingers.

The town nearly erupts in a "feud" because of the disagreement over who wins the contest. Alden published the story, illustrated by Remington's rival A. B. Frost, in *Harper's Monthly* for August 1897 and paid Wister two hundred dollars for it.

In mid-January 1897, Wister finally began the story he had promised the Bacheller Syndicate the previous October. For a week, from January 19 to 25, he worked on "The Jimmyjohn Boss" ("jimmyjohn" a corruption of "demijohn") about Dean Duke (renamed Dean Drake) and his no-drinking rule at Apache Tejo. The opening pages feature a pair of Jewish drummers traveling by stagecoach—and an anti-Semitic subtext. Wister referred in these paragraphs to the "two bulging Jews" and how "the Jews broke into clamorous snarling" and "the Jews cackled maliciously."

After he submitted the initial pages of manuscript to the Bacheller editors for their approval, he was told to stop "because the Jew is forbidden ground in Syndicate fiction." He began the story over "without Jews" on February 1 and changed the setting from western Oregon near Portland to southern Idaho near the town of "Silver City." Much as "Separ's Vigilante" seems to be set in Wyoming though the real town of Separ is in New Mexico, "The Jimmyjohn Boss" seems to be set in Idaho though the real town of Silver City is in New Mexico.

Whereas in truth the "saloon element" in Deming had hired a gunman to kill Duke for discouraging his employees from binge drinking in town, in Wister's version of events the cowboys in Duke/Drake's employ conspire to kill him for forbidding them to drink on the ranch. Although Wister was opposed to prohibition, he made an exception for cowpunchers. Max Vogel, the "biggest cattle man on the Pacific slope," modeled on Henry Miller, the German-American cattle baron, urges Drake to forbid "one drop of whiskey at the whole place." But a peddler smuggles whiskey to the cowhands, who in their stupor plot to kill their "boy superintendent." Drake reads "his buccaroos like the children that they were" and punishes them by, in effect, sending them to separate rooms. He divides them among many ranches owned by Vogel in order to "stir you in with decenter blood." The double entendre is deliberate: Drake both decenters them and introduces them to more decent ranch hands. According to G. Edward White, Dean Drake is "a pivotal figure in the development of Wister's protagonists" because he was committed to his employer's interests and preserving the social order. Or as John Cobbs adds, "In whatever form they appear, the authoritarians have Wister's unqualified approval"—except for Mormon clergy, as in "A Pilgrim on the Gila."

Despite Wister's efforts to tailor the story to the specifications of the Bacheller Syndicate, "The Jimmyjohn Boss" was originally published not in newspapers but in *Pocket Magazine* for June 1897. Duke wrote to congratulate Wister after reading the story: "That part where 'Vogel'-Miller was delighted because his 'boy' was safe is simply be-you-ti-ful." Tired of the "butterfly existence" of managing Apache Tejo, Duke had resigned in February 1896 and moved to California. He updated Wister on the sad fate of "the jolliest and best working lot of cowboys in the West," as he had once styled them. "Our poor old cowboy outfit in New Mexico went wrong—most of them are in jail now. Most of the outfit got mixed up in a train robbery and then got 'ketched.' . . . Those were a mighty good lot of boys that I had together in New Mexico, but they needed the right man to say 'Don't' occasionally and then back it up"—exactly as in Wister's story.

Two tables of contents for the novel about Lin McLean and the Virginian survive among Wister's notebooks. The first, compiled sometime after November 1895 and before November 1896, lists eleven stories in this order: "Em'ly," "How Lin McLean Went East," "Where Fancy Was Bred," "The Winning of the Biscuit-Shooter," "Balaam and Pedro," "Grandmother Stark," "Lin McLean's Honeymoon," "A Journey in Search of Christmas," "Separ's Vigilante," "Destiny at Drybone," and "With Malice Aforethought." The final two stories remained to be written. The second table of contents, compiled after November 1896 and before March 1897, lists twelve stories in substantially the same order, adding at the beginning "Hank's Woman," which introduces "Lin the young barbarian." In March 1897, however, Wister decided his decision to publish "a novel with both Lin McLean and the Virginian as the chief characters" was impractical. It "would be too long," he concluded, so he separated the narratives. As Neal Lambert speculates, Lin "became less and less satisfactory as a central figure" because he "was too much a Westerner, too much the vernacular hero and thus too subversive to many of Wister's own values." Richard Etulain echoes the point: "Wister is reluctant to allow Lin to become civilized." Lin was, according to White, "a perpetual adolescent, a fool for women, and a hopeless vagabond." In other words, he was a comic character who wasn't very funny, even an occasional target of Wister's condescension and satire, unlike the Virginian, who typifies popular faith in individualism and the beneficence of nature as well as commitment to civil order and social progress.

Later in March 1897 Wister updated his editors at Harper & Brothers on his publishing plans. At the time he had three books in progress—two novels and another collection of short stories. He submitted a proposal and most of the material for his novel *Lin McLean*—including two tales in which both the Virginian and Lin appear, "The Winning of the Biscuit-Shooter" and "Separ's Vigilante." He also listed the stories he planned to include in a second novel, nearly completed, entitled *The Virginian*, in which Lin and the Virginian would appear together in one episode, "Where Fancy Was Bred." Moreover, in revising "The Winning of the Biscuit-Shooter" for *Lin McLean*, Wister added a few cosmetic touches to his "gentle-voiced Southerner" the Virginian. No longer a run-of-the-mill cowhand without a future, the Virginian still tells Molly that cowpunchers "mostly don't live long enough to get old"—but in the revision he quickly adds, "But I have a reason, and I am saving."

Wister had only to add a final chapter to *Lin McLean* to complete it. Between May 19 and August 5, he wrote "Destiny at Drybone" (working titles "The Burial of the Biscuit-Shooter," "An Ill Wind at Drybone," and "The Funeral at Drybone") composed of equal parts slapstick and maudlin sentimentality and loosely based on an incident that Amos Barber had related when Wister passed through Cheyenne in December 1893. He made a note of it in his journal:

Man shot. . . . B[arber] had said 'He'll die in a few hours.' Jury
sworn—Got their $5—Coroner got his $10, drank $5—sent
over: 'Man dead?' 'Not yet.' Drank another $5—same game. Man
lingered unexpectedly long. Jury all drunk and dispersed over the
country. Finally when man did die, no jury. Coroner forged their
names to his finding.

In Wister's reconstruction of the incident, the *femme
fatale* Katie Lusk dies not from a gunshot but by suicide,
overdosing on six ounces of laudanum. The post physician—"Barber, actually"—was walking "the unhappy
woman up and down in the effort to save her life when her
husband broke in and made her death certain through his
drunken and blundering interference." "I'll not say there
was much chance for her," the doctor tells the offending
husband. "But any she had is gone through you. She'll die."
After the drunken coroner signs her death certificate, the
ex-soldiers with whom she partied bury her in a scene, as
one reviewer declared, "worthy to rank in humor with Mark
Twain's story of the famous Scotty Briggs" in *Roughing It*.
Remington wrote Wister that he thought "Destiny at Drybone" was a "great story—everyone says so & everyone
knows everything." Alden published it in *Harper's Monthly*
for December 1897 with a single illustration by Remington
and paid Wister six hundred dollars.

Lin McLean, with illustrations by Remington, appeared
on December 7, immediately after the issue of the magazine containing the final chapter hit the newsstands. Considered in the most charitable light, it was an experiment. Less
charitably, it was a novel without the necessary connective
tissue. As Wister explained in a new preface to the book
in 1907,

It was my aim to tell a long story, not through a series of chapters
in the usual way, but through a chain of short stories, each not only
a complete adventure in itself, but also a fragment of an underlying drama. Thus each new link inherited from its predecessor

a situation which it developed and passed on to its successor. I had hoped that this somewhat unusual device might be noticed, and possibly create a little interest; but I had overlooked the fact that matters of craftsmanship do not fall into the light of critical attention here as they do in Europe, where the writer is held as much accountable for his manner of saying a thing as for the thing he says.

Lin McLean was, like later story-cycles such as Stephen Crane's *Whilomville Tales* and Sherwood Anderson's *Winesburg, Ohio*, a mosaic, an attempt, as Wister put it, to narrate "a long tale through successive short ones which hit only the high spots in the central figure's career." It was also a resounding commercial flop. Wister's royalties on sales of both *Red Men and White* and *Lin McLean* for 1898 amounted to only about $180.

On the whole, the flawed structure of the novel was overlooked by reviewers. Once again, their overriding conclusion was that Wister was a realist in his treatment of the West. The *New York Tribune* ("invariably veracious") and the *Chicago Tribune* ("truthfully . . . drawn") led the pack. The *Boston Journal* thought *Lin McLean* "might almost be called an epic of the West"—high praise indeed for a book nearly forgotten today. The *St. Louis Herald* compared Wister, perhaps for the first time, to Remington in preserving "a picturesque phase of our country's history." The *Brooklyn Eagle* ("our foremost artist in the delineation of the life of the fast vanishing frontier") and the *Criterion* ("does for the cowboy what Harte did for the miner") joined the chorus of approval. Ironically, Howells again qualified his praise for the book. In an interview, he grouped Wister with Garland, Abraham Cahan, and Stephen Crane among the "good many promising" young American writers. But Howells worried that Wister was stuck in a proverbial rut in writing about the West. "I believe Owen Wister will get out of that purely local vein of his. He ought to. He was born here in the East among the fine linen—we don't have purple now—and he has written of that Western life just because he went out there and understood it and felt that he wanted to put it into stories. If he could do that he can do more. I hope to see him getting at something more broad and comprehensive."

Harper's vigorously promoted *Lin McLean* in England, and the reviewers there were as enthusiastic as their American counterparts, demonstrating again the potential market for the western overseas. According to the *Westminster Gazette*, Zola "could hardly have pictured anything with more relentless fidelity than Drybone." The *Manchester Guardian* averred that Lin McLean was "perhaps the truest presentment of an actual cowboy that American fiction has as yet given us," and *Literature* agreed it was "a faithful study of a curious and edifying human creature." Henry James contended that Wister limned "the manners of the remoter West" with "a hand of a singularly trained and modern lightness." Even the stuffy and tendentious *Saturday Review* of London praised the book: Wister's cowboys were "neither blood-and-thunder ruffians nor disguised evangelists. One of their distinctive traits is that they work. They do not spend all their time shooting each other through the lungs."

In fact, the American poet and journalist Robert Bridges was the only prominent critic to object to Wister's episodic construction of the novel. In his pseudonymous review in *Life*, Bridges expressed the wish that the stories had been

welded into a compact novel. The minor characters appear and reappear with all the familiarity of a continuous performance. And the last story winds up all human interest in the motley company as effectively as the last chapter of a novel. Standing separately, the episodes were good magazine stories, but Mr. Wister would have added to his excellent reputation by welding them into a homogeneous tale.

Wister thanked Bridges for his criticism. He would not repeat the mistake in *The Virginian*. In retrospect, moreover, he seems to have recognized his imaginative failures in *Lin McLean*. After completing "Destiny at Drybone" in August 1897, Wister never again wrote a word about Lin. "The only thing that we can finally say about Lin is that he loses the essential frontier characteristics of natural vitality, spontaneous response, and utter freedom without gaining others to take their place," as Neal Lambert has diagnosed the problem. "Wister could not make Lin civilized without destroying his essential nature, yet he seemed unable to develop Lin's character in any other direction." Nor was *The Virginian* nearly as ready for publication as Wister presumed in March 1897. Busy with *Lin McLean* and his second collection of short stories, and suffering from poor health, Wister did not return to the manuscript of his novel for more than two years.

4

1898–1902

Owen Wister, at the age of thirty-seven, proposed marriage to his second cousin Molly Channing Wister on New Year's Day 1898. They were married on April 21, the same day the United States declared war on Spain. Meanwhile, he wrote nothing for publication. "I am totally unable to think about [stories] at all, & they must wait—& I don't care!" he informed his mother. Remington wrote from New Rochelle that Molly had married "a pretty good fellow but she wants to keep a rope on you—you have been *bron-cho* so long." Though the couple had planned a wedding journey to the Wind River Mountains in Wyoming, Wister's Wyoming friends had been deployed to Cuba. Instead, in July the newlyweds embarked for the Pacific Northwest and Guy Waring's home in the Methow Valley. Wister took along a No. 4 Kodak folding camera, not a gun, to "shoot" antelope. They traveled via the Great Northern Railway to Wenatchee, Washington, downstream on the Columbia from Bridgeport, where Wister had crossed the river on a chain ferry in 1892. Then on July 25 they took a steamboat seventy miles upstream. Wister wrote that this stretch of the river was "the most dreadful thing I have ever seen. I thought it dreadful in 1892 when I only crossed it on a ferry; but after this journey it is something to have nightmares about for 20 years. . . . It lies in a rut away below the

Owen Wister carrying his camera (circa 1898). Owen Wister Papers, American Heritage Center, University of Wyoming.

world, and you look up at steep hills sometimes 2000 feet above you each side. . . . I would sooner climb along outside the Brooklyn Bridge than take that trip again."

When Sarah Wister learned that her son and Molly were lodged in a rustic cabin on Waring's property, she expressed her dismay. She doubted "the propriety of putting y[ou]r bride of less than three months into a one-roomed cabin." She was "completely horrified by the account of y[ou]r life at Winthrop; you are not yet fit to have charge of a woman; if I had had the slightest idea of the sorts of thing you were going to do I w[oul]d have opposed it to the utmost." Wister assured her that, not only did he and his "puritan damsel" wife maintain the proprieties in "our little cabin," it was all very snug and comfortable with "its fresh air, its clean swept floor, its bear skin rug, the shelf of books, the photographs on the walls, and the chintz screens that conceal our belongings." (For his part, Waring lived in a hand-hewn log house, nicknamed "Waring's Castle" by his neighbors. The house is still standing, and is listed on the National Registry of Historic Places.) "I told Molly she was seeing about as much West as there was left," Wister wrote his mother. He added four days later that their cabin was about twenty feet above "the clear current of the Methow," which was "about as large as the Brandywine, but oh! another sort of thing quite. It forks just here, and the two sparkling green waters ripple together over shallows." He assured his mother, too, that Molly "has gained flesh, & says her dresses are tight." In mid-August, Molly attested to her happiness and comfort in a letter to her mother-in-law: "I believe I have never liked anything as much as this new experience—certainly have never found anything as strange. I was not prepared for it in the least." Much as Molly Wood in the final chapter of *The Virginian* begs to remain at the bridal camp in the mountains with her new husband, Molly Wister relished "the sense of freedom, & repose & endless space" she shared with her new husband: "I should be happy here for a long time." They camped along Lake Chelan in mid-September and—after a detour through Seattle, Tacoma, and Yellowstone National Park in late September—returned to Philadelphia.

Wister finally resumed writing in March 1899 when, for the first time since completing "Grandmother Stark" in November 1896, he added a chapter to his story of the Virginian. In "The Game and the Nation," he repeated with a vengeance his defense of wealth and privilege, restaging the railway strike of 1894 and depicting the Virginian's defeat of a labor leader typified by Trampas. Five years after the strike, Wister's decision to set the "The Game and the Nation" in railcars and a train station was entirely in character. The narrator repeatedly alludes to the railroad, from an initial reference to Colonel Cyrus Jones's eating palace near the rail yards in Omaha to the caboose that "trundled on to Billings along the shingly cottonwooded Yellowstone" at the close. Since the railway strike, Wister's animus against organized labor had been exacerbated by the strike of 1899 in the coal fields of eastern Pennsylvania. As he wrote George Brett, a Macmillan editor, "perhaps this experience will open more eyes to the intolerable arrogance of united labor. This menace will have to be adjusted, and it will before many years have gone." In each crisis—the Johnson County War of 1892, the railway strike of 1894, and the coal strike of 1899—Wister consistently sided with capital.

In the story, Judge Henry sends the Virginian on a mission: first to sell twenty railcars of cattle in Chicago, then to negotiate with the directors of the Northern Pacific for cheap rates in the future, and finally "to lead his six highly unoccupied brethren . . . back in peace to the ranch." Gold has been discovered near Rawhide, however, and the cowboys employed by the judge must decide whether to remain with the Virginian or to mutiny with Trampas. Not only are they called "mutineers"—the same word Wister used to describe

118

strikers in "The National Guard of Pennsylvania"—they are described as "trainhands" and they occupy the caboose in which Pullman employees were normally quartered. That is, Trampas functions in these chapters as a strike organizer à la Debs.

The Virginian is forced to dismiss one of the cowhands, Schoffner the cook, a German and the only "mutineer" given a name. The detail is telling: Wister believed that "every race has some particular excellence & some pre-eminent inferiority. The Germans, for example, hear the music, but they make a poor hand at cooking." Elsewhere, he distinguished between two kinds of German immigrants—"the Prussians and the prussianized"—with "good" Germans such as Carl Schurz among the former type and "Huns" like Schoffner among the latter. Thus Schoffner is determined by heredity to fail both as a cook and as a cowboy. Wister conceded the need for immigrant labor; the Virginian allows, "Without cheap foreigners they [the railroad] couldn't afford all this hyeh new gradin.'" But some workers were preferable to others.

In the original manuscript of "The Game and the Nation," the Virginian is accompanied by Honey Wiggin, who doubles as his confidante. In the final version of the tale, however, Wister introduced an entirely new character. After the hero fires Schoffner, he hires Scipio Le Moyne, a native-born American of French ancestry. As Scipio announces, "Us folks have been white for a hundred years." (Wister was an unapologetic Francophile, fond of French wines and fluent in the language.) In effect, a German worker is fired and replaced by an assimilated strikebreaker of French descent, altogether to his credit in Wister's opinion. As Wister argued in his essay "The Land of the Free" (1904), the scab "stands for liberty, the right to live, the right to work, every right that we have all inherited."

Eventually, the train with the Virginian, Trampas, and the "mutineers" parks behind "four stalled expresses" and "several freights" at the washed-out Big Horn bridge. They are all hostages, stranded much as Wister and others had been stranded by the Pullman strike in 1894, and the stage is set for a showdown between Trampas and the Virginian. According to the narrator, the "dark bubble of mutiny swelled hourly beneath my eyes" in this "undercurrent of war." Wister used the same term to describe the 1894 Pullman strike: "Debs was beaten in this war—for civil war is the only name for it." When "the Trampas faction" threatens gunplay, the Virginian defuses the threat by spinning a tall tale about frog ranching in Tulare County, California.

This story within a story loosely recapitulates the recent history of the Wyoming cattle boom and bust. At first the frog ranchers, all of whom "had been cattle-men," invested "big capital and went into it scientific, gettin' advice from the government Fish Commission." The business prospered, with the owners some years netting 40 percent profit and paying "generous wages" to the frog-hands. Unfortunately, the "frawgs had enemies, same as cattle" were prey to coyotes. "I remember when a pelican got in the spring pasture, and the herd broke through the fence" of wire mesh, the Virginian says. The "herd stampeded right into the San Joaquin River," and "a frawg in a river is more hopeless than any maverick loose on the range." The stampede led to disputes over ownership because the frog barons "never struck any plan to brand their stock." In the end, however, the bubble burst in the frog market as the result of disease and the rivalry of two chefs, Peter Augustin of Philadelphia and Lorenzo Delmonico of New York, who collude to wipe "frawgs off the slate of fashion," much as the cattle boom went bust as the result of overgrazing, the economic depression of 1886, and the disastrous winter of 1887. Completely fooled by the tale, Trampas is intellectually crushed in this battle of wits, which wins the "mutineers" over to the Virginian and makes them "his captives and admirers." As one of Judge Henry's friends realizes back at Sunk Creek, the

Virginian "cajoled them into a bout of tall stories, and told the tallest himself. . . . I couldn't be a serious mutineer after that." The hero exercises a kind of moral suasion by proving he is more adept at lying than Trampas.

In all, the episode illustrates the triumph of benevolent capital over labor, exactly what had occurred (from Wister's perspective) in the railway strike. Why else are these chapters set against the backdrop of stalled trains? As if by miracle or magic, the blockade is lifted and rail traffic restored on the same page that the Virginian outwits Trampas. As the narrator notes, "Possibly the supreme—the most American—moment of all was when word came that the bridge was open, and the Pullman trains, with noise and triumph, began to move westward at last." The image evokes the end of the Pullman strike, with employees pacified and passengers back on board. The story appeared with drawings by Remington in the May 1900 issue of *Harper's Monthly*, and Alden paid Wister five hundred dollars for it.

The original manuscript version of "The Game and the Nation" included a two-page coda in which the narrator tells Judge Henry about the threatened mutiny and the Virginian's defeat of Trampas with his tall tale. Both a genteel cousin of Mrs. Henry's from Rhinecliff on the Hudson and the Reverend Bismus Hape (a faint echo of "abysmal hope") express their disapproval of western ways in general and the Virginian's brand of deceit in particular. As the minister declares, "Life, and death, and frivolity. . . . And lying apparently to decide the survival of the fittest. Great heavens, this Western country! Its future!" In the version of the story reprinted in the novel, the Reverend Dr. Alexander MacBride similarly deplores "the struggle between men where lying decides the survival of the fittest"—the only occasion when the phrase coined by Herbert Spencer appears in Wister's published work. The narrator adds in the manuscript draft that he would "try and tell you, perhaps, some day," how the "eminent divine strove later to convert the Virginian." Although Wister omitted these final two pages from "The Game and the Nation" when it appeared, he would write the sequel about the evangelist's attempt to convert the hero two years later.

Wister followed the polemics of "The Game and the Nation" with low comedy in "Twenty Minutes for Refreshments," drafted in August in the seaside village of Saunderstown, Rhode Island, where he, Molly, and their children had retreated for the summer. Ironically, the story again focuses on the railroad; the title comes from the call of the train conductor for passengers to dine at a rail stop, such as the Harvey Houses owned by the Fred Harvey Company in the depots along the Southern Pacific. Set again in "Sharon" or Deming, New Mexico, the tale is thematically indistinguishable from "Sharon's Choice" and is even written in the same tone of undisguised condescension toward the backward backwoods citizens. The narrator has "set out from Atlantic waters on the 30th day of a backward and forlorn April" and arrives in Sharon on May 4, much as in 1894 Wister left Philadelphia for the West on April 28 and passed through Deming on May 4. This time the hick town is abuzz not over a school declamation but about a baby contest, which the narrator is conscripted to judge. He expresses the same unflattering opinion of Sharon: "There, as of old, lay the flat litter of the town—sheds, stores, and dwellings, a shapeless congregation in the desert. . . . Little black Mexicans, like charred toys, lounged and lay staring among the ungraded dunes of sand." Wister takes another swipe at William Jennings Bryan, too: one of the babies is named Thomas Jefferson Brayin Lucas, who would have received at birth "a souvenir sixteen-to-one spoon" (the ratio of silver to gold favored by the free-silverites) from "the statesman for whom her child was called" but for the fact that too many children had been named after him and the supply was exhausted. Later, in *The Seven Ages of Washington* (1907), Wister compared Bryan to Thomas Jefferson, "the incomparable dabbler, the illustrious dilettante, of his day." Alden published the story in *Harper's Monthly* for January 1900 and paid Wister $295 for it.

Harper & Brothers had fallen on hard times, unable to repay a loan from J. P. Morgan, entering receivership in December 1899, reorganizing, and barely evading bankruptcy, with the family losing control of the company. Rivals circled like buzzards around a dying animal. "All their competitors in business hastened to profit" by their trouble, inviting authors "to leave the Harpers and come to them," Wister remembered. He was heavily recruited by Macmillan, Doubleday, Appleton, McClure, L. C. Page, and H. T. Coates, and he received offers for upwards of fifty dollars per thousand words to contribute to their magazines. However, he was offended by the crass commercialism: "This conduct on the part of so many firms decided me to express some visible allegiance to the Harpers." The head of the firm, J. Henry Harper, appreciated Wister's loyalty and wrote to thank him on December 1: "Your letter was so like you that it was a kind of personal presence and I seemed to feel the grasp of your hand of friendship which I value most highly."

Meanwhile, Wister knocked out another story for *Harper's Monthly*. In "Padre Ignazio," written the same month Harper & Brothers entered receivership, Wister depicted the Spanish mission past of California much like Harte in "The Right Eye of the Commander" and Helen Hunt Jackson in *Ramona*. He based the story on an anecdote he had heard during his 1893 trip to the West Coast and jotted in his journal:

> The old mission priest whose only contact with the civilized world was when the infrequent ship brought books and news, and whose taste for light popular music led him to send for it to Europe and when it came he set it to the mass and taught the Indians to sing it.

Remington declined to illustrate the story because, he said, "all the action is in men's minds, and not their bodies." In addition, however, the friendship between the two men had begun to deteriorate. The tale appeared without illustrations in the April 1900 number of the magazine.

Then, inexplicably, Wister took a detour from the trail leading to his next story collection. During the first week of January 1900, he wrote "The Patronage of High Bear," a title which first surfaces in his notebook for 1893. It is an anomaly in his career in more ways than one. Wister did not submit it to Alden for *Harper's Monthly.* He did not include it in *The Jimmyjohn Boss and Other Stories,* planned for publication later that year, the book he had been rushing to complete to help Harper's forestall bankruptcy. And though it features the Virginian in a minor role, the tale was not part of the narrative arc of the novel. Instead, it is a tale about competition among traders on Indian reservations with Scipio Le Moyne as protagonist. Wister submitted it first to the juvenile magazine *Youth's Companion,* whose editors rejected it, and he then sent it to *Cosmopolitan,* where it appeared in January 1901 and whose editors paid him $250 for it. He revised it a decade later under the title "Happy Teeth" and reprinted it in his collection *Members of the Family.*

Two months later, in March, Wister finally rounded out the collection he had planned with a revision of "Hank's Woman," originally published eight years before. "Hank's Woman was my first attempt at a Western sketch, and after its appearance in *Harper's Weekly,* I grew dissatisfied with it, and revised it," he explained. In the new version, Wister replaced Lin McLean with the Virginian. To "get all which was to be out of Hank's Woman, I needed a 'Greek chorus' of an intelligence more subtle than Lin's." In particular, he needed the Virginian to mock the social pretensions of a New York snob who dismisses her maid, Hank's future wife, with a remark Lin could neither have conceived nor expressed: "She was rich an' stinkin' lookin,' an' she'd discovered where all our Philadelphia servants have gone to. They've all joined New York society." Though Wister referred in the revision to "Em'ly," a tale not yet written when he published the original version, the story of Hank's murder was irrelevant to the larger plot he had in mind for *The Virginian* and so he omitted it from the novel. Instead, the revision appeared in *The Jimmyjohn Boss and Other Stories*, and in the novel, Wister twice alluded in passing to the deaths of Hank and his wife (chapters 7 and 31).

The collection finally appeared on May 3, 1900. Wister dedicated it to "Messrs. Harper & Brothers and Henry Mills Alden whose friendliness and fair dealing I am glad of this chance to record." It was published with the illustrations by Remington that had accompanied the first appearance of the stories—and almost simultaneously with Remington's own collection of western tales *Men with the Bark On*, also issued by Harper's. For the first time, that is, Wister and Remington were as much competitors as collaborators, perhaps one of the reasons for their estrangement. As Remington biographers Peggy Samuels and Howard Samuels observe, "Wister's book was soon out of print while *Men with the Bark On* ran through two editions in two months. The comparative success helped Remington to feel that he had equaled Wister in narrative skill and had overtaken him in the use of grander themes."

As a result of the publisher's financial crisis, Wister's book was poorly promoted and was a commercial failure. Wister's royalties from the sale of his first three western books—*Red Men and White*, *Lin McLean*, and *The Jimmyjohn Boss*—for the first six months of 1901 totaled only $45.75. Moreover, the new volume was rarely reviewed. Most of the printed notices, though favorable, were perfunctory and appeared without signature in daily newspapers. For example: the *Brooklyn Standard-Union* ("one of the classics of a stage of development which . . . is rapidly passing away"), *Brooklyn*

Eagle ("very faithful reflections of the queer life away out yonder"), *Louisville Times* ("Wister is just getting the place that he deserves"), *Minneapolis Times-Journal* ("a distinct addition to the summer literature"), New York *Sun* ("all admirable" stories), and *Springfield* (Massachusetts) *Republican* ("the ring of truth"). Richard Henry Stoddard in the *New York Mail and Express* pronounced *The Jimmyjohn Boss* "an amazing exhibition of sheer talent" and Robert Bridges in *Life* averred that Wister had "gained confidence and skill." George Hamlin Fitch insisted in the *San Francisco Chronicle* that Wister "in his way has the same ability as Remington" and the *Chicago Tribune* declared that he had "shown what good stories can be written without" the "love theme"—not exactly bait to hook women readers. But the *New York Tribune*, the most influential paper in the country, expressed disappointment. The anonymous critic thought the tales "uneven in quality" and found Wister in places "almost unreadable." Governor Roosevelt of New York, the hero of San Juan Hill, paid his respects privately: "Just a word to say how much I like the Jimmyjohn Boss and your other stories. But then I always do like your stories."

Wister had abandoned his law practice by 1899, though he continued to keep an office in the building where he might write. He left Molly and their new son in mid-August to travel alone to the West Coast. He declined reporters' requests for interviews in Denver on August 12, though he remarked for their benefit that theirs was "the most beautiful city in the United States," earning him "column upon column of taffy" or free publicity. Denver "seems to strive after Ruskin's ideal of how people should build," he declared—"artistically all around, or rather with architectural splendor." On August 14 he traveled from Truckee in western Nevada to Verdi in eastern California. "This is not at all the country of Padre Ignazio," he noted in his journal. "It is more approximately that of [Harte's] Mr. Oakhurst."

He registered at the Palace Hotel in San Francisco the next day and set about finding Dean Duke, who had recently received a contract to furnish eleven hundred horses and five hundred mules to the army. Together they traveled north to Heppner, Oregon, where Wister met a local journalist and former soldier, J. W. Redington, who had contacted him after the publication of *Red Men and White*. Redington had been a printer's devil for Howells at fourteen and a scout for Generals Nelson A. Miles and Oliver O. Howard at seventeen. "After a roaming life," Wister later wrote, "he married & became an editor. . . . He is a singular person."

Redington and Wister had been corresponding for years about the Bannock Indian War, and Wister seemed ready at last to write the novel about the war that he had contemplated since at least 1895. He walked the battlegrounds, listened to Redington's reminiscences, traveled to Malheur Lake in central Oregon, took "some very long stage journeys through the less settled parts of Oregon," and made copious "notes and drawings of the lay of the land." He shelved this material beside the notes he had taken during conversations over the years with Edwards and other soldiers "about the Bannocks and Buffalo Horn, their evil medicine man, and Chief E-egante." Though he readily conceded that the "tragic tale" would "make a thrilling page in our frontier history," Wister eventually abandoned the project for reasons of poor health, much to Redington's disappointment. He finally returned to Philadelphia in early October, pausing in Boise en route for a few days to rest.

A few months later he began yet another ill-fated project. The grandson of Shakespearean actress Fanny Kemble, Wister was born with the proverbial greasepaint in his veins. He had written and performed in amateur theatricals for years, in college and at the Tavern Club in Boston. In the spring and summer of 1901, he experimented with a pair of collaborators on a dramatization of *Lin McLean* that included the usual ensemble cast—Shorty, Chalkeye, and Hank—

but no Virginian or Molly. Script-writing was potentially much more lucrative than novel-writing: a popular play might earn many thousands of dollars more in licensing fees per season than a best-selling novel. Wister read a finished act to his mother, who was delighted with it: "I know of nobody but [George Washington] Cable & Mark Twain who c[oul]d write with as much power," she averred. But the play was never completed. Wister concluded after months of frustration that his collaborators were "utterly unequal to their task of dialogue," though in June 1902 he briefly corresponded with the theatrical impresario Kirke La Shelle about the script. La Shelle advised Wister that he "did not find this play the best of dramatic products" but "thought with some amplification and elaboration it might find a market" in working-class theaters such as the Fourteenth Street Theatre in lower Manhattan.

At first glance, Wister's next installment in his saga of the Virginian, "In a State of Sin," written in May 1901 and originating in the unpublished coda to "The Game and the Nation," seems like a digression. The story opens with a glance back at the resolution of the cowboys' threatened mutiny, how the hero quelled "their revolt at the railroad" with his tall tale about the Tulare frog ranch. He had "utterly confounded them, playing with them the kind of war they themselves had chosen, and killing them with the own attempted weapon of ridicule, which is more fatal than pistols." In "the final pitched battle of wits he had marshaled his words like a general who plans flank movements and designates reserves. Then with a sudden final charge he had routed the enemy."

The final two sentences, in which Wister compares his hero to a general—even though they would be omitted from the novel—are key to a reading of the saga of the Virginian. Much as he characterized both Judge Henry and Molly Wood as atavists, reflecting the character and

strengths of their forebears, Wister conceived the cowboy hero of "In a State of Sin" as a throwback to the true
American aristocrat—more specifically, to George Washington of Revolutionary War fame—through whose agency
the national character (Wister hoped) would be revitalized.
In other words, Wister cast his hero as the male lead in a
revival of the Revolution staged in late-nineteenth century
Wyoming. Not only does Washington share the same state
of birth as the Virginian, he had once been a western hero
in his own right, as a military scout during the French and
Indian War. Wister owned a pair of letters Washington had
written Pierce Butler, Wister's great-great-grandfather,
which he framed and hung in the hallway of his home. His
grandfather, Charles Jones Wister, still alive when he was
a child, had actually spoken with Washington. Wister read
all fourteen volumes of Washington's writings edited by
Worthington Chauncey Ford before he began to compose
his own biography, *The Seven Ages of Washington* (1907).
Moreover, in his Washington biography he even referred
occasionally to the "captain and savior of our Revolution" as
"the Virginian." In Wister's original theatrical version of the
novel, Uncle Hewie (sometimes spelled Hughie) names his
newborn twins "George" and "Martha." In Wister's West,
in short, the spirit of '76 was alive and well and punch-
ing dogies west of Medicine Bow, and the story of Wister's
hero is a fable of renewal in which the Revolutionary War
is reenacted in Wyoming, with the Virginian in the role of
Founding Father.

The Virginian's similarity to Washington is underscored
by the visit of an itinerant evangelist to Judge Henry's
ranch. When the Reverend MacBride damns the Virginian
for quashing the mutiny by skillful lying, Molly Wood—
who shares the same initials as Martha Washington (and
Molly Wister)—defends her suitor: "It wasn't that George
Washington couldn't tell a lie. He just wouldn't. I'm sure if
he'd undertaken to he'd have told a much better one than

Cornwallis." When the narrator recounts the story of the threatened mutiny, the judge "brought his fist down on the table" and declares, "I'd make him a Lieutenant-General [Washington's rank during the American Revolution] if the ranch offered that position."

Reverend MacBride's stay at Sunk Creek Ranch in fact may be based on a similar visit of a group of clergymen to Washington, an incident that Wister recounts in his biographies of Washington and Theodore Roosevelt. Washington met the ministers during his presidency with a silence that "very plainly told them that he considered their attempt [to coerce a confession of faith from him] a piece of impertinence."

"Americans certainly began minding their neighbors' business very early," Wister adds in an aside. Washington "was what we call a religious man, very deeply so, but also very broadly, and had outgrown formulas." Or as the Virginian says to the narrator, "I ain't religious. I know that. But I ain't *un*religious. And I know that too." Much as Washington "ceased taking the Communion before he became President," the Virginian tells Molly in a scrap of dialogue Wister discarded, "I don't go to church because I don't care to hear nice ladies called miserable sinners. You're not a miserable sinner." Wister discarded three other lines in a similar vein from the final version of the tale, all spoken by the Virginian: "I always kind o' believed some man away back had invented Hell for the benefit of his acquaintances, an' now I know it." "Hell's a great comfort to his thoughts." "I wouldn't care to be a man that had nothing to be ashamed of. I'd sooner be a man that had something to be proud of." Had Wister included these lines of dialogue in the novel, however, he would have obscured the hero's method of ridding the ranch of the evangelist: he feigns a conversion experience that infuriates MacBride, who leaves after delivering only one sermon.

In the penultimate magazine installment starring the Virginian, "Superstition Trail" (working title "For Lack of Evidence"), written in Saunderstown during the summer of 1901, the hero, commissioned by Judge Henry, leads a posse that hangs a pair of cattle rustlers. By chance, the narrator is also on the scene, and in a passage deleted from the final draft he muses that "Sometimes I come near believing that a fate attaches to places. That in certain spots nature has sown in the ground and woven in the air a doom which neither spring floods can uproot nor autumn gales blow away." As David Mogen suggests, "Superstition Trail" illustrates the difference between Wister's two novels: "the heroic world of *The Virginian* is made of sterner stuff than the pastoral world of *Lin McLean*." Whereas the Virginian inhabits a "Darwinian arena of struggle where the noblest and strongest rise naturally to eminence," Lin occupies a "pastoral West" of "uninhibited, youthful camaraderie." Significantly, too, in an early note for the story Wister identifies the narrator with the author: "Perhaps Shorty's previous history [as a store clerk in the East] can be told [to] me by the Virginian." More than any other part of the novel, "Superstition Trail" chronicles the Johnson County War (and the American Revolution) in microcosm. The Virginian literally reenacts on a small scale the role of Washington as commander-in-chief of the Continental army. Wister justifies the extra-legal devices (lynching and the later gunfight with Trampas) as necessary to bring law and order to the frontier. As he depicts Wyoming, the territory in the 1890s was not savage but merely pre-civilized, requiring vigilantes acting in the public interest. As the narrator tells the story, however, one of the cattle rustlers is the Virginian's ex-best friend Steve, so the hero must repress his personal affection to perform his duty.

Some modern readers are not so sanguine about this turn of events. According to Christine Bold, for example, Wister "turned a brutal murder by a power elite into a democratic uprising" and "he converted an incident of mob violence into an image of heroic individualism." Louis Owens dismisses the Virginian as "a good middle-management tool" who hangs a friend "when his employer's interests are threatened." Bernard DeVoto, who long ago argued that "the themes of the novel are from the Johnson County War," describes the lynching of Steve as "murder in the interest of a master class." Eugene Manlove Rhodes, author of *Bransford in Arcadia* (1914) and other popular westerns, wrote a friend years later that he "never forgave the Virginian for helping to hang Steve." The posse has narrowly missed capturing two other rustlers, Trampas and Shorty, and at the close of the story Trampas kills Shorty to speed his own escape. Wister conceded later that "Superstition Trail" was

> the most difficult [chapter] to write of any in the book. I knew what was coming, and I rather dreaded it, to tell the truth. I knew it would be a hard one to handle, but before I got through with it I was disgusted with myself. The confounded thing wouldn't move any better than Balaam's pony Pedro. I worked on it like a man pounding rivets in a boiler factory. I fumed and sweated and stormed, and finally I got to the end of the chapter. Then the curious thing happened. The following day, when I took up the next chapter, everything was as serene as a June morning.

Despite his reservations, Wister believed he had never written anything as good as "Superstition Trail," and Remington also believed it was "artistically the best thing [he had] done." Remington had agreed to illustrate the story. The initial installment of the story appeared in the *Saturday Evening Post* in late October—the first part of *The Virginian* to appear outside *Harper's Monthly*. The second installment appeared in early November and contained the last illustration Remington drew for any of Wister's tales.

Their friendship and collaboration were over, for all practical purposes. Not only had they become competitors, their attitudes toward the West were simply incompatible. Wister's West was too good to be true from Remington's perspective, and Remington's was too dark and uninviting from Wister's point of view. Wister wrote introductions or verses for three of Remington's collections of sketches: *Drawings* (1897), *A Bunch of Buckskins* (1901), and *Done in the Open* (1903), but the latter two experiences in particular were not happy ones. As Wister explained to Remington's publisher R. H. Russell after the artist found fault with his preface to *A Bunch of Buckskins*:

> Remington is crazy as I expect to explain to him this evening at New Rochelle. Were he an unknown whom you were exploiting, and I much better known than I am, it might be of some avail to begin a preface in the spirit of a prospectus. But the public has known Remington for 15 years in about 15 magazines, & it knows him by heart. Any laudatory data about him would be promptly skipped by the average purchaser. This preface stands some chance of being read because it does not start off with the routine blowing of trumpets. It ends so. No higher praise can be given to Remington than the last sentence. But I will not have the praise come first. It must be led up to, and then people may believe it is not an advertisement.

The next year, while preparing a series of poems to accompany *Done in the Open*, Wister even critiqued Remington's skill with brush and pen: "He is the most uneven artist I know which you find out very much when you come to extract verse from each drawing. Some are full of meaning & some empty as old cartridges."

As Wister began to contemplate revisions to the separate stories about the Virginian, especially the connective tissue needed to stitch them together, "Superstition Trail" posed a question: who was Steve? Wister needed to include Steve's backstory. In the original magazine version, the narrator is "ignorant who Steve might be" though they have met before.

"You don't remember me," [Steve] said, and as I did not he recalled the occasion of our meeting. "You got out of the stage at Signor's. I was tending bar."

Then I recalled the usual midnight change of horses and how I had taken the usual chance to stretch my legs and to drink some beer. He had sold me the beer on that particular journey. I had shared the quart bottle with him, and we had talked about elk hunting until the stage took me on through the midnight. It came back to me that I had thought him pleasant to talk with. I had never thought of him since but here was a man I had known a little, gossiped a little with over a friendly glass of beer, and tomorrow—it gave me a new shock, very chill and painful.

On the reverse side of the galley proof, Wister penciled a possible revision:

And then I looked harder at him, and suddenly remembered. "Last July a year," he added. "You got out of the stage at Rongis." Yes, that was it. Rongis. My stage journey came back to my memory; the midnight change of horses; the great darkness outside; the small lighted saloon; this man with whom I had drank a glass of beer while waiting; his pleasant face, his friendly talk, his wishing me good luck on my hunting trip; and then the going on in the stage, never seeing or thinking of this wayside acquaintance again. Yes, I now remembered him & his pleasant face well, and our companionable glass of beer. And now, here he sat, sentenced to die. A shock, chill and painful, deprived me of speech.

In both of these passages, Wister was laying the groundwork for a short chapter, never written, to "mark [the] flight of time" in the narrative and to introduce the future cattle rustler. Tentatively entitled simply "Steve," Wister

Chapter headings for *The Virginian* (December 1901). Owen Wister Papers, American Heritage Center, University of Wyoming.

planned to insert it between "When Fancy Was Bred" and "The Game and the Nation."

As late as April 10, 1900, A. V. S. Anthony of the House of Harper assured Wister that when *The Virginian* "is able to leave his nursing bottle send him to me and I will give him such tender care as I am capable of." But in October

1901, Wister wrote William Stone Booth at Macmillan & Co. that he was "contemplating a temporary, and possibly a permanent, change of literary domicile. I have of late feared that my old home was losing its identity beneath the rule of its housekeeper." He was disenchanted with the new staff at Harper's led by Colonel George M. Harvey. The first installment of "Superstition Trail" appeared three weeks later in the *Saturday Evening Post*, and he offered Macmillan "*my next volume of Western tales*. It lacks one story of being ready"—not including all the revision, backfilling, and writing of new material that remained. As Bold notes, publishing with Macmillan held some advantages for Wister. The firm "was more aggressively transatlantic in its reach. Whereas Harper's vaguely promised Wister 'some English publisher,' Macmillan had a secure contract with its parent company in London, providing simultaneous publication" on both sides of the Atlantic. He soon contracted to publish his novel with Macmillan and forwarded a tentative table of contents to Booth and George Platt Brett, president of the company, on the last day of 1901. In the long run, Wister's defection from Harper's was fortuitous. In the throes of financial distress, the new regime there was unreasonable, Wister thought, demanding ten thousand dollars for reprint rights to his first three western books, even though the company was only paying him about $100 a year in royalties on them. His writing would rarely again appear from its press.

Few books have had a longer gestation than *The Virginian*, Wister's tour de force of western fiction. The seeds of the novel planted in his journal germinated over the course of many years. He once admitted that he invented the character of the Virginian by "pure accident" in "Balaam and Pedro" after experimenting with such flawed western prototypes as Chalkeye, Specimen Jones, and Lin McLean. He had originally planned to publish *The Virginian* with the same episodic design as *Lin McLean*—its working subtitle was "a tale of sundry adventures"—but he realized "that to have any chance of success it must appear" as a more cohesive narrative. He needed to integrate the seven installments of the novel published piecemeal and one other forthcoming in the *Saturday Evening Post* into a continuous plotline by adding "much supplemental narrative about smaller events." The "missing links" that the reader was left to infer in *Lin McLean* "were supplied; and during this process, many happy thoughts occurred and were woven forthwith into the fabric" of the novel.

Wister moved temporarily with his family to Charleston, South Carolina, in January 1902 to finish the novel—to revise the completed episodes, weld them together, edit them for continuity, and write the climactic chapter about the hero's duel with Trampas. In the end, Wister wrote *The Virginian* not in linear fashion but haphazardly, as if he were editing a film from raw footage. Wister's problem in integrating the intertwined "love" and "hate" stories may be put this way: the first and second published installments ("Em'ly" and "Balaam and Pedro") have nothing to do with either plot. The third and fourth published tales ("Where Fancy Was Bred" and "Grandmother Stark") take up the love story and touch lightly on the hate story. The fifth and seventh tales ("The Game and the Nation" and "Superstition Trail") focus on the hate story. Only in the sixth and eighth tales ("In a State of Sin" and "With Malice Aforethought") do the two plots significantly intersect, and only the final episodes that appeared in magazines were incorporated into the larger novel in the sequence in which they were written and published.

For three months, Wister "pegged away" at the manuscript, working every day on it, sometimes nine hours at a stretch, nearly doubling its length to about 130,000 words. Before he began wholesale revisions, Wister had to address a technical problem: five of the eight published or forthcoming installments had been written from an omniscient point of view ("Balaam and Pedro," "Where Fancy Was Bred," "Grandmother Stark," "The Game and the Nation," and "With Malice Aforethought"), the other three from the perspective of the tenderfoot ("Em'ly," "In a State of Sin," and "Superstition Trail"). When he reread *Madame Bovary* in December 1901, however, he discovered that Flaubert's first person narrator "simply dissolved away into the third" and so he decided to leave untouched his own inconsistent point of view. The decision was nothing if not controversial.

Wister initially considered opening the novel on a note of comic pathos with a revision of "Em'ly." A fragment of this aborted beginning survives in his notebooks:

> But from here he rose in flights of novelty that appalled & held me spell-bound, & which I grieve to be unable to print. Then he came down to indulgence again and ended with an expression of sympathy for it because it could never have known a mother.
>
> "Do you expect it would reckonize its male parent?" a slow voice inquired.
>
> "Not it!" replied my friend, wheeling to see who had spoken. "Why the son-of-a-gun was sired by a whole dog-gone Dutch syndicate." I had also turned; and thus my eyes rested for the first time upon the Virginian.

By February 9, after about forty days, Wister had written the opening chapters of the novel, totaling about twenty thousand words, and he had rewritten "Em'ly" and "Where Fancy Was Bred" according to his "present standard." He was surprised "how much of my old writing offends me for various reasons, and whenever I can't sand it, out it goes." In the opening chapters, the greenhorn narrator arrives in Medicine Bow much as Wister had visited the town in late July 1885 on his first trip to Wyoming. At least to this extent, *The Virginian* is a type of romanticized *roman à clef*.

In the second chapter, Wister introduces the hero and his friend Steve, precluding the need to devote a chapter to the narrator's encounter with Steve at a way station as he had anticipated in "Superstition Trail." In the second chapter, too, Trampas calls the Virginian "a son-of-a-b———" over a game of cards. Wister based the incident on notes he jotted in his journal in 1894 about events at Fort Fetterman when Amos Barber was army surgeon there:

> Card game getting on. Big money. Several desperadoes playing. One John Lawrence among others. A player calls him a son-of-a-b———. John Lawrence does not look as if he had heard it. Merely passes his fingers strikingly up and down his pile of chips. When hand is done, he looks across at the man and says, "You smile when you call me that." The man smiled and all was well.

According to the chapter outline Wister had mailed Macmillan a few weeks earlier, the Virginian replies, "When you say that to me, *smile!*" In the final revision, he responds with the more felicitous "When you call me that, *smile!*" Wister also worked "one of Skirdin's actual practical jokes" into chapter three of the novel in which the hero tricks a drummer into surrendering his bed.

In revising "Em'ly" for the novel, Wister made three noteworthy changes. First, the Virginian no longer wears bib overalls befitting a hired man. Second, Wister underscored the hero's atavism. "I have many letters from him now," the narrator notes, and his spelling from the beginning "was little worse than George Washington's." Later, in his biography of Washington, Wister again referred in passing to the general's "uncertain spelling." Finally, much as Wister eroticizes the Virginian in the opening chapters, the narrator and the hero unsex the wayward hen (and by implication the virginal schoolmarm en route from Vermont) by contrasting her to "the eating-house lady at Medicine Bow." Or as the hero says with a "hilarious chuckle," Em'ly "knows nothing o' them joys."

Wister's revision of "Where Fancy Was Bred" emphasized Molly's reincarnation of her great-grandmother. "If the ancestors that we carry shut up inside us take turns in dictating to us our action and our state of mind," he added to the text, "undoubtedly Grandmother Stark was empress of Molly's spirit" the day she left Bennington for Wyoming. Molly also refuses to permit Sam Bannett, Molly's stuffy Vermont suitor and a new character, to accompany her as far as Rotterdam Junction and so "his golden moment [was] gone like a butterfly."

Midway through the three months required to whip *The Virginian* into final shape, Wister compared his work on it to climbing a mountain. In a letter to his mother, he reported, "Each time I think I have reached the last rise another unfolds."

> What I have is satisfactory; and some I think is good, some of the dialogue ahead of any, I think, in the way of lightness and immediacy; wholly new work I don't mind, and at time greatly enjoy. It is the revision and interpolation that I do certainly hate. If you look at this sheet of paper you'll see cuts—knife cuts. Those are where I have sliced my short stories and pasted them in pieces with the interpolations between. Sometimes a page needs a change for consistency; sometimes it needs an addition for clearness and emphasis; sometimes it needs some elision.

The pasted sheets of "A Stable on the Flat," "The Cottonwoods," and "Superstition Trail" survive among Wister's papers in the American Heritage Center at the University of Wyoming.

Predictably, Wister's original version of "Balaam and Pedro," the first episode he wrote to feature the Virginian, required more substantial revision for the novel than any of the other published installments. At an annual meeting of the Boone and Crockett Club in New York in 1894, Roosevelt, at the time a U.S. Civil Service Commissioner, assailed Wister's depiction of the eye-gouging in "Balaam and Pedro," but Wister defended his story.

Page of revised proof of "The Stable on the Flat" (early 1902). Owen Wister Papers, American Heritage Center, University of Wyoming.

The thing had actually happened, I replied; I had seen it with my own eyes, and it was not an isolated case, but typical of a certain streak of cruelty which belonged to that life. Quite true, he asserted; he knew that; but life every day offered degrees of repulsiveness which were utterly inadmissible in Art, where violent extremes and excrescences had no place. I stood up for myself; I had seen it, I insisted. What if I had? he asked. That didn't justify repeating it in fiction. Still I stood up for myself. The incident had made a deep impression on me, to strike it out would weaken the story. And I reminded him that we had never liked tea-cup tales. He twisted his mouth and puckered his brow, and looked as if he was going to purr; and intensity came out all over his face. And he let me have it: "I'm perfectly aware," he replied, "that Zola has many admirers because he says things out loud that great writers from Greece down to the present have mostly passed over in silence. . . . There's nothing masculine in being revolting. Your details really weaken the effect of your story, because they distract the attention from the story as a *whole*, to the details of an offensive and shocking *part*. When you come to publishing it in a volume, throw a veil over what Balaam did to Pedro, leave that to the reader's imagination, and you will greatly strengthen your effect."

Roosevelt and Wister debated the propriety of the passage for years. In December 1897, TR reiterated his objections in a letter to the author: "I have never changed about that eye incident. It should be done in the same way as Stevenson did the incident of the torture of the squirrel" in his short story *Olalla* (1885). In the end, Wister capitulated. He decided not to reproduce the passage that had appeared in *Harper's Monthly*. After "thinking and talking it over I decided that it must be left out of the book." In dedicating *The Virginian* to Theodore Roosevelt, who had succeeded to the presidency upon the assassination of William McKinley the year before, Wister allowed that he had rewritten one page "because you blamed it." In the original draft of the dedication, he made the point even more explicitly:

Dear T.R. Some eight years ago, when the chapters which unite to form this Romance began to appear in the guise (or disguise) of short stories, no better news of them came to me than to find you were giving them your attention without my having asked you for it. If you read them again as they stand here, you will find one page that goes differently now because of a protest which you made, not against its truth but its literalness.

Revised for the novel, the eye-gouging is obscured behind a scrim.

"I'll have to take your horse," he said, "mine's played out on me."

"You ain' goin' to touch my hawss."

Again the words seemed not entirely to reach Balaam's understanding, so dulled by rage were his senses. He made no answer, but mounted Pedro; and the failing pony walked mechanically forward, while the Virginian, puzzled, stood looking after him. Balaam seemed without purpose of going anywhere, and stopped in a moment. Suddenly he was at work at something. This sight was odd and new to look at. For a few seconds it had no meaning to the Virginian as he watched. Then his mind grasped the horror, too late. Even with his cry of execration and the tiger spring that he gave to stop Balaam, the monstrosity was wrought. Pedro sank motionless, his head rolling flat on the earth. Balaam was jammed beneath him. The man had struggled to his feet before the Virginian reached the spot, and the horse then lifted his head and turned it piteously round.

Then vengeance like a blast struck Balaam. The Virginian hurled him to the ground, lifted and hurled him again, lifted him and beat his face and struck his jaw. The man's strong ox-like fighting availed nothing. He fended his eyes as best he could against these sledge-hammer blows of justice. He felt blindly for his pistol. That arm was caught and wrenched backward, and crushed and doubled. He seemed to hear his own bones, and set up a hideous screaming of hate and pain. Then the pistol at last came out, and together with the hand that grasped it was instantly stamped into the dust. Once again the creature was lifted and slung so that he lay across Pedro's saddle a blurred, dingy, wet pulp.

While it is clear that the Virginian punishes the rancher Balaam, the events here have been so veiled that what happens to the horse is virtually unintelligible. Wister's inaction in his original journal account is replaced in this final version of the episode with the hero's "sledge-hammer blows of justice." That is, Wister mythologized the western hero as a type of avenging angel who metes out justice. As Larzer Ziff concludes, Wister "produced a literature fit for the followers of Theodore Roosevelt, leaving his realism to smoulder in his journals while his fiction spoke of other things."

Wister also revised the conclusion of the magazine version of "Balaam and Pedro" to account for Molly's rescue of the hero in "Grandmother Stark." In the original printed version, Balaam takes sanctuary at Sunk Creek to avoid giving the impression he is a coward. In the revision, after the hero disappears in the woods Balaam returns immediately to his ranch, too embarrassed to face the judge.

> To Balaam the prospect of going onward to the Sunk Creek Ranch became more than he could bear. To come without the horses, to meet Judge Henry, to meet the guests of the Judge's, looking as he did now after his punishment by the Virginian, to give the news about the Judge's favorite man—no, how could he tell such a story as this? Balaam went no farther than a certain cabin, where he slept, and wrote a letter to the Judge. This the owner of the cabin delivered. And so, having spread news which would at once cause a search for the Virginian, and having constructed such sentences to the Judge as would most smoothly explain how, being overtaken by illness, he had not wished to be a burden at Sunk Creek, Balaam turned homeward by himself. By the time he was once more at Butte Creek, his general appearance was a thing less to be noticed. And there was Shorty, waiting!

Balaam breaks the news to Shorty that Pedro is dead, ostensibly killed by Indians. More importantly, unbeknownst to the other characters, the Virginian is wounded but alive beside Bear Creek, where the schoolmarm soon discovers him.

In revising "Grandmother Stark," Wister made only one significant change. In his delirium, the Virginian addresses

Steve—this sequentially after Steve has started to rustle cattle but before the hero has led the posse that lynches him in "Superstition Trail":

> "Steve!" the sick man now cried out, in poignant appeal. "Steve!"
> To the women it was a name unknown,—unknown as was also
> this deep inward tide of feeling which he could no longer conceal,
> being himself no longer. "No, Steve," he said next, and muttering
> followed. "It ain't so!" he shouted; and then cunningly in a low-
> ered voice, "Steve, I have lied for you."

Wister also decided in revision to downplay the Virginian's sophistication before the schoolmarm arrives at Sunk Creek. In the original "Grandmother Stark," the Virginian mentions that he has attended a performance of Shakespeare's *Henry IV*, but in the novel he is familiar with the play only because he has read it on Molly's recommendation.

In revising "The Game and the Nation" Wister also inserted an elitist political credo. In its earliest and crudest formulation in his journal, it read simply: "All America is divided into two classes: the Quality and the Equality. The Declaration of Independence can't help it. This is a story about both." In a deft rhetorical move, that is, Wister insisted that the opposite of equality is not inequality but quality. In a new chapter titled "Quality and Equality" that leads into "The Game and the Nation" sequence, the Virginian tells Molly that "equality is a great big bluff." The narrator echoes the point in the new paragraphs Wister added to the beginning of the sequence:

> It was through the Declaration of Independence that we Ameri-
> cans acknowledged the *eternal inequality* of man. For by it we
> abolished a cut-and-dried aristocracy. We had seen little men arti-
> ficially held up in high places, and great men artificially held down
> in low places, and our own justice-loving hearts abhorred this
> violence to human nature. Therefore, we decreed that every man
> should thenceforth have equal liberty to find his own level. By this

very decree we acknowledged and gave freedom to true aristocracy, saying, "Let the best man win, whoever he is." Let the best
man win! That is America's word. That is true democracy. And
true democracy and true aristocracy are one and the same thing. If
anybody cannot see this, so much the worse for his eyesight.

As this passage makes clear, the Virginian is a natural aristocrat of virtue and talent and Trampas a despicable social
leveler.

Wister's changes to "In a State of Sin" were more minor.
In the preface to the novel, he claims that in revising he had
been obliged to change the verbs in the chapters "published
separately at the close of the nineteenth century" from the
present to the past tense, so that "verbs like 'is' and 'have'
now read 'was' and 'had.'" Not exactly. Only in revising "In
a State of Sin" did he revise verbs, and then from past perfect to past tense (for example, "the talking part of him had
deeply and unbrokenly slept" to "the talking part of him
deeply and unbrokenly slept"; and "Official words had of
course come from him as we rode southward" to "Official
words of course came from him as we rode southward").
Wister also deleted a pair of paragraphs from the magazine
version of "In a State of Sin" that subtly denigrate Molly
Wood. Though on the surface she may seem superior to the
Virginian, the narrator asserts that "from him she would
inevitably learn" about love and that "the woman who
should get him for lover and husband" would "know a passion and a protection of not the every-day kind." That is, in
omitting these passages Wister qualified the male chauvin-
ism of the original version.

In a late interpolation to the story, a sequel to "Superstition Trail" entitled "The Spinster Loses Some Sleep,"
Judge Henry, a former federal judge, must justify to a distraught Molly the lynching of Steve and Ed. He explains
that in Wyoming "the law has been letting our cattle thieves
go for two years. We are in a very bad way, and we are try-

ing to make that way a little better until civilization can reach us." When government fails to protect the rights of a sovereign people, Judge Henry continues, ordinary citizens "must take justice back" into their own hands "where it was once at the beginning of all things. Call this primitive, if you will. But so far from being a defiance of the law, it is an assertion of it—the fundamental assertion of self-governing men, upon whom our whole social fabric is based."

As Wister tells the story, John Locke is on the side of the vigilantes. But as Jane Kuenz protests, "the 'we' Judge Henry repeatedly invokes in his argument to Molly is not the 'ordinary citizens' he claims they are, but the 'we' of cattle barons like himself who have considerable interest in seeing the West won in their own way. 'Ordinary citizens' were more like the homesteaders trying to settle on the same land large ranchers had always used without ever bothering actually to claim." The judge in effect justifies the Johnson County War from the cattlemen's point of view.

In truth, moreover, Wister's defense of lynching at the turn of the century, despite his attempt at fine distinctions, might as easily have applied to the South as to the West—this in a year (1901) when a hundred and five blacks and twenty-five whites were lynched, a ratio of more than four to one. The next year, when *The Virginian* was published, eighty-five blacks and seven whites were lynched, a ratio of more than twelve to one. The vast majority of all lynchings—some 90 percent, according to Gunnar Myrdal—occurred in the South, and most of the victims there were black.

Wister composed the coda of the novel, "At Dunbarton," in which the Virginian and Molly honeymoon in the mountains and then visit Molly's relatives in Vermont, before writing the preceding chapter, "With Malice Aforethought," in which the Virginian kills Trampas in a gunfight. That is, Wister had decided before writing the climactic scene that his hero would shoot the villain, marry the heroine, and meet the heroine's family. He considered an alternative ending: the death of the Virginian at the hands of Trampas. "My pen paused suspended over that solution," he claimed, "and I saw all the reasons for so doing but more for not so doing. It took a year before I was certain that killing would be merely a bow to the ritual of the higher banality and then the first class thing was just the marriage." Sarah Butler Wister was convinced, however, that "At Dunbarton" was superfluous even if the Virginian survived the duel. Her son defended the ending: "I should write it the same way over again." (He echoes here the Virginian's insistence, after hanging Steve, that he "would do it all over again the same this morning" and Molly's insistence, in an early draft of "The Sincere Spinster," that she would travel alone two thousand miles to the West "right over again tomorrow!") He believed it "desirable to have some serene closing cadences" after the drama of the shootout, that it was "essential the hero should meet the Great Aunt" and "desirable his unromantic future" should be foretold. The final chapter also serves again to contrast Lin McLean, who in "How Lin McLean Went East" fails to adapt to eastern manners, with the Virginian, who demonstrates his capacity to adapt to circumstances when he visits Dunbarton. That is, the hero proves he is equally at home on the range and in the effete and sophisticated East. Wister thought that the final chapter of *The Virginian* contained "the best pages I have ever written," though modern readers are not so sure. John Cobbs sniffed that the schmaltz was aimed straight at female readers. In any case, the blessed union of the Southern hero and Yankee heroine at the close of *The Virginian* gestures in the direction of the post-Civil War "reconciliation novel" of North and South invented by John W. DeForest in *Miss Ravenel's Conversion* (1867) and featured in Albion Tourgée's *A Fool's Errand* (1879).

Ironically, Wister purchases his happy ending with an ominous silence about its implications. The Virginian, soon to become the judge's partner and "an important man" in the territory, explains to Molly's great-aunt at Dunbarton that, if necessary to protect his herd, he will fence "big pastures" and haul in "hay and shelter" for winter. "What we'll spend in improvements," he avers, "we'll more than save in wages." In other words, he will become exactly the type of cattle baron who fires cowpunchers when they become obsolete. With infallible foresight, moreover, he will forestall the crash in cattle prices when the thieves prevail in Wyoming "by driving his herds to Montana." But Wister fails to mention, as Max Westbook explains, the reason that Montana, unlike Wyoming, is safe territory for the cattle: "In that state, the cattle barons cooperated with small ranchers and devised a fair system for handling new-born (therefore unbranded) calves, the major source of potential disputes." In Montana, that is, a cattle war had been unnecessary.

The chapters Wister added to the manuscript during the winter of 1902 also betray the influence of Walt Whitman. Though they lived in close proximity for many years—one in Camden, New Jersey, the other across the Delaware River in Philadelphia—Whitman and Wister probably never met. The poet died just as Wister was launching his literary career, but the younger writer certainly read and admired *Leaves of Grass*. He discovered the Good G(r)ay Poet as a fifteen-year-old prep school student; he sent his mother a copy of "To a Locomotive in Winter"; he selected both "When Lilacs Last in the Door-Yard Bloom'd" and "Pioneers! O Pioneers!" for particular praise; he ranked Whitman with Emerson, Poe, Hawthorne, and Mark Twain "at the highest level of American literature"; and he commended the chapter on Whitman in *Understanding America* (1927) by his fellow Philadelphian, collaborator, and cousin Langdon Mitchell.

Not surprisingly, Wister repeatedly alluded to Whitman's verse, albeit without attribution, in the final chapters of his novel. In chapter 35, to cite a minor example, the hero walks around the town of Medicine Bow "aloof in the open air," a phrase that parrots lines in "Song of the Open Road." Even more obvious allusions to Whitman have puzzled critics since the original publication of Wister's novel. In chapter 30, the narrator, a former tenderfoot able to travel alone in the wilderness for the first time, yearns to be initiated into the guild of western horsemen: "I wanted no speech with any one, nor to be near human beings at all. I was steeped in a revery [*sic*] as of the primal earth; even thoughts themselves had almost ceased motion. To lie down with wild animals, with elk and deer, would have made my waking dream complete," but "such dream could not be," given the narrator's obligations. Still, "to leave behind all noise and mechanisms, and set out at ease, slowly, with one packhorse, into the wilderness," he reflects, "made me feel that the ancient earth was indeed my mother and that I had found her again after being lost among houses, customs, and restraints." Similarly, during his wedding journey in the Wyoming mountains in chapter 36, the hero of *The Virginian* drifts into a Whitmanesque reverie. He and Molly Stark Wood spy

a little wild animal swimming round the rock from above. It had not seen them, nor suspected their presence. They held themselves still, watching its alert head cross through the waves quickly and come down through the pool, and so swim to the other side. There it came out on a small stretch of sand, turned its gray head and its pointed black nose this way and that, never seeing them, and then rolled upon its back in the warm dry sand. After a minute of rolling, it got on its feet again, shook its fur, and trotted away.

Then the bridegroom husband opened his shy heart deep down.

"I am like that fellow," he said dreamily. "I have often done the same." And stretching slowly his arms and legs, he lay full length upon his back, letting his head rest upon her. "If I could talk his animal language, I could talk to him," he pursued. "And he would say to me: 'Come and roll on the sands. Where's the use of fretting? What's the gain in being a man? Come roll on the sands with me.' That's what he would say." The Virginian paused. "But," he continued, "the trouble is, I am responsible. If that could only be forgot forever by you and me!"

Put another way, in chapters 30 and 36 of *The Virginian* Wister seems to allude to Whitman's "Song of Myself," especially section 32:

> I think I could turn and live with animals, they are so placid and
>   self-contain'd,
> I stand and look at them long and long.
> They do not sweat and whine about their condition,
> They do not lie awake in the dark and weep for their sins,
> They do not make me sick discussing their duty to God,
> Not one is dissatisfied, not one is demented with the mania of
>   owning things,
> Not one kneels to another, nor to his kind that lived thousands of
>   years ago,
> Not one is respectable or unhappy over the whole earth.

In chapter 36, moreover, Wister anticipates the final apotheosis of the cowboy in a merger with nature. "Often when I have camped here," the Virginian tells Molly, "it has made me want to become the ground, become the water, become the trees, mix with the whole thing. Not know myself from it. Never unmix again." He echoes here Whitman's declaration in section 31 of "Song of Myself" that "I find I incorporate gneiss, coal, long-threaded moss, fruits, grains, esculent roots" and Whitman's final resolution in section 52 to "bequeath myself to the dirt to grow from the grass I love." Read in the context of Wister's admiration for Whitman, the Virginian expresses neither a death wish nor a yearning to regress to childhood nor an urge to escape but simply a desire to dissolve in nature the poet describes in "Song of Myself."

By early March 1902, Wister was working on "the last, long chapter" of the novel, "With Malice Aforethought," published in two parts in the *Saturday Evening Post* in May. He had struck on an idea for the end of the novel while hunting in Wyoming in the summer of 1897. The Virginian is challenged by Trampas to a duel at sundown; Molly threatens to end their engagement if he accepts the challenge; and the hero, compelled by a masculine code of honor, shoots and kills Trampas in the street. Wister worried that the editor and publisher of the *Post*, George Horace Lorimer, would not understand that the Virginian slays Trampas on the ground of "justifiable homicide." Lorimer assured him on March 11 that this was not the case, however. "You certainly could not find a jury South of Mason and Dixon's line who would convict your hero," Lorimer advised him, "and I do not see how he could get more than five years even in New England. It is a rattling good story." Nevertheless, as a concession to the law, Wister has the Virginian declare, after killing Trampas, that "if anyone"—meaning the sheriff— "wants me about this . . . I will be at the hotel."

Of course, all ends happily. After the hero has disposed of the villain, Molly capitulates to love and accepts her social and economic dependence on a man. She and the Virginian wed as planned on July 3—significantly, the anniversary of the day in 1775 that Washington assumed command of the Continental militia—and together they watch the sun rise over their bridal camp the following morning—appropriately, the Fourth of July. Symbolically, at least, a new era has dawned. In effect, *The Virginian* offers an unapologetic defense of vigilante justice in the Johnson County range war against small farmers in 1892.

Lorimer was delighted. "I think it one of the best stories that we have ever had for the Post," he wrote Wister. The author sent the final corrections to the second part of "With Malice Aforethought" to the magazine on March 28, drafted a preface to the novel dated March 31, and mailed the entire manuscript to Macmillan on April 1. "I hope you may have the time (sometime) to read *The Virginian*," he wrote in his cover letter to the editor George Brett. "It has—or will have when all the proof is pulled off—about 490 pages—209 of which are wholly new!" On May 10, the second of two installments of "With Malice Aforethought" appeared in the *Post*, and on May 16 he wrote Lorimer to express his relief that no one had complained about the Virginian's street-style execution of Trampas: "I have now 4 letters from strangers about that story! None object to its morals. Isn't that re-assuring! But I now discover that I had been hoping you would get some protest from the sewing-circle & am disappointed. Of such perverse material are writers composed."

The same day, Wister received an advance copy of the novel from Macmillan and wrote Brett to express his pleasure. "It looks as I have always wanted my books to look," he avowed, "and as they never have looked until now. The cover is admirable—just right; the weight and bulk of the volume equally so, to my thinking; I have always liked the type extremely, and now that I see the page it makes, I like it more, if possible." He soon conceded to his mother that he wished the novel "was 20 times better than it is. I'd already like to have it back to make certain things better. But I think it is very much of an advance" on his earlier books. And he never expected again to "light on a character so engaging" as the Virginian. "That only happens once, even to the great ones of the earth." *The Virginian*, marketed as summer reading, was issued on schedule on May 30 and, as Wister reminisced later, "caught all the rush to the New England coast and mountains."

5

1902–1911

At the age of forty-one, Owen Wister became one of the most famous and successful writers in America. *The Virginian* unexpectedly took the book market by storm. More by chance than design, Wister caught a trend in the trade toward popular historical romances epitomized by such books as Weir Mitchell's *Hugh Wynne, Free Quaker* (1897), Charles Major's *When Knighthood was in Flower* (1898), Maurice Thompson's *Alice of Old Vincennes* (1900), and Mary Johnston's *To Have and to Hold* (1900). The "bones" of *The Virginian*, as John Seelye has argued, "were those of the historical romance, the grand tradition of Sir Walter Scott and Fenimore Cooper." That is, Wister was not a true realist but a local-colorist who shared a romantic sensibility with the most popular novelists of his generation.

The first printing of *The Virginian* sold out within three days. In the first week, as Wister wrote Brett, it earned two-thirds of what *Red Men and White, Lin McLean*, and *The Jimmyjohn Boss* combined "have done in two, five, and seven years." Macmillan issued a third printing on June 25, by which time *The Virginian* topped the best-seller lists in New York City. It sold fifty thousand copies during its first two months in print, another fifty thousand in August, was the best-selling novel of 1902, and Wister earned about thirty thousand dollars in royalties in less than a year. He bragged later that "by January 1903, it had been reprinted 15 times; by January 1911, it had been reprinted 38 times," and "by January 1928, fourteen various editions of it, here and in England, had been published." As late as 1932, it still sold about thirty thousand copies annually. It had also been translated into Swedish, Finnish, Danish, French, German, Spanish, Polish, Serbo-Croatian, and Arabic. It was such a sales success that George Brett tried to persuade Wister to follow it immediately with another "cow-boy story," though Wister declined. "I told him this was precisely what I did not intend to do," Wister remembered. "I had written four volumes about the West; I expected to write more, but not just then; I wished to turn to other themes for a while."

The Virginian was no less a critical than a commercial triumph. Virtually every reviewer extolled it, among them the *New York Times* ("Wister has come pretty near to writing the American novel"), the *Atlantic Monthly* ("The Virginian wins his successes fairly by force of character"), the *San Francisco Chronicle* ("by far the most striking picture of a genuine cowboy that has yet been painted"), the *Brooklyn Eagle* ("does with the pen what Remington achieves with brush and crayon"), and the Philadelphia *Public Ledger* ("will live as the epic of a day and conditions unique, but forever gone, in the development of our nation"). Elia W. Peattie declared in the *Chicago Tribune* that books like *The Virginian* "make the true Americana." A few reviewers singled out "Superstition Trail" for particular praise; for example the *New York Tribune* ("The lynching especially is treated as we believe no other living writer could have treated it, in a tone which is as far removed from that of sensationalism as the most fastidious critic could desire"), and the poet Harriet Monroe in the *Chicago American* ("In that last breakfast of captors and captives at dawn away up in the lonely mountains Mr. Wister has reached his highest point of simple and tragic art"). The *Nation* noticed the similarity of the hero to the first president ("As a cow-puncher of Wyoming he is . . . a historical personage, as genuine as George Washington"). As usual, Wister's writing was hailed for its realism, albeit mistakenly, as by the *Boston Advertiser* ("a faithful picture of a western day and generation") and the *Philadelphia Record* ("The realism of his type and manners is pushed almost too far by the author"). Not surprisingly, given the fascination with the American West abroad, *The Virginian* was also well received in England, though the *Spectator* averred that the humor of the tall tale about frog ranching told by the Virginian was totally incomprehensible to the British mind. According to the London *Daily Graphic*, in tracing "the growth of character through a long novel" Wister did what Harte had been "unhappily unable to do." Joining the chorus of praise were the *Athenaeum* ("a particularly well-constructed story"), the *Saturday Review* ("adds to the resources of American fiction"), and the *Academy and Literature* ("an importation from America which we can welcome without reservation").

To be sure, some readers found trifling reasons to carp. Predictably, several reviewers complained about the title, insisting that buyers were liable to confuse Wister's novel with Thackeray's *The Virginians* (1857). Julian Hawthorne, whom Frederick Macmillan had dismissed as a contributor to his magazines in 1883, opined in the *New York American* that he was "not quite so enchanted" with Wister's novel "as I expected to be." The *Baltimore Sun* asserted that Wister's "faulty character-drawing militates strongly against the claim that this book ranks as literature." True to his reputation for pedantry, William Lyon Phelps, professor of English at Yale University, wrote Wister to report an inconsistency in the text: the narrator paradoxically reports near the end of chapter 23 that "Shorty could not read" but near the end of chapter 32 he notes that when he and the Virginian lift Shorty's dead body "we saw the newspaper that he had been reading." Wister never corrected the error.

Several critics slighted Molly Wood's charms, and Wister conceded the force of the complaint: "I agree that the heroine is a failure," he wrote his mother. "She seems to me without personality." Six months after publication, he reiterated the point to Richard Harding Davis: "To me the heroine is nobody and nothing. Merely some remarks and petticoats labeled with a name." As late as 1929, Wister reiterated that "I don't like the girl. Never did. Tried hard to. Failed. She was really just a little self-righteous Puritan with all her nature under lock and key. The Virginian did unlock what there was of it, but she wasn't good enough for him. I don't think he ever found that out."

More serious were the objections to Wister's fumblings in the novel over issues of race. The critic for the *Sewanee Review*, published in Tennessee, censured the "inartistic and untrue" scene in which Judge Henry insists on a distinction between the lynching of cattle rustlers in private and the lynching of "Negroes" in public. A chagrined citizen in Wilmington, North Carolina, insisted in a letter to the author that "negroes" did not read newspapers, so lynchings and burnings of black rapists and killers were perforce public spectacles necessary to deter future crimes. Wister was piqued by the criticism and offered to address it in an appendix to future editions of the novel. After living in Charleston, South Carolina, he explained to Brett, "I am in a better position than almost any writer in our midst to say things about the negro [*sic*] question. I have a *lot* to say. Shall I?" Brett approved the suggestion, to Wister's relief. "What I have to say is not new—but has not been anywhere said by one man. It will find favor with all Southern & most Northern people—but it would highly displease the Evening Post & the Boston Transcript, should they deign to notice it." Fortunately, nothing came of the idea, though

Wister set his novel of Southern manners, *Lady Baltimore* (1906), in Charleston and commented at length on racial politics in it.

Predictably, too, a few reviewers qualified their high opinion of *The Virginian* by criticizing its episodic quality. Despite Wister's efforts to connect the chapters, it was, according to these readers, structurally similar to *Lin McLean*. Like the earlier book, declared the New York *Sun*, it was "really a collection of separate tales." Frank Mather complained in *Forum* that the novel betrayed, "in a certain episodic character and lack of unity, the marks of its composition from isolated sketches," and Lucy Monroe, while admiring it, lamented in *Critic* its inconsistency in point of view: "The effect is as if the book were written by two different hands—partly in the first person and partly in the third. It is a method which cannot be defended as art, for it brings in the outsider and his impressions too rudely for symmetry." Sarah Wister also complained to her son about the piecemeal structure of the novel, though he replied in his own defense that the "unflagging and developing personality" of his hero unifies "the book quite fundamentally, rendering the ordinary construction unnecessary." The fact "that every critic (who speaks of it at all) explains . . . that the *interest* holds from the first page to the last" is "proof of a very deep kind of unity," he insisted. Wister might have been referring to a trio of reviews in New York newspapers: the *Herald* ("a series of sketches . . . held together by the fascinating personality of the hero"), the *World* ("The chapters are sufficiently linked . . . by the personality of the tall, gentle-voiced Southerner"), and the *Commercial Advertiser* ("The central figure, the 'Virginian,' possesses an individuality and a strength which would give unity to episodes far more disconnected than these"). The *Philadelphia North American* put the most favorable spin possible on the novel's lack of formal structure: "Wister does not concern

himself with problems of art." This the reviewer intended
as high praise.

The novel was also lauded by several of Wister's friends
and fellow authors. Among the fan letters Wister received
was one from Roosevelt, who wrote on White House sta-
tionery that he thought *The Virginian* "a remarkable novel.
If I were not President, and therefore unable to be quoted,
I should like nothing better than to write a review of it. I
have read it all through with absorbed interest." Roosevelt
had doubted that Wister could "combine those short stories into a novel without the loss of charm and power. Yet
I think you have greatly increased both their charm and
their power." John Hay, the secretary of state, who had met
Wister through Roosevelt, also wrote him an appreciative
note. "Mrs. Hay has just finished reading 'The Virginian'
aloud to me," Hay reported. "I have to thank you for a
great and stimulating pleasure. It is good all through—not
a false note in it. It is *seen* from beginning to end; one of
the few genuine bits of art I have enjoyed in recent years."
Jack London thought *The Virginian* "*the* book about the
cowboy," that Wister had "justified and explained" his
personality. Despite their obvious political differences, the
socialist Upton Sinclair also congratulated Wister. He had
read *The Virginian* while sitting in a meadow, and when "a
deer came out in front of my nose" Sinclair "never turned a
hair," so fixated was he on the novel. Wister's friend Henry
James similarly regarded the novel as "a rare and remarkable feat. . . . You have made [the hero] *live* with a high,
but lucid complexity, from head to foot & from beginning
to end; you have not only intensely seen & conceived him,
but you have reached with him an admirable objectivity."
However, James tempered his praise with reservations, especially about Molly ("the little Vermont person") and the
happy ending. He "would not have let [the Virginian] live
& be happy; I should have made him perish in his flower &

in some splendid somber way," presumably in the gunfight with Trampas. That is, James bemoaned the romantic elements that mar the final chapters. He also urged Wister not to revive the hero in a sequel.

The critical response to *The Virginian* was not limited to friendly letters and published reviews, however. At least three western novels were also written in direct reply to it. The first of them, and the most benign, appeared from the pen of the African American poet Paul Laurence Dunbar, best known for his dialect verse. In 1899, while living in Denver, Dunbar wrote a western novel entitled *For the Love of Landry.* Apart from a cameo appearance of a Pullman porter, the novel contains no black characters. Instead, it betrays the influence of the earliest stories in *Harper's Monthly* featuring the Virginian, especially "Where Fancy Was Bred" and "Grandmother Stark." Mildred Osborne, a genteel easterner, goes west for her health to a ranch "situated somewhere between Denver and the setting sun"—a region that presumably includes Wyoming. On the ranch she meets and falls in love with a western cowhand with mysterious antecedents known merely as Landry, who despite his low station exhibits the polite manners and language of a gentleman inherited "from some old Virginia grandfather." As in Wister's novel, Landry defends the heroine's reputation from the insinuations of a Trampas-type, saves her from stampeding cattle much as the Virginian saves Molly from an overturned stagecoach, and woos her for months before his proposal of marriage is finally accepted. In each novel the vestal of eastern civilization, Mildred or Molly, is exactly twenty years old and resists the romantic overtures of the hero because she considers him of inferior caste. Much as Mildred's aunt "fainted at the first lines of the letter" announcing her engagement to Landry, Molly's mother must "gather her senses after the shock" of her daughter's letter announcing her engagement to the Virginian. Mildred receives a condescending letter from her sister in New York, who asks if Landry "wore many pistols"; Molly receives a letter from her sister in New England commending her for choosing a lover "so scrupulous" that he has "never killed for pleasure or profit." In the end, much as the Virginian is a natural aristocrat who proves his mettle, Landry turns out to be the scion of a distinguished family who rebuilds the ancestral fortune through mining and ranching. If imitation is the sincerest form of flattery, Wister had every reason to feel flattered.

Frederic Remington, Wister's onetime friend and former illustrator, also published a novel in reply to *The Virginian*. Privately, Remington derided Wister's story as "slop" and "without truth." He ridiculed the eastern narrator as a "thin-chested, cigarette-smoking dude." He declined the opportunity to illustrate Wister's novel and, in apparent response to the insult, Wister failed even to send Remington a copy of it. In *John Ermine of the Yellowstone* Remington virtually parodied *The Virginian*. As the *New York Times* fairly noted in its review, *John Ermine* "makes one think of *The Virginian*, and yet it is *The Virginian* with a thousand differences." It was published six months after Wister's novel; both stories are set at least in part in Wyoming, and both contain a love story. Like Wister's hero, John Ermine falls in love with a genteel eastern woman. Much as the Virginian rescues Molly Wood from an overturned stagecoach, Ermine saves Katherine Searles's life after her horse steps in a gopher hole and throws her to the ground. She even permits him to kiss her. But here the comparisons end. Wister's white-bre(a)d hero was a much more idealized figure than Remington's uncouth scout. The Virginian incarnates the conflict between the natural West and the civilized East, resolves it, marries the heroine, and becomes a rich rancher. John Ermine, who is raised by Indians, incarnates the conflict between western or naïve honesty and eastern or white duplicity, fails to resolve it, is spurned by the anti-heroine, and is killed. *The Virginian* is a romantic, optimistic success story that anticipates a prosperous future for the West; *John Ermine* is a tale of decline and failure pervaded by a sense of doom. Whereas Indians appear only offstage or in the margins in Wister's novel, Remington depicts a West populated by Mexicanos, Irish soldiers and servants, mixed-bloods, and many tribes of Indians. Whereas the Virginian serves as an agent of civilization, lynching cattle rustlers and gunning down the villain, John Ermine is a primitive man who ends his life a martyr to civilization. In the end, both Wister's and Remington's heroes prefer death to dishonor. The difference is that Ermine actually dies after he has been robbed of his self-respect, forced into outlawry, and rejected by the woman he loves. In effect, Remington wrote the final chapters of *The Virginian* in a way Henry James would have approved. On the eve of the publication of *John Ermine*, Remington forewarned Wister that his "little old story comes out soon" but it "wont interest you. However if you read it tell me what's what and spare not." There is no evidence that Wister replied, and Remington's "little old story" effectively ended their correspondence.

Charlotte Perkins Gilman, a leading American feminist intellectual early in the twentieth century, also read *The Virginian* soon after its publication in 1902. A copy of the first edition survives among the books in her library, and she alluded to it in her autobiography—in particular to the baby-swap scene in "Where Fancy Was Bred"—but from a point of view very different from Wister's. In *The Living of Charlotte Perkins Gilman* (1935), she compared Wister's barbeque and dance to a ball she had attended in Utah in 1888: "The bedrooms were all occupied by sleeping babies, as described in *The Virginian*." She singled out this episode for special mention because, by permitting his hero to disrupt a kindergarten, Wister mocked the practice of efficient and cooperative child care that was a centerpiece of her reform agenda.

Much as *The Virginian* is sometimes described as a cowboy novel without cows, moreover, Gilman later wrote a western, *The Crux* (1911), without a male hero. Morton Elder, the character who might have filled that role, is instead a rake and syphilitic coward. Nor does Gilman's western feature either adventure or a compelling love story, staples of the formula. To be sure, the fair New England heroine, Vivian Lane, like Wister's Molly Stark Wood, has inherited "a store of quiet strength from some Pilgrim Father or Mother." If Molly is Wister's type of independent woman, then Vivian is Gilman's. While Molly and the Virginian eventually marry and live happily ever after, however, Vivian eventually breaks off her romance with Morton Elder when she discovers he is afflicted with venereal disease.

Both the Virginian and Vivian are agents of civilization. They even have similar names—both begin with a "Vi" and end with "ian"; that is, their names are alliterative and they rhyme. Each of them "wins" the West, but in distinctively different ways—the Virginian with revolver and rope, Vivian with pencil and pen. Gilman described not a "regeneration through violence" as in the typical male narrative of the period, but a regeneration through literacy. In other words, according to Jennifer Tuttle, *The Crux* is "a middle-class white woman's answer to the Western," specifically Wister's western. Jane Bellair, a woman physician, persuades Vivian and a group of other New England women to pull up stakes and move to Colorado. "Break away now, my dear, and come West. You can get work—start a kindergarten or something." (Like Molly Wood, Vivian is a teacher.) Bellair's surname suggests the health benefits to women in the West, and she diagnoses the medical conditions from which the women in New England suffer: "arrested development" or "an advanced stage of *arthritis deformans* of the soul." Her role as the heroine's mentor in Gilman's novel is analogous to the role of Judge Henry in *The Virginian*. Whereas

Henry commissions the hero to lynch a gang of cattle rustlers, however, Bellair leads women to a peaceful West where she founds a prosperous community governed by women who are reinvigorated. Or as Tuttle again explains: "Vivian experiences the kind of personal transformation in the West that Wister had reserved for his male narrator. . . . Vivian's West Cure and new life in Colorado are central to Gilman's plot and are clear rewritings of Molly Wood's role in Wister's Western."

Both Wister and Gilman depict the West in similarly racialized terms, however. As in the male western, Gilman's western reflects conventional ideas about race and racial conquest. Their Wests are dominated by Anglo-Saxons, and neither novel portrays ethnic minorities. As Tuttle observes, "the reinvigorated 'race' of Americans in Gilman's Edenic West is white, and is to be saved and 'improved' by 'clean' New England women—the 'good people' and 'best civilization.'" Gilman thus aligned her belief in eugenics with her feminist rhetoric. Like Wister's whitewashed West, her West presumes Anglo-Saxon superiority and so her ideas are in this sense as passé as his. But at least she understood the extent to which conventional westerns were gender-biased.

Scarcely two weeks after submitting the completed manuscript of *The Virginian* to George Brett, Wister was contemplating his next move. First, strangely enough, he wanted to prove that he was more than a one-trick pony by writing a novel about Saunderstown and vampires. "Would you believe," he asked an interviewer, "that within sound of the whistle of the New York, New Haven and Hartford locomotives there are people, many people, who believe in vampires?" In October he assured Lorimer of the *Saturday Evening Post* that the "bloodthirsty" novel was "now fairly organized in my head, and will be quite full of Rhode Island. I shall certainly show it to you before any other editor, but am doubtful about serial publication." Nothing more than a few penciled notes survive of the project. Then he decided to write a long-planned, monumental novel about the West, tentatively entitled "The Star of Empire," set in "a somewhat earlier day than *The Virginian*. It will be a broader story, too—taking in the whole of pioneer life—Indians, hunters, first settlers, cowboys, desperadoes and all." It would be "a very large proposition," as he informed Brett,

indeed I have a chance to make it by far the greatest piece of Western fiction that has been done & I must sweat blood to 'get there.' It will be a canvas as big as our map, taking in as it does Arizona, New York City, the Missouri River, & Oregon, and I must make my boy & his friends & his loves so interesting to the reader that he will want to read every word. I cannot tell at all how long I shall need for such a job.

He had told Remington years before that "I should do it when I knew enough about writing: & now I do." At the time, Remington had offered to illustrate the story: "Mind, nobody but me is to do that with you." In December 1899, in fact, Remington had urged Wister to return to the West and "do the 4 volume novel about a South Western Natty Bumpo." Despite the success of *The Virginian* and the luxury it afforded him, Wister never wrote either novel, and he did not even visit the West again until 1910.

Instead, he picked up a few odd writing jobs for *Outlook* and the *Saturday Evening Post*. "I am doing 2 or 3 short things that never could be worked into long ones, & which bring me 10 cents a word," he explained. "Our small town house needs a new furnace & these are going to pay for it, and leave me some change." One of them, "How the Energy Was Conserved," written in the early summer of 1902, was based on an anecdote Wister recorded in his journal during his 1895 trip to the Southwest. Captain Jug Wood, "large, swearing, and bibulous" and stationed at Fort Huachuca, Arizona, marries the daughter of the Episcopal minister at Tucson. She takes "great interest" in the spiritual welfare of "some recruits from the South of the shouting Methodist persuasion" and plays the melodeon, a primitive organ, "for them at their praying-bees. It seems that the Captain was not aware precisely how deeply religious these gatherings had become." One evening "a young soldier came through his gate" and asked for "Sister Wood," whereupon "the furious officer" kicked him over the fence and "the shoutings were no longer rendered harmonious by the organ playing of Sister Wood." Wister's retelling of the story ends as the secretary of war, a professed champion of the enlisted man who once addressed the troops at the fort, ignores the soldier's letter of complaint.

Wister finished another story in September, "The Vicious Circle," featuring Scipio Le Moyne, based on an anecdote J. W. Redington told him in Oregon in the autumn of 1900. Redington "was carrying dispatches for Howard in the Bannock Campaign of 78, was directed to follow a fence, & follows a circle." In Wister's retelling of events, set chronologically not long after "The Game and the Nation," Scipio has been entrusted on an errand with payroll money by Judge Henry. He is robbed, but convinces the thief to follow a trail until he can ambush him and retrieve the cash. Wister was paid $450 for the story by George Horace Lorimer and it appeared in the *Saturday Evening Post* in December 1902.

On June 9, 1902, scarcely a week after publication of *The Virginian*, the theatrical producer Kirke La Shelle contacted Wister with an idea, or at least the seed of one.

> It has occurred to me that your book 'The Virginian' might afford subject matter for a play which in the hands of a dramatist like Augustus Thomas would develop into a play for the higher class market. I have briefly touched upon the matter with Mr. Thomas and am in a position to say that should, upon a further examination of the subject matter referred to, my impression be borne

out, I can command Mr. Thomas' services in the making of such a play.

La Shelle took a ninety-day option on the project. Three months later, however, Thomas reported to La Shelle "that he could not make a play" from the novel. Undeterred, the impresario wrote Wister in late September. He still wanted to produce a play based on *The Virginian*, perhaps even one based on *Lin McLean*, but he needed Wister's help. "In case we strike a bargain," he advised the author, "I would of course desire such a co-operation from you as may be necessary for it is possible that some new bits might become desirable in filling in the chinks and nobody could do that so well as you." La Shelle invited Wister to develop his own scenario, though he also offered some thoughts: "The plan I have will carry the first, second and fourth acts and I will require some invention for a third act leading up to the wounding of the Virginian by Trampas." La Shelle wanted to telescope the plot—by replacing the Indians, who shoot the hero in "Balaam and Pedro," with Trampas, who shoots the hero after he leads the posse that lynches Steve.

In the wake of the sales success of *The Virginian*, George Brett also urged Wister to adapt the story for the stage. After all, the titles to chapters one ("Enter the Man") and five ("Enter the Woman") are stage directions, and "The Game and the Nation" sequence (chapters 13 to 16) is divided into "acts." Wister protested in early October 1902, about a week after La Shelle urged him to draft a script, that he was "not going to write a play when I don't know how on a book which contains only one act of a play"—the hanging of the cattle-rustlers. He initially concurred with Thomas that it was impossible "that any play at all could be made from a story which, by a long-cherished plan, was so deliberately picaresque." Three weeks later, however, he had changed his mind. "During my rides," he reported to Brett on October 28, "I have shaped a play of five acts, the

167

scheme of which is not yet committed to paper." In December he began to block out the play. In early January he wrote Lorimer that his work on the script was "oppressing me so heavily that I feel as if I'd never write anything again," and two months later he declared that he would "not be happy until two things happen: Thing 1, 200,000 [copies of the novel] sold; Thing 2, Play finished and accepted." On a happy note, he reported on March 3 "that Act 4 is propitiously begun." He completed a fifth act on March 18 and he considered it "so effective a play that I can't imagine it's not proving a thing managers would jump at."

He was mistaken. His myriad experiences in amateur theatricals notwithstanding, Wister was not a professional dramatist. He was ignorant of the requirements of the well-made play. As he explained later, "If a play arouses my interest at the start and holds it until the finish, I ask no questions about the craft with which it has been constructed." In his original script, the Virginian is already foreman of the Sunk Creek Ranch. Wister introduces a chorus of cow-punchers, including Trampas, Honey Wiggin, Steve, Dollar Bill, and two new characters, Razorback Charlie and Educated Simpson. Lin McLean does not appear. Wister later admitted that "the five acts which I originally wrote" were "pretty grim entertainment: no babies changed, no Emily, no Elk head [saloon]."

Wister focused the action in the play around the events of the Johnson County War, or as he explains in the stage directions: "Cattle are being stolen. Somebody will have to be lynched. Trampas is the suspected ringleader of the thieves. He is converting several young men, hitherto honest," including Steve. Much as Black Henry Smith had in fact tricked a friend into paying for his travel to South America and Europe in the 1880s, Trampas promises the rustlers they will dine on "patty de parly voo. . . . We'll take in the world. London, Paris, Vienna, Timbuctoo." In other words, the romance of the Virginian and Molly is subordinated to, in Wister's phrase, the "main plot" of the cattle war.

Wister set his five acts—eventually compressed to four—in the eating house in Medicine Bow, Uncle Hewie's cabin (the dance and barbeque), Horse Thief Pass (the lynching), Molly's cabin (the Virginian's recovery), and again in Medicine Bow (the gunfight between the hero and Trampas). In act 1, the Virginian defends his friend Steve, who is suspected of cattle-theft: "Steve and me has worked together, and we have holidayed together. I expect we have broke most all the ten commandments together. But (very slow, and taking one step forward) if anybody said 'thief' concerning Steve, it would be about the same—no, not *about* the same, it would be *exactly* the same—as saying 'thief' concerning me." Lest Steve succumb to the temptation to steal cattle, the Virginian offers him a steady job at Sunk Creek for forty dollars a month, which he declines. For his part, Steve repeatedly refers to the Virginian as "Jeff," the name given him only once in the novel. As if to prove his depravity, Trampas has earned his nickname "Sorghy" because he pours sorghum "on every blamed thing he eats. Pours it on his fried beef." Both Steve ("The whole of Johnston [*sic*] County's on our side") and Trampas ("Johnston County is about tired of these big ranch-owners and swell-heads like Judge Henry") rationalize their crimes. In act 2, which stages the barbeque to celebrate the christening of Uncle Hewie's twins, not the end of fall round-up with cattle at seventy-five dollars a head as in "Where Fancy Was Bred," the cattle barons compile a blacklist and commission "a secret expedition to catch these Cattle Thieves." In act 3, Wister dramatizes the lynching of Steve and his accomplice offstage to the sound of wind. As he wrote in the stage directions, "After the lynching, the moon rises, throwing upon a flat face of rock the black shadow of Steve as he hangs in mid-air." Wister also revises the note Steve writes to the Virginian on a newspaper. In the novel, it simply read "Good bye, Jeff. I could not have spoke to you without playing the baby." In the script, Wister added a line: "Keep my belt and six-shooter." As a result, Wister's final act, otherwise a faithful adaptation of the Virginian's duel with Trampas, ends with a twist: the Virginian kills Trampas on the street in Medicine Bow with Steve's revolver in a stroke of poetic if not theatrical justice.

Wister also wrote music for the play. A musical prodigy, he had occasionally composed songs inspired by his travels in the West, such as "A Frontier Symphony," arranged for four-handed piano and originally performed at the Manuscript Music Society of Philadelphia on January 15, 1896. He composed overtures for each of the four acts in the theatrical version of *The Virginian* entitled "American Medley," "Young Lochinvar," "Emily," and "Dawn of Love." He also included in the play a tune entitled "Ten Thousand Cattle Straying," which he had originally composed in 1888. "When it came to producing a dramatization of my book *The Virginian*," he remembered in 1928, "it struck me that the song would make a good point in the play, if used the way of what is now called a theme song." He taught the song—four stanzas and a chorus—to Frank Campeau, the actor who played Trampas, who, according to the script, hums the melody or sings the lyrics to it in every act. The sheet music for "Ten Thousand Cattle Straying" was published in 1904 along with a theatrical edition of the novel with a new, brief foreword by the author. The song also is played, without attribution to Wister, during the opening credits of the western movie *My Darling Clementine* (1946).

Wister sent his script first to Charles Frohman, owner of the Empire Theatre in New York and the Duke of York's Theatre in London, and a prominent producer of plays in both the United States and England. Frohman rejected it, though he offered to buy theatrical rights to the title and characters. But, as Wister put it, "I declined Frohman's terms, Frohman declined my terms." Fortuitously, La Shelle continued to be interested. The two men met in New York on June 10, 1903, "to talk . . . about both pieces"—*The Virginian* and *Lin McLean*. In mid-June, while awaiting La Shelle's verdict on the viability of the project, Wister also contacted David Belasco, another prominent producer, because he feared that La Shelle, like Frohman, would find "making the new version of the play harder than he anticipated." Wister noted that La Shelle was already producing "The Earl of Pawtucket" by Augustus Thomas, Remington's neighbor in New Rochelle, at the Manhattan Theater on Broadway—"a sure thing, & doesn't want a bird in the bush."

Again he was wrong: La Shelle was enthusiastic about staging *The Virginian*. He had rewritten Wister's script by late June, omitting Wister's opening act and so cutting the number from five to four, broadly adapted from the novel and organized according to this outline:

- Act I: Uncle Hewie's Cabin. "Where Fancy Was Bred" and "When You Call Me That, Smile."
- Act II: Judge Henry's Ranch. "The Game and the Nation" and "Em'ly."
- Act III: Horse Thief Pass. "Superstition Trail," "Grandmother Stark," and "The Spinster Loses Some Sleep."
- Act IV: Street corner in Medicine Bow. "With Malice Aforethought."

La Shelle read his first two acts aloud to Wister in New York, and within a few days he sent acts 3 and 4 to Philadelphia so that Wister might edit the dialogue, "as his in some places is not as good as I could write," Wister recalled. Overall Wister was delighted. La Shelle's "construction is very clever, the interest flows steadily, he keeps wonderfully close to the book, and he had introduced Em'ly with admirable ingenuity!" La Shelle even managed "to change the babies" in act 1 "without making it farce or horse play."

His new collaborator, Wister concluded, was "an *extraordinary* person, a mixture of subtle critical talent & shrewd business sense, and all hands say—more honest & square than anybody." The two men reached contractual agreement on June 25, 1903: as producer, La Shelle would stage the play before November 1 and pay Wister about 3 percent of the box office on the first four thousand dollars of gross receipts, about 6 percent of the next four thousand dollars, and 10 percent of the box office receipts after eight thousand dollars. Wister would advise "in the matter of dialogue, supervision of details in dress, manners and character usage" and would travel with the company during tryouts to assist, if necessary, in rewrites.

Wister checked into the Players Club in New York in August to help La Shelle punch up the script while La Shelle hired a cast. The draft they developed retained elements of both their earlier versions. They drew much of the dialogue directly from the novel, though they combined some of the characters (Lin and Scipio, Steve and Shorty, and the narrator and "Mr. Ogden," a tourist in the West). La Shelle and Wister also cut a few corners in their adaptation to enhance its theatricality. Although Molly doesn't appear until the eighth chapter of the novel, for example, she appears in the first act of the play. As the theater historian Richard Wattenberg observes, Trampas justifies cattle-rustling "by means of working-class revolutionary rhetoric" drained of nuance:

> Who says it's stealing? Why should Judge Henry make a pile out of the work you and me do for him? Who does the work? You and me, and how are the proceeds divided? You get $40 and the Judge 5000. Out' what? Cattle. Did God make the cattle for Judge Henry? They're as much yours and mine as his aren't they? Then why shouldn't we take what's our own?

Whereas fugitive Indians ambush the Virginian in the woods in "Balaam and Pedro," Trampas shoots the hero in the play, just as La Shelle had planned. For their part, the

Original cast of *The Virginian* (1904). Publicity still. Owen Wister Papers, American Heritage Center, University of Wyoming.

rustlers are explicitly identified—or stigmatized—as Mexicans in the dramatization. In addition to his Spanish name, Trampas in the adaptation is dressed as a Mexican vaquero. His accomplice, known as Ed Rogers in "Hank's Woman" and simply as Ed in "Superstition Trail," is renamed Spanish Ed in the play. The melodrama ends with Molly rushing into the hero's arms after his gunfight with Trampas; that is, it omits the events in both "Balaam and Pedro" and the second part of "At Dunbarton," while incorporating the major events of the rest of the novel.

Rehearsals began the last day of August and continued "briskly" all through September, Wister reported. "I began to get the following impressions: leading man good— and good in appearance, and good in accent." According to reviewers, although Dustin Farnum was a native New

Englander, he impersonated "an ideal Westerner—stalwart, strong and with the bearing, almost slouch, that is characteristic of men who live in Mexican saddles." At Wister's suggestion, La Shelle had sent Farnum to Richmond, Virginia, to study the part and "get the lingo" and accent. Campeau as Trampas was also "very good—the real thing; all the punchers good; most of the ranch men good; most of the women good." But Lucille York in the role of Molly was "awful," according to Wister. La Shelle assured him that "she'd come all right," but York "didn't get better but worse" in rehearsals. Finally, the play premiered at the Hyperion Theater in New Haven on September 30, 1903. Wister afterwards wrote his friend Dean Duke: "Big house. Acts 1 & 4 successful. Acts 2 & 3 cold. Girl fearful." The next night "she was worse. Third night, Friday, she fell all to pieces" and La Shelle fired her, admitting to Wister that he had been wrong. York's dismissal was an omen of things to come: for the first two years that the play was staged it continually limped on the casting of Molly.

La Shelle postponed the scheduled opening of the play in Boston for a week, and he and Farnum traveled to New York to find a new leading lady. While they auditioned actresses, Wister supervised rehearsals. The play opened at the Majestic Theater in Boston on October 10 with Nanette Comstock in the role of Molly. Although Wister thought Comstock "did very well indeed" under the circumstances—that is, after only four rehearsals—the reviews were brutal. The critics "damned the play up hill and down," he reported. The *Boston Transcript*, for example, griped that the play was "sluggish in action and wearisomely monotonous." Wister agreed. It "struck me as dull," particularly La Shelle's third act, which "was good in itself—but coming after a very gentle second act (also Kirke's) it was monotonous." This first staged version of the play skipped Wister's lynching scene, which both La Shelle and Sarah Wister judged too vulgar and violent for audiences. Instead, La

Shelle's act 2 ends as Judge Henry commissions the Virginian to lead the posse charged with executing the rustlers, and his act 3 begins after the hangings, which apparently occur during the intermission. "It became clear to me the play was a failure as it stood," Wister remembered later. To address the objection that the play was boring, the lynchings needed to be dramatized. La Shelle was blind "to the fact that his third act killed the play, and that my original act with the lynching was of vital importance to save us. We played [Boston] for two weeks. But always it grew plainer we were a failure."

Finally, La Shelle agreed to allow Wister to have his "day in court" with his third act "written over again with some new ideas." While still in Boston, Wister and John Stapleton, the director, began to doctor the script, and Wister soon decided not only that act 3 had to be rewritten, but also that acts 1 and 2 "required a tremendous lot of overhauling." Wister explained to Stapleton "how the 2nd Act could be made much better and he said go on and get at it." After La Shelle left the company for health reasons in late October, he wired Stapleton to make any changes his judgment approved; "Want play to have every chance." Stapleton then wrote Wister, "That gives us a clear field, and I am most anxious to have the first and second act changes all ready for rehearsal" when the company arrived in Syracuse on November 1. Wister joined Stapleton there "and we worked at new scenes in Act I day and night. . . . I sat at my table, in my shirt sleeves, writing until midnight or one o'clock, and getting up at 7.30 and taking copy to the typewriter and going on. Thus I had to do Whiskey while awake and then I had to take bromide to sleep." When the company arrived they "rehearsed the new stuff by day and played the old stuff by night." The new first act debuted in Geneva, New York, on November 4 and was, Wister boasted, a "big success—thanks to Stapleton and also to me. He taught me a lot about the play business."

While the company continued to stage the play across New York and Pennsylvania, Wister and Stapleton settled in Harlem to revise acts 2 and 3. They worked from November 8 until November 13 "in a little spittoon of a hotel, and got Act 2 (which I had re-written in Boston) still more re-written—all this time while Stapleton distrusted my lynching act as much as Kirke." Then "one night I read Act 3 to Stapleton and won him. He admitted that now for the first time he began to have faith in my scheme." Wister joined the company in Scranton, Pennsylvania, and "gave them their new parts for Act 2." Stapleton caught them at Wilkes-Barre, Pennsylvania, to rehearse the new act, and they staged it for the first time in Rochester, New York, on November 18 with "great success." Wister and Stapleton traveled to Buffalo, New York, ahead of the troupe to "polish up my Act 3" with the lynching scene in shadow, and after rehearsing it for a week they staged it for the first time during the Saturday matinee in Buffalo on November 28. "The house was reduced to tears," Wister reported, "and a better vindication no man ever got." He only regretted that La Shelle and Stapleton had failed to recognize "the pathos in that situation at first. For here was a man's whole Autumn used up in a wasteful way." Wister averred later that act 3 was the only act in which La Shelle "had no hand," and Wattenberg agrees that "it is perhaps the most effective scene in the play."

On December 3, the play finished its out-of-town try-outs in Erie, Pennsylvania, and the company was laid off for a month. Ironically, Nanette Comstock quit the company during the hiatus. The second Molly was haughty and imperious and, as Payne records, "as big a problem . . . as her predecessor." Farnum and Campeau both hated her, and Stapleton was "afraid of her." She was irritated, it seems, by the constant changes in the script, went to pieces in Buffalo while rehearsing the new third act, and gave her notice six weeks before the New York premiere. According to Payne, "Wister and the rest of the company were relieved at the news." Meanwhile, La Shelle had time enough to recruit and rehearse a third Molly, Agnes Ardeck.

On January 5, 1904, *The Virginian* opened at the Manhattan Theater on Broadway. It was popular among theater-goers from the first, even if the critics were luke-warm. The cast received five curtain calls after the second and third acts, though the *New York Herald* sniffed that "the play still needs pruning before it can expect lasting favor. There is too much unnecessary dialogue and the action lags in the earlier parts." Ardeck was the target of special scorn: William Winter of the *New York Tribune* complained that she "made Molly Wood a tongue-tied damsel, with a lisp, and expressed all her emotions by gasping." The *Herald* groused that she was "weak and monotonous" in the role. Acton Davies, drama critic of the New York *Sun*, executed the coup de grâce: "Agnes Ardeck was very blond as the heroine." Wister responded acerbically in his private jour-nal: "Mr. Acton Davies writes something like a critic. It is a pity he does not also write something like a gentleman; but this, I take it, is beyond him."

The playwrights enjoyed the last laugh. On January 18, Wister wrote Brett that he was "feeling surer and surer about the play. Bigger money second week than first." On the 23rd, the *Dramatic Mirror* declared *The Virginian* "is one of the few great successes of the season," and Zona Gale soon reported that it was "one of the financially suc-cessful plays of the winter." With his salary, Farnum bought a yacht in mid-April that he christened the *Wister*. The play was performed 138 times at the Manhattan before closing on April 30 to move to the Garrick Theater in Chicago. It opened there, with Gretchen Lyons in the role of Molly, on May 2 to enthusiastic audiences and warm reviews. Cam-peau wrote Wister on May 10 that the play "seems to be the hit of the season here" and the company "could stay here for three or four months and do a big business." He enclosed a notice by Amy Leslie, the distinguished theater critic of the *Chicago Daily News*: "Wister and La Shelle have achieved that which [Clyde] Fitch shot so short of in 'The Lady and the Cowboy.'" *The Virginian* was, Leslie crowed, "a triumphantly enjoyable American play and full of the life we know and love and believe in as a nation." It played Chicago for a month, with an average attendance of about seven hundred per night, before closing for the season.

The play cemented its success in 1904–05. With Helen Holmes as Molly, the fifth actress to perform the part, the company opened in Providence, Rhode Island, in October and performed week-long engagements in Philadelphia, Newark, and Brooklyn that month, and Manhattan, Baltimore, Washington, and Norfolk, Virginia, in November, with closing-night audiences in the larger cities often numbering more than two thousand. The troupe then marched across the South to the provinces—Atlanta, Montgomery, New Orleans, and in Texas Galveston, Houston, Austin, Corsicana, and Fort Worth before Christmas. After the holidays the play opened in St. Paul and headed west to Grand Forks, Spokane, Seattle, Portland, San Francisco, San Jose, and Los Angeles before touring Salt Lake City, Colorado Springs, Denver, Omaha, and Chicago.

Unfortunately, the production was not without its problems. Farnum became identified with the title role in *The Virginian* just as Joseph Jefferson and James O'Neill had been identified with the leads in the theatrical versions of *Rip Van Winkle* and *The Count of Monte Cristo*, respectively—and in the middle of the second season he demanded more money. La Shelle was paying him $375 a week, and after the success of the melodrama in New York in January 1903, the producer had offered him a ten-year contract to replace the four-year contract they already had. Farnum verbally agreed on the condition his salary was raised to $400 a week. When La Shelle sent him a written contract, however,

Farnum claimed he had been "offered more money" to act in another play and refused to sign. La Shelle replied, as he notified Wister in mid-January 1905, "that I was sorry to know that he was turning out like all other actors." La Shelle pointed out to Farnum "that in this matter he was trading on a value which was not his own" and that "I was quite satisfied to revert to my four years' contract with him and pay him the face value thereof. He refers to this as cutting his salary, whereas he has been receiving more than his salary under the verbal agreement with me which he now repudiates." La Shelle was infuriated by Farnum's ingratitude: "There is no actor in the world whom you can depend on after he has made a hit." Farnum had been "a wholly unknown proposition" before La Shelle cast him in the role, much to

> the surprise, not to say the amazement, of everybody 'in the know.' Of course he was the right man. That was the result of my judgment, and had nothing whatever to do with the value that I handed him. Also I paid him a larger salary than he had ever had and am still doing so. But the success of the piece following the New York engagement has swelled him up and made him think he ought to have half the profits. I shall stand, of course, upon the contract, and, if he leaves the performance, enjoin him from playing with anyone else.

Farnum remained with the company for the remainder of his four-year contract, at least in part because Mary B. Conwell was cast as the female lead in the third year. "I think we have the best 'Molly' that has ever played the part," Farnum wrote Wister in mid-December 1905. Farnum and Conwell eventually married.

But La Shelle was not mollified. In early March 1907, in the closing weeks of Farnum's contract, La Shelle wrote Wister that the actor seemed to harbor the hope "that he might continue with the company another year." But the producer had already decided to allow the contract to expire.

"Evidently Farnum appreciates the fact that he is getting a lot of money this year," he continued. "Between ourselves, I personally fancy that Farnum will receive more money for his current season's work than he will ever receive during any other single year of his life." The first week in March alone the play earned nearly $8,700 in Los Angeles and it was staged forty-two and a half weeks during the year. As La Shelle told Wister, "Not so bad for a piece now in its fourth season!" Farnum was succeeded in the role the next season by William S. Hart, not that his career suffered. He remained a popular stage and screen star until his death in 1929 and, in 1914, he was cast as the lead in the first film adaptation of *The Virginian*, directed by Cecil B. de Mille. The part has since been played on stage or in movies by such actors as Gary Cooper, Henry Fonda, and Joel McCrea. Nor did the production suffer appreciably from Farnum's departure. In 1911, a columnist in Denver, during an engagement of the play at the Tabor Grand Opera House there, described it as "actor-proof," an "old standby," and a "western classic." As late as 1942, four years after her father's death, Marina Wister Dasburg boasted that the play had made a fortune for the playwrights and their families and that "it is still acted by stock companies all over America."

The years between 1904 and 1909 were a fallow period in Wister's career as a western writer. When he traveled he crossed the Atlantic Ocean, not the Missouri River, though he bought a Shetland pony for his children to ride during their summers in Saunderstown. As Payne notes, it "kept Marina, a promising horsewoman, happy from dawn till dark." After Sarah Wister died in June 1908 he moved his brood—Molly and their four children—to her estate in the Germantown section of Philadelphia.

At about the same time, Wister's army friend from Arizona, Charles Skirdin, also turned up in Philadelphia—and in trouble. After being wounded in the Philippine-

American War, Skirdin had retired from the army, moved to Philadelphia and joined the local police force. In 1908, he was charged with murder in what was an accidental death and Wister testified on his behalf. "That man embodies all the characteristics of the hero of my novel, 'The Virginian,'" Wister declared under oath. "While no person was the actual prototype of the character, Skirdin, more than any man, embodies the type." Skirdin was exonerated. In 1916 Wister supported Skirdin's petition to Congress for a military pension on the ground of physical disability, and in 1918 the retired soldier was awarded twelve dollars per month.

After collaborating with La Shelle on the theatrical version of *The Virginian*, Wister wrote nothing about the West for publication for more than four years. Under the most favorable circumstances he was a slow and meticulous worker, but his productivity was dramatically curtailed by poor health during these years, when he otherwise might have been in the prime of his career in the heyday of the mass-media magazine. As he wrote Garland in March 1904, he had "been sick abed with a doctor & a surgeon watching me." A few months after the publication of his novel *Lady Baltimore* (1906), Wister finally returned to western fiction in the short story "Timberline." Based partly on his journal account of an electrical storm he had experienced in the Washakie Needles in Wyoming in September 1888, it recounts a hunting trip by the narrator (aka "The Professor," apparently the tenderfoot of *The Virginian*) and Scipio Le Moyne. Coincidentally, they also stalk a murderer. It appeared in the *Saturday Evening Post* for March 7, 1908.

It was soon followed by "The Gift Horse," which anticipates by thirty years the plot of Walter Van Tilburg Clark's *The Ox-Bow Incident* (1940). In this tale, set during the Johnson County War, the narrator is falsely accused of horse theft on the basis of circumstantial evidence, and Scipio Le Moyne must rescue him. The "big cattlemen were going to demonstrate" their authority on Powder River, a stage driver explains, and the narrator "perceived 'demonstration' to be the driver's word for the sudden hanging of somebody without due process of law." Wister here again betrays his ambivalence about lynch law. "I know lynching must be where there is no other law," the narrator declares. "But look what it does to those who practice it." The narrator barely escapes so-called "natural justice." In effect, Wister recants the views so emphatically expressed by Judge Henry in *The Virginian*. "The Gift Horse" was published in the *Saturday Evening Post* for July 18, 1908.

He next wrote a thin sketch, "Extra Dry," in which Scipio robs a con artist of money he has won in a crooked shell game. Unable to find honest work, broke, his clothes in tatters, Scipio rationalizes his theft as a way to punish an outlaw. The story appeared in the *Saturday Evening Post* for February 27, 1909.

Wister planned to include these three tales, along with "The Patronage of High Bear" (aka "Happy Teeth"), "The Vicious Circle" (revised under the title "Spit-Cat Creek") and "How the Energy Was Conserved" (revised under the title "In the Back"), in a new collection of his short fiction tentatively titled *Members of the Family*. On September 24, 1908, George Brett advised the other editors at Macmillan that Wister reported "that he had 6 stories" finished "and that he contemplated 6 more, making 12 for the book." Brett expected the volume "to be ready for spring publication 1909." After the 1908 publication of *The Whole Family*—a so-called "collaborative" novel by twelve prominent authors—he considered changing his title to *Beggars and Choosers* to avoid confusion, but Brett persuaded him that his original choice was better. In short, Wister seemed to be charging ahead with his first new western book since *The Virginian*.

Then, as he put it later, his health fell "down stairs all the way to the cellar." The problem was a recurrence of his old malady, nervous prostration. He took to his bed in spring 1909 and spent one of every three days there for the next several months. He wrote Brett in late September 1909 that he expected "to be West all this winter in some dry and bracing climate." He, Molly, and their youngest son William left for California via New Orleans on January 26, 1910, and traveled leisurely. In El Paso on April 2, he suffered a public embarrassment. After crossing the border from Juarez, Wister was arrested and taken to the U.S. Customs Office and searched on the suspicion that he was an opium smuggler. After his release, he filed a complaint with the customs collector, who told him that "under civil service rules the offending subordinate could not be disciplined." The Wisters immediately left Texas for Deming and Tucson—where the local press reported on April 5 that his health had improved "appreciably" in only a couple of days—before continuing to Maricopa, Phoenix, Yuma, Arizona, and San Bernardino, California. After three weeks in the Loma Linda Sanatorium, Wister retreated with Molly and William to the Hotel del Coronado near San Diego before they began their slow trek eastward, first to the Grand Canyon. On May 26, they stayed the night at the swank Alvarado Hotel in Albuquerque, New Mexico, where Wister was interviewed by a local reporter. He bragged that he had long been familiar with the southwest part of New Mexico Territory around "the neighborhood of Deming, Silver City and Fort Bayard. When Bayard was a garrison, and before it was converted into a hospital, I spent a great deal of time at the fort with military friends." Asked whether he had researched any new stories on the trip, Wister replied that he had enough material in his notebooks to keep him busy "for ten or fifteen years." The next day, the Wisters left for Lamy, New Mexico, eighteen miles south of Santa Fe, where they registered for a week at El Ortiz Hotel, a boutique Harvey House that had opened the year before. Designed by Louis Curtiss and

Mary Colter, El Ortiz was "absurdly tiny," with only ten sleeping rooms, a dining room and lobby, and a patio. But Wister was charmed by it.

Wister returned with his family to Philadelphia in early June. But he had not yet recovered his health and, as in 1885 at Weir Mitchell's orders, he again tried the West cure. On August 4 he left again, this time alone, for Wyoming via Chicago, St. Paul, Fargo, North Dakota, and Billings, Montana. He arrived in Cody, Wyoming, on August 13 and at the Aldrich Ranch near Ishawooa, on the south fork of the Shoshone River in the northwest corner of the state, three days later. He remained at the health resort for nearly four months. He initially consumed a diet of raw eggs, milk, and the health food panopepton, though he no longer required a barbiturate to sleep, and on doctor's orders he spent three hours daily smeared with icthyol ointment "lying without a stitch in the glaring sun." As he wrote Brett, "I begin to resemble a meerschaum pipe or a russet shoe from top to toe." He also performed light exercise—trout fishing, walking, horseback riding. "When I came here Aug. 16," he wrote Brett in early December, "I couldn't walk for 30 minutes without having to lie down for a couple of hours—& I could not ride at all. Now I can walk a couple of hours and ride for three. It tires me, but I am rested by next day." He had also "written a short story! It took me a month;—for an hour a day—not by any means every day—was the most I could work at it at a time. But only imagine being able to write at all after nearly two years!"

Inspired by a white drake and two ducks he observed on a nearby pond, "The Drake Who Had Means of His Own" was another story, like "Em'ly," about anthropomorphized fowl. Like Em'ly, Sir Francis the drake has two crooked feathers in his tail, which this narrator associates with sexual attraction. Unlike the gender-confused chicken, however, Sir Francis devotes most of his time in sexual negotiations with his two mates, the Duchess and the Countess. Wister's narrator, like the author, is "a paying boarder in that new-established Wyoming industry which is locally termed dude-wrangling." The eastern dude, he speculates, "is destined to replace Hereford cattle" as a growth industry in Wyoming. The tale appeared in the *Saturday Evening Post* the following March.

Wister reported to Brett on December 3 that, after long delay, he hoped to publish *Members of the Family* in spring 1911. The collection would contain seven stories—the six he had completed by September 1908 plus "The Drake." He left Wyoming six days later, retraced his route through Cody, Billings, St. Paul, and Chicago, and arrived in Philadelphia on December 15. In Chicago, he was forced to deny a published report that he was ill. But he also turned the interview to account by endorsing a movement to have the government provide a better range for elk. Wister expressed the fear "that unless measures were taken soon to provide a winter range for elk that game will be extinct in five or six years."

Brett was enthusiastic about the prospects for *Members of the Family*, Wister's first western book since *The Virginian* nearly a decade earlier. "Unless I am much mistaken," he assured the author, the volume "is going to appeal to all the readers" who bought the novel. Wister was much less sanguine. "Don't you flatter yourself or flatter me that his new book is going to be a great big huge success," he cautioned Brett. "I hope that enough people will like it to make it profitable and enough critics will perceive that so far as skill goes there is a development." Moreover, as he noted on February 17, there was "no love interest, & none can be put in." But at the last minute, Wister injected a little love interest by adding an eighth story. He resurrected from his files a manuscript he had completed in May 1893 but never published, "The Falling Out of Kultus Jake and Uncle Pasco" (working titles "The Twenty-Fifth Hour," "Skookum Joe

& Uncle Pasco," "Skookum Pelz & Frisco Baldy"), revised it between February 19 and March 15, published it under the title "Where It Was" in the *Saturday Evening Post* for April 22, and added it to the collection. The sketch features a pair of grandees, an eastern schoolmarm, and a character named Edmund modeled on Guy Waring, who owns a trading post in the Methow Valley. The narrator observes that he "was the squarest man I have ever known. Too square. And about the finest. He was from an Eastern college and entirely wasted on the Thowmet Valley, where nobody but him had any education or understood honesty as he understood it." The tale ends with Edmund's marriage to the schoolmarm and Scipio's announcement that "they was sure a happy two!"

Members of the Family was finally published on May 11, 1911, four years after Wister first conceived it and more than two years behind schedule. Seven of the eight tales, excepting only "In the Back," include Scipio Le Moyne in the cast, if only in a minor role. Wister summarized the difference between his old tales and these new ones this way: "The nomadic, bachelor West is over, the housed, married West is established." He had originally planned to tie the episodes together to form a more continuous narrative, as in *The Virginian*, but he had been forced by illness to abandon the plan. H. L. Mencken carped in *Smart Set* that the collection was a "queer composition."

Still, most of the reviews were laudatory. The New York *World* ranked Wister with Mérimée, Howells, Kipling, and Henry James among writers of short stories. The *Philadelphia Press*, his hometown newspaper, declared that the stories "not only show Mr. Wister at his best, but may be said to represent in full flower a tradition" of fiction "which is indigenous to America," and his friend Hamilton W. Mabie asserted in the *Ladies' Home Journal* that "during his long silence Mr. Wister has lost nothing of his skill and freshness of style." Both the *Brooklyn Eagle* and the London *World* nominated "The Drake Who Had Means of His Own" for best story in the collection. "His characters are the perfect successors of his former ones," the *Salt Lake Tribune* asserted, and "are just as good in their way" though "tamed down to some extent." Several critics singled out Wister's characterization of Scipio for special praise. According to the *New York Tribune*, he was "the most beguiling personality in the book" and "nearly always in the centre of the stage." The *New Orleans Picayune* ("The Scipio of these pages is a real hero of the West, a man of true impulses and loyal friendships") and *Outlook* ("The central figure of these tales is Scipio, whose resourcefulness, humor, pluck, and loyalty are dramatized with Mr. Wister's first-hand knowledge, artistic integrity, and vital skill") echoed the point.

Most English reviewers compared Wister to Harte, sometimes likening Scipio to Harte's Yuba Bill (*London Morning Post*) or Jack Hamlin (London *Times*). The *Edinburgh Scotsman* pronounced Wister "the natural successor to Bret Harte" and the *Pall Mall Gazette* even regarded Wister a superior writer to Harte ("He never oversteps, as Bret Harte sometimes did, the thin borderline that divides true sentiment from mere sentimentalism"). Only the *Los Angeles Times* ("Wister never shows the sordidness of the West") and the *Nation* ("the relative thinness of most after-gleanings") expressed reservations. Privately, Roosevelt wrote the author that "Mrs. Roosevelt loved 'The Members of the Family,' and so did I. I think I especially liked 'Timberline,' 'The Gift Horse,' and 'Extra Dry.'" Eugene Manlove Rhodes considered Scipio "better characterization than the Virginian and more interesting."

Unfortunately, sales of the book were mediocre. Brett wrote Wister six weeks after publication that if Wister "had been able to do for this book what you hoped to do for it in the first instance, i.e., work it over into one continued tale, there is no doubt that it would have had a sale approximate to that enjoyed by 'The Virginian,'—it is so good, but the dealers fight shy of short stories because of the competition of the cheap magazines." Wister had not entirely lost his audience, but his brand of historical romance was fading in prestige and popularity.

6

1911–1938

In mid-June 1911, a month after the publication of *Members of the Family*, Wister and his family left Philadelphia for an extended summer vacation in the West. They traveled first to Wyoming. He had conceived of a sequel of sorts to *The Virginian* to be entitled *The Marriages of Scipio* (with apologies to Mozart) that would update the adventures of his hero's sidekick. Scipio "should appear as a young man in the early stories dealing with frontier life before it was changed, and as a man of 45 or 50 in the later stories," he notified George Brett. The novel "will present the roving man of 1878–1895, surviving into the new state of Western things, and not able to adjust himself to them. I grieve to tell you it will be very tragic." But, after all, he had "'established' Scipio as a popular favorite" and so he expected "the whole novel I have planned about him . . . to meet a success if I can write it as I see it."

He visited Wyoming "to see again certain country & people & brush up some Western material I need for Scipio's further adventures." He "was shocked by the changes" that had taken place since he was last there. "I found farms where formerly there were cattle ranges, and crops on the once unsown trails," he told an interviewer. "My cowboy acquaintances were many of them gray haired men; some had prospered and some had not, but they all united with me in missing the West of other days." Among the old friends he consulted was Amos Barber, who was "anxious that I should carry" out the plan for the new novel. Meanwhile, Roosevelt urged caution: "When you come to your cowboy tragedy . . . don't leave it in such unrelieved blackness. Let in some sunlight, somehow. Leave your reader with the feeling that life, after all, does—go—on." Roosevelt need not have fretted. Nary a fragment of the tale survives, if any of it was written. It became yet another of the projects Wister aborted or abandoned over the years. Twenty years later, in the midst of the Great Depression, he lamented his failure to complete *The Marriages of Scipio*. "I wish very much that one obstacle after another hadn't prevented my carrying out the plan," he mused. "I am too old now, too far away from that mood, too steeped in the mood which the predicament of our country induces."

After retreating to the Hotel del Coronado across the bay from San Diego, where Wister celebrated his fifty-first birthday, the family again ventured to the mountains, first to Salt Lake City for three weeks in July, then to Medicine Bow, Wyoming, where the author was the guest of honor at the dedication of the Virginian Hotel on the site of the old Elk Saloon. His return to Wyoming was prompted by another reason besides recreation, however: he had decided to buy a 157-acre ranch near Jackson's Hole with a view of the Grand Tetons for $2,700. "I first started passing vacation time in the Jackson's Hole country in 1887. It was then a hunter's paradise, but of late years it is getting to be a 'next-to-nature' resort," he explained.

> With the exception of the canyon and geysers in Yellowstone, Jackson's Hole is so far superior in beauty to the park that after seeing it, one goes away and forgets the latter. I have traveled this country for twenty-five years and I think Jackson's Hole is the most beautiful spot in the Rocky Mountains. Nothing but its inaccessibility

has prevented people from enjoying it, and I am told that an auto road is being built into it.

That is, travelers "don't have to depend on the pack animal as formerly" to reach the valley.

Wister built a cabin in Jackson's Hole, where he "lived a very tame existence. Very quiet." His daughter Frances remembered the bucolic life the family enjoyed the summer she was ten.

> Mostly we rode, I bareback for miles each day. Fording Snake River, loping through the sagebrush with no trail, we went into the foothills as far as our laboring horses could climb. We were not too young to be stunned with admiration by the Tetons, and we loved the acres of wild flowers growing up their slopes. . . . We were not awed by the wilderness, feeling that the Grand Teton was our own mountain and the most wonderful mountain in the world, and the Snake River the fastest, longest river in America. We could ride all day and never get past the Tetons. When we returned to the ranch in the late afternoon, we would ride up the brief slope and suddenly Phelps Lake would appear in front of us.

Ironically, after finally establishing a home in Wyoming, Wister's passion for roughing it dissipated. The purchase of the ranch also sparked rumors of his ill health. The Associated Press and United Press even reported on October 13 that he had died, a story printed in newspapers across the country. Wister didn't learn of the report—and so did not issue a public correction—until he left his ranch a few days later to return to Philadelphia. "I am much stronger than when I went to Wyoming," he assured an interviewer in Salt Lake City. He had finished no "literary work during my period of rest and recreation," though he had three books on the boards "and may shortly write another concerning the West."

His first order of business at home was to prepare a "Rededication and Preface" for a new illustrated edition of

The Virginian. At Wister's suggestion the previous April, Brett had recruited the cowboy artist Charlie Russell to contribute some new drawings, and Wister's new introduction was nothing less than a political endorsement of Roosevelt, who was contemplating another run for the presidency in 1912. "Ten years ago, when political darkness still lay dense upon every State in the Union," Wister began, "this book was dedicated to the greatest benefactor we people have known since Lincoln. Today he is a benefactor even greater than he was then; his voice, instead of being almost solitary, has inspired many followers." Wister reiterated that "Our Democracy has many enemies, both in Wall Street and in the Labor Unions; but as those in Wall Street have by their excesses created those in the Unions, they are the worst." But then he qualified this gloomy judgment: "After nigh half-a-century of shirking and evasion, Americans are beginning to look at themselves and their institutions straight." If his novel was "anything more than an American story," it was "an expression of American faith."

The Wisters followed much the same travel itinerary the next summer—a vacation in California followed by a couple of months on the ranch in Wyoming. They arrived in Santa Barbara in early July 1912 and soon moved south to the Hotel del Coronado. While in San Diego, Wister visited J. D. Redington, his friend from Oregon days, and he bought a summer house at Grossmont and a half-interest in nearly 3,300 acres of an old Spanish land grant, Rancho El Cajon in La Mesa, for twenty-five thousand dollars. After two weeks in southern California, they left for their ranch in Jackson's Hole. While in the vicinity, Wister traveled some eighty miles to speak in St. Anthony, Idaho, on behalf of Roosevelt, who after losing the Republican nomination for President to William Howard Taft in June was running as a third-party candidate. The family returned to Philadelphia via Salt Lake City in early September. Wister wrote a friend that his "children, I think, would like to live in the

West altogether, which I naturally shall not allow them to do. They must get their education and they must grow up where they really belong, but I am glad enough to think that they care every bit as much as their father did for that life. The only pity is that the cream of that life which you and I knew twenty and twenty-five years ago has all been skimmed off." Meanwhile, he wrote next to nothing for publication.

In 1910, Wister had agreed to pen a brief biography of Frederic Remington, but he backed out of the project in late 1912 and sent a telegram to Remington's widow Eva that "he c[ould] not possibly write the book." He had been working intermittently on a novel about Philadelphia society for several years, but as he admitted in the spring of 1913, "it goes slowly" after his health problems. He could only write for an hour or two at a time before he had "to 'knock off' because my carcass is patched up only so-so." He never completed the novel, entitled *Romney*, though the surviving fragment was published in 2001. In it, Wister referred in passing to Fort Bayard, New Mexico, "to which no railroad had come yet; it was a safe, epic distance away . . . a journey full of sands and shores and desert wildernesses, with a sprinkling of hostile Indians and cactus."

His life changed irrevocably on August 24, 1913. That day Molly Wister died after giving birth to their sixth child. He afterwards suffered a prolonged depression, with a succession of nannies and in-laws caring for the children. As a result of Molly's death, Wister never built a house as planned on the tract of land he owned near San Diego. He began to sail more often across the Atlantic on vacation. As his daughter Marina explained in 1942, "As he grew old, he turned more and more to Europe. Wyoming as he knew it was a young man's country; fences, highways and dude ranches had banished the life" he had known as a young man. On the occasions when he went west, he traveled in the style of an affluent summer tourist, staying exclusively in upscale hotels. Wister later explained, "Some bad grief, some bad health, the war and three books about that, suspended all thought of fiction from 1913 to 1915 or so."

His friends in the West had slowly been winnowed by death and disease. Wolcott had died in 1910; the military officers Wister knew, including Edwards, had mostly retired or been transferred; George West had married and quit ranching; Charles Skirdin, disabled during the Spanish-Philippine War, lived in Philadelphia. Amos Barber died in May 1915 in Cheyenne—according to John W. Davis "the only place in Wyoming where he was not publicly reviled"—and with him, Wister wrote, "has gone out of the world unrecorded as great and picturesque a treasure of lore about the Ranch Era as any I have ever known." Wister had planned "for many years to settle down in Cheyenne" for a few months "and write down all the extraordinary things he used to tell me" about Fort Fetterman in 1885–86, when Barber was a medical officer there, "and thus make a book of them" entitled *Chronicles of Fetterman*. Instead, "my health went to smash. And now that it's mended sufficiently for me to be able to write a little each week," his confidant had died. The only story based on Barber's reminiscences that Wister had completed by this date was "Destiny at Drybone."

He finally returned to the West in spring 1915 when, with war raging in Europe, he went alone on holiday. He left Philadelphia in late June and celebrated the Fourth of July at the Pace Hotel in Gallup, New Mexico. During the next month he registered at El Tovar on the south rim of the Grand Canyon, the Hotel del Coronado near San Diego, and the Fairmont Hotel in San Francisco before returning to Philadelphia in early August. He spent a similar summer in 1916 in British Columbia and the U.S. Pacific Northwest. Interviewed in Seattle in early July, he admitted that he hated "to see the country grow up with railroads and farms doing what the wire fence did in Wyoming to end the cattle days." During the summers of 1917 and 1918 he vacationed at the Trapper Lodge in Shell, Wyoming, with his son Owen, and in August 1919 he vacationed on Dean Duke's ranch in Modoc County, California; but he suffered a riding accident and, with the war in Europe over, he didn't return to the West again for nine years. In February 1920, after his cabin in Wyoming was vandalized, he sold the ranch there for fifty dollars more than he paid for it. He lived on his investments and the income from his writing, especially the continuing sales of *The Virginian*. He sold film rights to *Red Men and White* and *Members of the Family* in 1919 and to *Lin McLean* in 1920. In 1920–21, he received about twelve thousand dollars from the sale of movie rights to *The Virginian* to Douglas Fairbanks—two-ninths of the fifty-five thousand dollars that Fairbanks paid. The Famous Players-Lasky Corporation received half the amount, and Kirke La Shelle's widow Mazie the balance.

Still, Wister's interest in the West had atrophied, replaced by issues of immigration, the armistice in Europe, civic corruption in Philadelphia, the Atlantic alliance, foreign debt, and Prohibition. He had even run on a reform party platform for a seat on the Philadelphia City Council in 1912 and lost in a landslide to the machine candidate. Later, he vehemently opposed Franklin D. Roosevelt and his New Deal. As he wrote his friend Redington in January 1923, "I have gone away from all that sort of subject [the West] and what compels my attention and interest now are these public matters of the world." He had published no fiction, let alone western fiction, since *Members of the Family* in 1911. Much to Wister's consternation, his fellow curmudgeon H. L. Mencken compared him at the time to W. D. Howells as "a wart succeeding Ossa," an allusion to *Hamlet*. Wister never forgot or forgave the insult.

"Then one day" late in 1923 "a very pleasant fellow, an editor," almost certainly Ray Long of *Cosmopolitan*, contacted him

and said, how about more stories? I wasn't sure that I hadn't lost
the trick of it. But I tried—it was all Western. Well the consequences of that was that I had a hard time writing the first two
yarns; re-wrote them in fact, two or three times, and then each
yarn after that came easier and easier until the 9th (which would
have been impossible to bring off at the beginning) was written in
very few days, & needed but trifling amendment. All we've been,
known, and done remains in us but most of it has to be evoked.
[But] as I had grown very distant from the West, the evoking of it
took long.

Wister found the sources for most of these tales in his old
diaries and notebooks, publishing all but two of them first
in *Cosmopolitan* and then polishing them for his final collection of western stories, *When West Was West* (1928). But
their tone was so new it might have been titled "the waning
of the West." In the style of Damon Runyon, they feature
colorful ne'er-do-wells, deadbeats, and down-and-outers.
As John Cobbs observes, "Systematically Wister takes the
character types of his early stories and etches their sad transformation into the 'new' West. The Indian, the cowboy, the
doctor, the soldier, the hunter, the rancher, the preacher,
and even the dude—all reappear in diminished and cheap-
ened forms in these sad stories."

Wister stumbled out of the gate. The first of the nine
stories written for the collection, "Lone Fountain," originally written in 1923, revised in 1926, but not published
until 1928, recounts the life of a latter-day pagan. With its
labored prose and an element of the supernatural, it is one
of Wister's weakest tales. His next story was "Sun Road"
(working title "Little Chief Hare"), first published in *Cosmopolitan* for July 1924 and subsequently rewritten under
the title "Bad Medicine." It is the tale of a noble Shoshone,
Sun Road, caught between the tragic past of his people and
modern consumerism—the vacationing hunters, summer
mob of tourists, and souvenir collectors—that was shaping

the future of the West. That is, Wister allegorizes the disappearance of the so-called "vanishing American," whose culture is ostensibly incompatible with white "civilization." The eastern narrator remarks that, though the son of a chief, Sun Road was "heir to nothing any more save the extinction of his race because it lay in the path of my own." When Sun Road learns that the narrator and his party plan to camp in Yellowstone National Park, he refuses to guide them. Much as Dick Washakie had quit Wister's hunting party in 1891 because, he said, "he must cut his hay," Sun Road insists he must stay behind with his father who "is an old man" and "cannot cut [his] hay field." Dick Washakie "never gave the real" reason, though the narrator guesses at it in "Sun Road"—superstition. The natives believed the Yellowstone "was the home of devils and believed that the geysers were the open doors that let the devils out on earth." The narrator finally persuades Sun Road to join the excursion. Unfortunately, the story is marred by a hamhanded conclusion. Like many other tourists, the narrator goes to see Old Faithful. The ground around the geyser "sounded hollow when we crossed the channels beneath the crusty surface." Sun Road, posing for tourists near the vent, collapses into the steaming cavern beneath the geyser as it erupts, a victim of the "bad medicine" of the title. The third of Wister's new stories, "Captain Quid," one of his poorer sketches, features a hen-pecked roué nicknamed "Quid" for his tobacco-spitting skill. It was first published in *Cosmopolitan* for September 1924.

Finally, two years after resuming his career as a writer of fiction, he hit his stride. "Once Around the Clock," completed in August 1925 and published in *Cosmopolitan* for July 1926, was a distinct improvement on the earlier three stories. Based on notes in Wister's 1893 Texas journal, this tale introduces an ensemble of characters he portrayed in several subsequent sketches. First among them was Doc Leonard, a graduate of Harvard Medical School, modeled on General Leonard Wood, whom Wister had met through Roosevelt. Wood completed his medical degree at Harvard in 1884, joined the U.S. army as a surgeon stationed at Fort Huachuca, Arizona, in 1885, was active during the pursuit and capture of Geronimo in 1886, received the Medal of Honor for bravery, and helped his friend Roosevelt organize the Rough Riders in 1898. He later served as chief of staff of the army, military governor of Cuba, and governor general of the Philippines. As Wister explained, Wood was the model for "a character in three of my tales"—all of them written shortly after Wood's death in 1927—"as I imagined he might have been in the days when he was a young army surgeon, not yet at the threshold of a splendid career." Other recurring characters who first appear in "Once Around the Clock" are a *bruja* or witch named Salamanca and a local politician, Colonel Steptoe McDee, the putative hero, who is as eccentric as a bent wheel.

Set in the fictional "O'Neal City," named for one of Wister's Texas friends, "Once Around the Clock" depicts violence with slapstick humor. "I have heard more stories of cowardly murders here than I have ever heard before," Wister had noted in his journal. "And it is a serious thing to be a witness against any man, for he, or his brother or cousin will shoot you sooner or later. In fact a man who is likely to be a witness at a trial not yet come off is likely to be killed by some unknown person as he sits by his lighted window in the evening." In the story, McDee warns Doc Leonard, Salamanca's professional rival, to "never place yourself in a lighted window. That's a habit it costs little to acquire, while failure to acquire it in Flanagan County has cost acquaintances of mine a high price." Similarly, a few days before Wister's arrival in Texas in 1893, an acquaintance there was shot "while he was unsuspiciously walking away with his back turned," though luckily "the bullet merely grazed his scalp, making a rut as long as one's finger, chiefly to be detected by a strange width in the parting of [his] thick hair." In "Once Around the Clock," a character is also shot but the "bullet just kind o' parted [his] hair." While in Texas, Wister also heard an anecdote about a

> versatile doctor who was helping dig a well. He was down at the bottom and just beginning to be raised out by the man at the windlass, for he had lighted the fuse of a heavy blast. But the man at the windlass had some months previously assisted at a lynching, & the brother of the lynched man had ascertained the names of all the parties, & come into the country from up north, and just at this particular moment was watching the man at the windlass from behind a bush. It being a good chance, he shot him dead, and the doctor halfway up the well plumped down again on the hissing fuse. His screeches produced no effect on the parties above; but he had a happy thought and bit the fuse off in time.

Wister worked the incident into the story without significant change.

He also alluded to an actual scheme to displace Texas landowners. "About three years ago this part of the country was in a high state of disorder through cattle stealing and other crimes," he noted in his Texas journal. "In 18 months there were 34 murders"—the exact statistic Wister mentions in the story. "It began to be a common thing for people to receive a paper giving them 10 days to leave the country," especially if they were known to eat beef without owning any cattle, and "thus many people left land behind them which they would not be likely to return to, and from this quite a business grew up. The owners of lands so vacated would receive a letter from their district written by some well wishing citizen who 'supposing they had no further use for their domicile' wrote to say he would pay them so much for the land and improvements.'" At the end of the story, Doc Leonard leaves Texas after receiving such a letter from the *bruja* Salamanca.

Among the best short stories Wister ever wrote, "The Right Honorable the Strawberries," first appeared in *Cosmopolitan* for November 1926. The lead tale in *The Best Short Stories of 1927*, it was followed by Ernest Hemingway's "The Killers" and Sherwood Anderson's "Another Wife." It was based on two versions of an anecdote about events in Fort Fetterman in 1885–86 that Amos Barber had related to Wister, once in 1895 and again in 1911. Or as Wister conceded in 1933, "Into the tale about Strawberries I did spill many old memories." In his notes for the story taken in 1895, Wister described "a young man from the East" who

> came to Fetterman because his family desired him out of sight. He had in some way disgraced himself, and was given an allowance of $150 a month on condition he remain out of sight. Once a month a letter with the money would come for him to the Fetterman P.O. & other correspondence he had not. He boarded at the hotel, bought him a good horse & saddle, and encountering for the first time in his life the game of Stud Poker, fell fascinated.

He became a favorite mark of the professional card sharks at the fort, who "plundered him every month regularly" upon the arrival of his remittance. Eventually his parents, suspicious of his increased demands for money, "stopped all income. This of course was a blow to several people: the youth, the hotel keeper, and the gamblers. . . . The youth grew despondent, & playing no more, sat about the saloon looking on" and soon realized that the gamblers conspired "against all strangers & that he had been plundered. After this he was to stand about Fetterman and warn newcomers against the professionals." The card sharks might have murdered him. Instead, "they saw a smoother way to rid themselves of him."

> There was, they told him, in the graveyard a woman buried with a quantity of jewelry. They could go by night, dig her up & get this, and pawn it. . . . He and two or three others went to the

graveyard after dark, and just as they had begun operations a furious crowd rode out of town up the hill. "We're dead men" said the youth's fellow diggers—leaped on their horses & dashed away southeast—one by one they turned off the road, telling him that if he could rely on his horse—which was a good one—to keep on down the road—that the superstition & feeling in that community about robbing graveyards was so strong that he & all of them would be lynched if caught. All this while the pursuing party was following up hill & down, shooting (in the air) when a rise brought the pursued in sight. Finally the last conspirator bade the youth good bye, his horse could not go on—he must take a gulch & hope to gain the mountains—but let the tenderfoot keep the road because his horse could stand it. He did. And he rode out of the country, & was never seen or heard of them [*sic*] again. The gamblers returned to Fetterman and divided his trunks and possessions among them equitably.

In addition, Wister had met a prospector in Duncan, Arizona, in May 1895 whom he worked into the story. The old man was attired in a "frayed but respectable tail coat," his silver hair "flowed nearly to his collar," and, as Wister describes him, he was slightly addled. "I cannot reproduce his conversation, but he spoke with mild tones and the speed of lightning—running one sentence into another. My name is Henry Murphy, said he, and I've been up and down rich and poor, Earl Marquis, walking the track, and again come out with a jackass load of money. I've been from hell to Cape Horn." Though his talk "was almost too incoherent," Wister thought "his character is a good suggestion" for a story and "not like any I have met before."

Sixteen years later, Barber told Wister a story about an Englishman who had once lived at Fort Fetterman that was substantially the same as the one he related in 1895. The Englishman's "only activity" was gambling. He was welcome among the card sharks so long as he lost to them, but when he realized they were cheating him "he began very properly to warn newcomers not to play. The gamblers found this out, and concluded they must get rid of the Englishman." Rather than kill him, they persuaded him to help disinter a bejeweled corpse and, to save himself from a lynching, he fled "the country & was never heard of again."

In Wister's retelling of the anecdote, a minor English peer, nicknamed "Strawberries" by the cowboys on account of his fondness for the fruit—the eleventh son in his family and unlikely ever to inherit a title—long resists the lure of the flesh and the gambling saloon in Drybone. On a hunt, he even kills "a white-tailed deer with one bullet, well-placed just behind the shoulder," a "better job than any of my attempts, in spite of my three months' start," as the narrator remarks. That is, Strawberries initially proves his ability to survive and even prosper in the West. But he suffers a slow deterioration in character and principle when he begins to gamble. When he realizes the other cowboys cheat at cards, he begins to cheat better than they. The narrator encounters him "in this hour of his luck." He had been transformed by hardship, and "if you did not look twice, you would hardly see that he had been a gentleman." The narrator last meets the decaying aristocrat in 1910 in Drybone, now a virtual ghost town, where he lives in the squalor of a dilapidated hotel. Hemingway was so impressed by the story that he wrote his editor Maxwell Perkins that it was "wonderfully good" and "a lesson to our generation in how to write." One of the few stories Wister did not revise after magazine publication, he reprinted it in *When West Was West* without the change of a word.

"The Right Honorable the Strawberries" was also in effect a retraction of Wister's argument in "The Evolution of the Cow-puncher" more than thirty years before. Then he had asserted that "the polished man in London and the man unpolished in Texas" were but "the same Saxon" in different environments. But, as Neal Lambert explains, the fictional crux of "The Right Honorable the Strawberries" is "the problem of whether or not the British gentleman can find in the West a way of life that will sustain him away from cultured, traditionalized civilization." Wister's final answer was no. While at first Strawberries successfully adapts, he eventually suffers a moral and mental collapse befitting his rude circumstances.

In mid-August 1926, as the sixty-six year old Wister was working on "At the Sign of the Last Chance"—a dirge for the West as he had known it in the 1880s and '90s—he suddenly "had to stop," as he wrote George Brett. He became dizzy when he tried to write, another apparent recurrence of the psychosomatic illness from which he had suffered on-and-off for years, in this case prompted by imagining his requiem for the Old West. Wister didn't finish the story for a year, and it was not published in *Cosmopolitan* until February 1928.

In it, Wister simply depicts a circle of old storytellers around a poker table, raconteurs with shallow memories engaged in a cacophony of absurd conversation. Nothing any of them says registers with any of the others; each of them talks and none of them listens. Like them, the West is exhausted, too. The rivers have been fished out, the forests depleted of game. Only the narrator makes any sense:

> I had begun to see those beards long before they were gray; when no wire fence mutilated the freedom of the range; when fourteen mess-wagons would be at the spring round-up; when cattle wandered and pastured, dotting the endless wilderness; when roping them brought the college graduate and the boy who had never learned to read into a lusty equality of youth and skill; when songs rose by the camp-fire; and the dim form of the night herder leaned on his saddle horn as under the stars he circled slowly around the recumbent thousands; when two hundred miles stretched between all this and the whistle of the nearest locomotive. And all this was over. It had begun to end a long while ago.

The decline began "with the first wire fence," was accelerated "by the winter snows of 1886," and "received its mortal stroke in the rustler war of 1892." Of the nine tales in *When West Was West*, "At the Sign of the Last Chance" was the sixth to be written—but Wister wisely printed it last in the book. It was, at least figuratively, his final word about the West.

Wister completed the seventh story, "Skip to My Loo," during the last week of January 1928 while vacationing in Palm Beach, Florida. Like "Once Around the Clock," it was based on notes in his Texas journal for 1893. There he "grew familiar with many of the doings and most of the conventions of a wide, wild farm and ranch community, spotted with remote towns, and veined with infrequent railroads." More particularly, Wister depicted with comic irony the "breezes of hypocrisy in the air." He was "inclined to think that Virtue in in Texas is not more rampant than in other states." For example, in his journal he joked about a fellow named Philpot forced to change his name to Price "because Texas ladies could not possibly say Philpot and feel pure." He also scorned the young Texans "who will watch . . . the burning of a negro" yet "shrink from using such words as bull or stallion in polite society." In "Skip to My Loo," Colonel Steptoe McDee similarly advises the narrator to "take care to say *male cow*, *male hen*, when a lady is present."

In his journal, Wister records several similar examples of "the fetid curse of hypocrisy," as Colonel McDee puts it, that he encountered while in Texas. "Many families here are so religious that they cannot possibly dance," he learns. "But they have assemblings of young men and maidens that are called Play Parties" where they skip and sing such lyrics as "Skip to My Loo" (hence the title of the story) so that "it seems that if you are religious and cannot dance, still a Play Party has its consolations." Or as the narrator observes in the story, the action at a Play Party "grew gayer and more energetic, and not so very unlike a Virginia reel—only it was not dancing; the singing saved it from being this forbidden fruit." Gambling is also prohibited by law in the town of San Saba, near Brownwood, Wister observed. But as he recorded in his journal

a suspicious elder climbed on a roof and looked down through a window at night & saw inside the saloonkeeper, a professor of the [high] school, & other worthies playing poker. At his insistence they were indicted. But being revengeful they kept an eye upon him, and caught him playing progressive euchre for prizes. So he is now also under indictment.

This paragraph appears almost verbatim in "Skip to My Loo." In the final pages of the tale, Wister hints at a situation he describes more fully in his journal: A pimp named Brock in Brownwood

had been employed as messenger between a man and a certain married woman. This got him the woman's confidence, and she employed him to gather cavaliers for her. She seems to have been both gregarious and mercenary. One evening she had told him to supply her with a companion, and finding a likely young male in a saloon, he struck a bargain and brought the male into the lady's presence. She screamed, and the male immediately filled Brock full of bullet holes, for he was [her] husband. But where poetic justice fails is that this husband and wife are now peaceably housekeeping together. Boccaccio or Balzac could have used this theme and embellished it to advantage.

As the tale ends, Colonel McDee introduces Doc Leonard to a Texas couple who fit this description—though he never uses the words "pimp," "prostitute," or "cavalier."

Like an extinct insect preserved in amber, Wister stubbornly resisted the inroads of literary modernism, with its experimentation and challenge to convention. Still, "Skip to My Loo" was remarkably risqué, given the social norms of the time. Its ribaldry—and the offense it would doubtless have given to readers in Texas—explains why it was not printed in a magazine prior to its appearance in *When West Was West*. If Wister was discouraged by his failure to place it with an editor, he was undaunted. "It was amusing to plan and spin according to accepted specifications, observing at the same time the only rule I never break:—'Never mind the rules. Absorb, digest, prehend your subject. Then try to interest your reader at the start, and keep him interested to the finish.'"

Wister's next tale originated in an anecdote he had heard in San Francisco in 1887 about Leonard Wood, who "took hashish once in Huachuca" to "fill the vacuum" or relieve the monotony of a frontier posting. Forty years later, "I put it into a story, with some other actual incidents at our old frontier army posts, to paint the infinite ennui of that life." Set before marijuana was criminalized and written after the International Opium Convention of 1925 restricted international trade in Indian hemp, "Absalom and Molting Pelican" is a pastiche of entries from Wister's journal, particularly this one:

> Leonard Wood and [Hugh] Tevis at Huachita agreed to take Hash-Heesh. Wood was a doctor and undertook to look after Tevis. The drug came like paste in tin foil. . . . They . . . agreed to take it simultaneously. Each took 1 grain. Sat. No result. Feel anything? No. you? No. 2 grains—no result. 2 more. Same. And so forth. Tevis and Wood, disgusted, then retired to bed. Beds in same room. T[evis] woke up and heard W[ood] sobbing bitterly. Sat up. W. said: 'Take him off me!' and began to dive under his bed and come up the other side, round and round. O Lord, thought Tevis, he's only taken 8 grains and I've taken 12. What will I do when it strikes me. Just then something in his head went Bing! and he immediately took to pursuing W[ood] round and round the bed. Every now and then they would have a sane moment—

They'd wring each other's hands and say, too bad, old man! and
then continue circling round the bed.

Finally, Tevis found "a bottle on the mantel piece, which
was ipacach [ipecac, a plant that can be used as an emetic
or expectorant] and began swallowing it—and instantly
foamed out the mouth. The foam came out in ribbons like a
conjuror. This sight sobered Wood, and he rushed for help.
The post doctor came—gave him an injection of brandy
and he got well." In the story, as James T. Bratcher notes,
Tevis and Wood are readily identifiable "as the actual hashish experimenters."

The comedy about their drug use is anticlimactic to
the tale as a whole, however. The focus of the first part of
"Absalom" is on a wig-wearing chaplain who ultimately has
his bald pate exposed in public by an Apache elder. Wister
had been told the story by the commanding officer at Fort
Bowie in 1893, and he repeated the anecdote to Rudyard
Kipling in April 1895. They had dined with Roosevelt at
his home in Washington, D.C., and they traveled north the
next morning in the same Pullman car. "During the journey, we talked some 'shop' in the smoking compartment,
and among other striking incidents of the old frontier,"
Wister told the story about the bald chaplain whose wig
was lifted. Kipling "urged that it be transmuted to fiction. I
said that it was too slight an anecdote as it stood, and that
I should have to wait until some happy thought occurred
which would give it more substance." As Wister recalled,
Kipling replied "You must do it, and when you have done
it, you must call it 'Absalom.'"

Not long after the Pullman journey, Wister, then in San
Francisco, received a letter from Kipling "suggesting an
admirable notion for the motive" for the story he had told
him in the train. He "had chanced upon a curious book"
by the Cherokee author and editor Elias Boudinot entitled

A Star in the West (1816) "written to substantiate Mormon claims about the final reunification of Israel and the origins of the Native peoples in America" and "conclusively proving that the Redskins generally are the lost tribes" of Israel. It "*supplies a motif*" for the story, which was "too good to be lost in a smoker," Kipling insisted. And it was. In yet another use of biblical types, in Wister's story an army missionary tries to teach an Indian some principles of psychology and a Hebrew dialect that will enable him to reclaim his repressed ancestral memory—"How his Hebrew forefathers got up into China, and how at last after many centuries they wandered across the Aleutian isthmus to America, long before it was discovered by Columbus." But even after Kipling supplied the donnée for the story, as Wister admitted, "Absalom" incubated for more than thirty years before it was finally written.

Wister also added a couple of new details to the narrative gleaned from his 1893 journal. He had met another post chaplain—"a good one," as he put it—who named his first child Alpha and his last Omega. "When asked by an officer how he knew Omega would be the last," Wister noted, "he said that he himself and his wife felt that their family was large enough. 'But if it had pleased Providence to ordain otherwise and give us another child to name, I should have commenced on the diphthongs.'" Similarly, the chaplain in "Absalom and Molting Pelican" has fathered three children named Alpha, Epsilon, and Iota, and when he has used all the Greek vowels he says he "will then begin on the diphthongs." Wister also satirized government bureaucracy in the tale. In his journal he recounted an anecdote about the secretary of war on an inspection tour, "visiting Yuma—no ice machine—officers buy ice—and make a punch. Afterwards they make a requisition for ice machine—and refer to Secretary—He says nonsense. Why I remember the water there was excellently cold!" In "Absalom," similarly, the

secretary of war visits Fort Huachuca and is regally entertained. The officers buy delicacies for him from their own
"slender purses," stage a minstrel show, and so forth, thinking he would then approve "anything we ask for." But when
they submit a petition to the War Department "for a second
ambulance and other improvements, the secretary of war is
greatly astonished and refused it promptly. 'Never at any
frontier Post that I have inspected,' said he, 'have I been so
well entertained. They've nothing to complain of.'" "Absalom and Molting Pelican" first appeared in *Cosmopolitan* for
May 1928, and Wister revised it for inclusion in *When West
Was West*.

In the last tale he prepared for his final collection of western
fiction, Wister returned to Texas and the characters Steptoe
McDee and Salamanca. In "Little Old Scaffold"—the title
refers to a horse on which a victim sits when he is lynched—
the *bruja* Salamanca conspires to drive out or murder landowners and then to buy dirt-cheap all the lands where the
railroad may locate its right-of-way. Wister based the story
on yet another anecdote he heard while in Texas in 1893:

> About this same period there lived a pony whose history is not
> a common one. He was ridden by a negro named Jim. Jim was
> on the blacklist for being suspected. Nothing was definitely (or
> legally) known against him, but his reputation was bad on many
> counts. Jim rode the pony out one morning, and in the afternoon
> the pony returned in good order, but without Jim; and the saddle
> was bloody. Some few days later the remains of Jim were found;
> and it looked as though he had been shot on the pony's back.
> Then Ace Brown [another suspect in land fraud] took him and
> rode him. And again one day, the pony returned in good order,
> but Ace was not in the saddle. They found Ace hanging to a tree
> which overhung the road he had traveled. And later it grew plain
> that he had been adjusted as he sat on the pony, which had been
> driven from beneath him.

"Little Old Scaffold" was originally published in *Cosmopolitan* for June 1928.

All nine tales were collected in *When West Was West*, and George Brett was optimistic about its prospects. Wister was sent a $2,500 advance on royalties and he received advance copies of the book on June 8. It was released the last week of June, and the reviews were almost universally favorable, if tempered in their enthusiasm. Wister's artistry, the critics declared, was still "sure and certain" (New York *Evening Post*); he related his stories "with his customary skill and tranquility" (*Spectator*); all of them were "well worth reading for their grace of manner and their restrained, if sufficiently lively plots" (*New York Herald-Tribune Books*); "all showing plainly that the writer knows the time and the people" (*Boston Transcript*). As usual, some readers were needlessly hyperbolic; for example, "Reading this collection of short stories is like turning a herd of trail-weary longhorns out into a desert oasis of rich bunch grass and spring water" (*Philadelphia Public Ledger*), and "It belongs . . . on the shelf with *Life on the Mississippi*" (*Atlantic Monthly*). Only a few reviewers were hostile; for example, "Nearly all the stories are spun out to too great length and not one is destined to live beyond the year in which it is published" (*Catholic World*), or Wister "forswears good taste when he indulges in political diatribes" (*Philadelphia Record*).

As early as January 1926, Wister had proposed to Brett that Macmillan issue a collected edition of his western writings "upon the completion of the volume of short stories on which I am at present at work." The idea would bear fruit more than two years later, when Macmillan included *When West Was West* as volume six in an eleven-volume set of Wister's works, not only books about the West but his biographies of George Washington and U.S. Grant, his novel *Lady Baltimore*, and his political essays: *The Pentecost of Calamity* (1915), an indictment of German militarism; *A Straight Deal* (1920), an ostensible exposé of the anti-British propa-

ganda machine; and *Neighbors Henceforth* (1922), an appeal
for a closer alliance with Great Britain. Wister was tempted
"to expand, to condense, to polish these old pages, as well as
many others of *Lin McLean* and *The Virginian*," he admitted, but in the end he allowed them to remain "pretty much
as they stood." He wrote new introductions to all of the
reprinted volumes and made only a few significant changes
to the texts. For example, Harper's had disapproved of the
title when *The Jimmyjohn Boss and Other Stories* had first
appeared in 1900, and Wister had long wanted to change
it. He rechristened the story "The Boy and the Buckaroos,"
and the volume in which it appeared *Hank's Woman*.

Wister also made his last changes to the text of *The Virginian* for the 1928 edition. For the first time, he no longer
needed to omit vulgarities. Steve and Trampas say "son-
of-a-bitch," not "son-of-a-b————," and "damned," not
"d————." In accordance with his conservatism, Wister
was an outspoken opponent of censorship. In 1919, for
example, he signed a petition sponsored by the Emergency
Committee Organized to Protest against the Suppression
of James Branch Cabell's *Jurgen*. "I never had any sympathy for censorship," he insisted to an interviewer. "If a man
would say a thing like that, there is no sense in using a blank
when you write about it. After all, if a word expresses an
idea and only that [word] will do, it should be used." Still,
he harbored few illusions about his creative achievements.
Thirty years after the first publication of *The Virginian*, he
conceded that "I don't pretend it is a 'permanent or indispensable addition to literature.'"

Immediately after publication of his collected writings,
as was his habit after completing a project, he left Philadelphia with his youngest son Charles for his final trip to
the West—to Trapper Lodge in Shell, Wyoming. In late
August, he met Ernest Hemingway and his wife Pauline,
who drove there from their vacation home in Sheridan.
The four of them spent several days fishing the Snake River

and hiking in the Tetons. The meeting of the two writers blossomed into a friendship and correspondence that lasted for eight years. Wister blurbed Hemingway's *A Farewell to Arms* upon its publication in 1929: "This astonishing book is in places so poignant and moving as to touch the limit that human nature can stand, when love and parting are the point." He might have added—but did not—that his wife Molly had died sixteen years earlier after giving birth, much as Catherine Barkley dies in the closing pages of the novel and much as Pauline Hemingway had nearly died in giving birth to their son Patrick in June 1928. As Hemingway's editor Maxwell Perkins wrote Wister when the book appeared, "I cannot but express the gratitude I so strongly feel for the help your support of Hemingway has also given me." Four years later, Wister offered Perkins and Hemingway some editorial advice about *Death in the Afternoon*. Many years after Wister's death, in fact, Hemingway remembered Wister as one of "the most unselfish and most dis-interested and the most loving" people he had known: "When my father shot himself" in December 1928 "and things were not good at all and I was making trust funds and having to discipline my bitch mother and put it all out of my head and do the re-write on *A Farewell to Arms . . .* he wrote me and sent me a very huge check and said for me not to have any money worries and he would back me all the way."

In 1929, Wister began to write a memoir of Theodore Roosevelt, who had died a decade earlier. He contracted with Lorimer to contribute six excerpts from the manuscript to the *Saturday Evening Post*," with a payment of $2,500 for each piece. After their publication in the *Post* in March and April 1930, Wister published the entire manuscript under the title *Roosevelt: The Story of a Friendship, 1880–1919*. Though he might still demand and receive lucrative stipends from the "slicks," however, Wister was unhappy with the intellectual compromises such commercial articles required. As he explained to Langdon Mitchell, "in writing for magazines one becomes false to oneself. True. True. True. Most horrible. In late years I have felt this in my bones so acutely, that I simply don't write for 'em anything that expresses a conviction, unless I can do it so they don't catch on." Eugene Manlove Rhodes, for one, appreciated Wister's honesty. According to Rhodes, Wister's tales were among the few "truthtelling 'Westerns' that get by,' that is, that were not diluted and falsified by editors."

In the early 1930s, at the nadir of the Great Depression, dismayed by both economic collapse and the ostensible collectivism of the New Deal, Wister was taking in sail. "I find it difficult to write when one is disgusted and furious with one's country and despises current standards and finds that most people have never thought or known anything at all," he fumed to Langdon Mitchell. He admitted that "For many years—ever since I began to think without gloves—I have had the vision of the overpopulated planet like a raft adrift in space, and the human race locked in struggle pushing itself off. . . . Well, I can't help bothering. I think I have something to say, but I'm not sure it's worth saying: so much is being said—and well said. Fiction is always in my head. So I hover and do nothing!" He closed the letter by alluding to Whitman's "Song of Myself": "in these days who can loaf and invite his soul?"

No more western travel. He refused even to consider another trip. He seemed afraid of what he would discover. "Fort Washakie may be prettier than ever, but too many ghosts are there for me," he allowed in the fall of 1933. "I don't want to see any of that country again. Too much nostalgia for past happiness." He was content to rest on his laurels.

Only one more essay about the West. As if to close the circle, he printed a valedictory memoir entitled "Old Yellowstone Days" in the March 1936 issue of *Harper's Monthly*, the magazine in which he had published his earliest western stories two generations before. It was a flashback to Wister's journey to Yellowstone National Park in 1887, in company with Tighee, George West, Copley Amory, George Norman, and Jules Mason. Upon reading the diary he kept during these weeks, he realized "that I had forgotten more than I recollected of that first camping trip; so novel, so vivid, so charged with adventure and delight and lusty vigor and laughter, that to think of it makes me homesick for the past."

On July 21, 1938, a week after his seventy-eighth birthday, Owen Wister died from a cerebral hemorrhage at his summer home in Rhode Island. Four of his five surviving children were with him—his daughter Fanny and his three sons, Owen, William, and Charles. His oldest child, daughter Marina, lived in Taos, New Mexico, with her husband, the artist Andrew Dasburg. But she had visited her father for several weeks in 1935, the year before her marriage. "I'm crazy to take more & better pictures before the Boss dies," she wrote Dasburg from Philadelphia. "You never know. He looks just fine. He is still interested, and I know would do all I asked." She added, "I am still astonished & delighted by my apparently undiminished skill on horseback. The Boss says he can't understand it." She credited the "wonderful training" he had given her on the pony in Saunderstown and during family vacations in the West long years before.

Conclusion

Owen Wister was a self-proclaimed progressive Republican in the Rooseveltian mold, though from a modern perspective he seems like an unalloyed reactionary—a racist, sexist, and imperialist. In fact, he often disagreed with Theodore Roosevelt on issues of race; he thought Roosevelt was too open-minded and tolerant. TR privately scolded him for his racial recalcitrance in *Lady Baltimore*, though to his credit Wister reprinted Roosevelt's objections in his 1928 introduction to the novel. On a visit to the White House in January 1908, shortly before Roosevelt left office, Wister "managed respectfully (I hope) to tell him he made a mistake in appointing [William D.] Crum the negro as Collector of the Port in Charleston [South Carolina]. . . . This brought out his full views and heart about the insoluble problem."

Given his racial blind spots, Wister not surprisingly depicted the West from first to last as if through a warped lens. His West is almost entirely lily-white. He virtually ignored the Asian American population; he "thoroughly expunged blacks from his West," according to Christine Bold, even though an estimated one-fourth to one-third of all cowboys were black men who had immigrated from the South; and his only prominent characters of apparent Mexican or mestizo lineage were the villains Trampas and Spanish Ed. He also believed in a specious distinction between whites and Native Americans: "Most white men know when they have had enough whiskey—most Indians do not." In some of his early western stories, such as "Little Big Horn Medicine" (1894), Wister demonstrated his ability to portray Indians sympathetically. But the Indians who are "off the reservation" in "Balaam and Pedro" are also offstage in *The Virginian* as a whole. "The native is simply erased in the paean to the mythic West," as Louis Owens has argued. The only Indians who actually appear onstage in Wister's novel are playing the part for tourists—and readers. Their disappearance in general from the novel was a blunder that can be neither excused nor repaired.

Wister's racial views paralleled his condemnation of both miscegenation and immigration. As Cobbs remarks, "*Mongrel* and *half-breed* are two of Wister's favorite pejorative terms," as in his introduction to *A Bunch of Buckskins*, a book of Frederic Remington's drawings: "Having passed the time of day with such half-breeds long enough to be familiar with what I may call their symptoms, I recognize all the symptoms in Mr. Remington's successful mongrel." Wister's choice of the term "symptoms" was not accidental: miscegenation was a pathology in his opinion.

Similarly, Wister was sometimes virulently racist, especially after he joined the Immigration Restriction League and became its vice president in 1904. The league, as Bold explains, "was supported by the same network of 'blue-blooded' Boston families as invested in open-range ranching and cultural entrepreneurship" in Wyoming in the 1880s, and unlike other groups that "argued the anti-immigration case on economic grounds, the league was deeply racialist in its principles."

Put another way: if, as Henry Nash Smith suggests in *Virgin Land*, miscegenation is the secret theme of Cooper's

Leatherstocking Tales, then social caste is the unspoken theme of *The Virginian* and many of Wister's other stories. In his fiction, blood always tells, especially if it is blue (good) or mixed or foreign (bad). He strenuously opposed the direct election of U.S. senators, for example, because he believed the measure empowered the rabble. With ill-disguised condescension toward working-class westerners, Wister often defended patrician class privilege and noblesse oblige, a factor in his background that explains his loyalties toward the cattle barons in the Johnson County War. He was troubled during his 1891 trip west to learn that an officer at Fort Washakie, in violation of Wyoming game laws, "had allowed his Indians to slaughter 35 elk in one morning, besides deer & antelope!" What troubled him most, however, was not the violation of the law so much as the presumption that the Indians rather than eastern men on vacation were entitled to the meat and pelts.

As for gender: Wister was never a liberated man. The cowboys' attitude toward women was, he once reported, "medieval, to say the least. . . . A wife is a good thing for a man to have cook his meals for him and generally to look after the home." Wister's own attitude toward women was similarly patriarchal and traditional. Late in his life, he confided to his friend John Jay Chapman that he had never approved of women's suffrage. With the exception of *The Virginian*, moreover, he seems to have targeted a reading audience of eastern men. John W. Cawelti identifies the audience for westerns during this period as "lower and middle class working males." Almost all of the critics of Wister's westerns other than *The Virginian* who comment on his readership agree that, as Howells noted in his review of *Red Men and White*, the "book is a man's book throughout." In her essay "Development of the Literary West" (1900), Kate Chopin averred that Wister "gives the impression of a stagy fellow with an eye on his audience in the East." Edwin L. Shuman, in his notice of *Members of the*

Family in 1911, asserted that the stories would be enjoyed by "red-blooded men of all ages." Even in *The Virginian*, Wister directly addresses "gentleman reformers" in chapter 33, and William Morton Payne in his review avers, not entirely accurately, that it "is a man's book, with not one touch of sickly sentiment."

All of which may begin to explain the exceptional success of *The Virginian*. The demographics of the turn-of-the-century book trade were unambiguous: Howells estimated that women accounted for about 75 percent of the reading public, so many novelists felt obliged to appeal to them for commercial success. When John W. De Forest was asked in 1898 "why I always had a boy and girl in love in my books," he replied that "it was the only kind of plot a writer could get the public interested in." Wister understood this dynamic, and although he often ignored the romantic imperative, he sometimes bent to it, as when he injected some love interest into *Members of the Family* at the last moment prior to its publication. In *The Virginian*, more than any other story he wrote, Wister pandered to a readership of middlebrow women with a romance plot. The commercial appeal of the novel depended more on the feminine allure of Molly than on the virility of the hero.

Despite his race and gender biases, Wister qualifies as a modern progressive at least on the basis of his environmentalism. Like his friend Roosevelt, cofounder of the Boone and Crockett Club, Wister was both a hunter and a conservationist who sought to protect natural habitat and open space. As early as 1889, when the commander at Fort Washakie complained to him about "men from the East who come here and shoot our game," he replied only half-facetiously that the officer would not mind if he knew "how little of it I shot." After returning to Philadelphia from Wyoming in the fall of 1892, Wister mailed a sheaf of his photos of Yellowstone National Park to the U.S. Geological Survey; that is, hunting had become "a secondary consideration" in his travels. As he declared in 1893 in an essay for the Boone and Crockett, "The Yellowstone Park is a sanctuary for buffalo, elk, deer, antelope, and sheep. There (if anywhere) our big game have a chance of surviving" their threatened extinction. He was troubled by reports the next year that the Chicago, Burlington and Quincy Railroad had designs on the park: "I suppose they'll water the locomotives at Old Faithful. Damn this stinking money dredging prostituted country. Civilized! We're not so civilized as we were fifty years ago. Not nearly." After 1895 he never hunted game again except for meat, and instead stalked it with a camera. As he told Arthur Stedman in 1895, "I am not in the least a good shot and I suppose it is the outdoor life and riding that I go for. It has lately been my habit to let all animals go that are not needed for food." He was outraged by commercial development that destroyed land or restricted access to it. He lobbied both Roosevelt and Senator Henry Cabot Lodge on behalf of the bill to purchase land in California to preserve the Calaveras big trees (giant sequoias) in 1900. Even in *The Virginian*, Wister was disgusted by the amount of trash that littered the West. The narrator remarks on "the empty sardine box . . . rusting over the face of the Western earth" and the "thick heaps and fringes of tin cans, and shelving mounds of bottles cast out of the saloons" on "the ramparts of Medicine Bow." During his trip west in 1910 he expressed his concern about the dearth of winter range for elk and urged the Department of the Interior to address the problem, even though years later he excoriated the New Deal and big government. He railed in 1931, fifteen years after his last visit to the park, about "the garbage piles in the Yellowstone." Like one of the Monkey Wrench Gang protesting construction of the Glen Canyon Dam, Wister repeatedly condemned the "commercial vandals" and "exploiters" who built the Jackson Lake Dam in 1910–16 "to irrigate some desert land away off in Idaho." Before the dam was built, he remembered, "long marshes spread above its inlet, where wild geese spent the night." But the vandals "stretched out a secret hand to seize the Yellowstone Park for its water power to deface and degrade a people's pleasure ground for the money in it." He invoked the same verbs in his essay "Old Yellowstone Days" (1936), his last word about the West: the dam "has destroyed the august serenity of the lake's outlet forever; and it has defaced and degraded the shores of the lake where once the pines grew green and dark. They stand now white skeletons drowned by the rising level of the water." That is, Louis Owens is not entirely correct when he asserts that "Wister's West is not the frontier. It is a profit-making enterprise for establishment America, a capitalist resource in which stability is a highly desired commodity." Wister criticized overgrazing, even as he defended the right of the privileged class to graze their herds on public land, and he condemned commercial development when it destroyed irreplaceable natural resources.

In February 1939, a year after Wister's death, the National Park Service named an 11,495-foot granite peak in the Grand Tetons of Wyoming after him. It was a fitting tribute to one of the leading western American writers of his generation.

Bibliographic Essay

The following guide to primary and secondary materials I consulted in the preparation of this biography should establish a baseline of sources for the reader interested in more detailed information about Wister's life and career. This commentary should address most questions related to the subject. As I also note in the acknowledgments, however, I have deposited a fully documented manuscript of the biography in the University of New Mexico English Department library in Albuquerque for scholars who wish to verify the accuracy of any of my specific statements.

Wister manuscripts, including his diaries and letters, are located in more than thirty archives in the United States. The four major repositories are the Library of Congress, the University of Wyoming in Laramie, LaSalle University in Philadelphia, and the New York Public Library. These archives are:

- Papers of Owen Wister, 1829–1966, Manuscript Division, Library of Congress. The single most important Wister archive, with more than 41,000 items. A search aid to the collection is available online. Wister's nine scrapbooks (boxes

40–48) have been microfilmed. The collection also includes
copies of Wister's journals for 1885–96 from the originals at
the University of Wyoming and Wister's manuscript journals
for 1900 and 1919–21.

- Owen Wister Papers, American Heritage Center, University
  of Wyoming. Manuscript scans and transcriptions of Wister's
  western journals for the period 1885–96 as well as other
  items, including "Chalkeye," several other stories, and many
  letters are available online. The journals are the basis for *Owen
  Wister Out West*, ed. Fanny Kemble Wister (Chicago: University of Chicago Press, 1958); however, this volume contains
  only about a third of the material in the journals. For example,
  the volume selectively omits entries from each of the journals and ignores entirely "Cinnabar and Return, 1892," the
  journal Wister kept during his brief trip to Wyoming in July
  1892, soon after the Johnson County War, as well as "Frontier
  Notes, 1893," "Frontier Notes, 1894," and "Journals of 1896
  and 1900." Moreover, it is haphazardly edited, with virtually
  no annotations and some mistranscriptions.
- The Owen Wister and Family Collection, Connelly Library,
  LaSalle University. Scans of several dozen Wister manuscripts,
  including many letters to George Horace Lorimer, the publisher and editor of the *Saturday Evening Post*, are available
  online.
- Manuscripts and Archives, New York Public Library. The
  papers of the New York branch of the Macmillan Company
  include both sides of Wister's nearly forty-year correspondence
  with editor George P. Brett. The Langdon Mitchell Papers
  contain Wister's letters to his distant cousin, one-time collaborator, and the son of S. Weir Mitchell, the physician who
  originally recommended that Wister travel west for his health.

In addition, small but valuable collections of Wister manuscripts are located at the State Historical Society of Pennsylvania, Philadelphia, (34 letters); the Alderman Library,
University of Virginia, Charlottesville (22 letters); the Hun-

tington Library, San Marino, California (6 letters); Butler Library, Columbia University, New York (29 letters); the Mark Twain Papers, Bancroft Library, University of California, Berkeley (10 letters); the Beinecke Library, Yale University, New Haven (22 letters); and the Doheny Library, University of Southern California, Los Angeles (18 letters).

Wister's most valuable correspondence has also been published in the following venues: Fanny Kemble Wister, "Letters of Owen Wister, Author of the Virginian," *Pennsylvania Magazine of History and Biography*, 83 (January 1959), 3–28; *My Dear Wister: The Frederic Remington-Owen Wister Letters*, ed. Ben Merchant Vorpahl (Palo Alto: American West, 1972); John M. Solensten, "Richard Harding Davis, Owen Wister, and *The Virginian*: Unpublished Letters and a Commentary," *American Literary Realism* 5 (Spring 1972), 132–33; *That I May Tell You: Journals and Letters of the Owen Wister Family* ed. Sarah Butler Wister (Wayne, Pa.: Haverford House, 1979); and Alan Price, "'I'm Not an Old Fogey and You're Not a Young Ass': Owen Wister and Ernest Hemingway," *Hemingway Review* 9 (Fall 1989), 82–90. Wister also published many of the letters he exchanged with Theodore Roosevelt over the years in *Roosevelt: The Story of a Friendship, 1880–1919* (New York: Macmillan, 1930).

Though Wister often sat for interviews, he rarely commented at length or in detail about his writing. The exceptions are "Has Come Out in the West," *San Francisco Examiner*, July 15, 1894, 13; "Charmed with Green Lawns," Denver *Rocky Mountain News*, August 12, 1900, 4; David Graham Phillips, "Owen Wister," *Saturday Evening Post*, January 3, 1903, 13–14; and "Owen Wister Makes a Brief Stay in Albuquerque," *Albuquerque Journal*, May 26, 1910, 5. Perhaps the most valuable interview of all, conducted by Arthur Stedman soon after the publication of Wister's *Red Men and White* and distributed nationwide by the Bacheller, Johnson & Bacheller newspaper syndicate, was printed under the title "Owen Wister Talks" in the *Dallas Morning News*, December 7, 1895, 6, as "A Talk with Owen Wister" in the *San Francisco Examiner*, December 8, 1895, 33, and under other titles elsewhere.

Wister slightly revised and collected virtually all of his published work for the eleven-volume *The Writings of Owen Wister* (New York: Macmillan, 1928). The first six volumes contain his western fiction, and the first five feature new introductions:

Volume 1, *Red Men and White*: "The Evolution of the Cow-puncher," "Little Big Horn Medicine," "Specimen Jones," "The Serenade at Siskiyou," "The General's Bluff," "Salvation Gap," "The Second Missouri Compromise," "La Tinaja Bonita," "A Pilgrim on the Gila."

Volume 2, *Lin McLean*: "How Lin McLean Went East," "The Winning of the Biscuit-Shooter," "Lin McLean's Honey-moon," "A Journey in Search of Christmas," "Separ's Vigilante," "Destiny at Drybone, "Autumn on Wind River" (aka "In the After-Days)."

Volume 3, *Hank's Woman*: (Reprint of *The Jimmyjohn Boss and Other Stories*) "The Boy and the Buccaroos" (aka "The Jimmyjohn Boss"), "A Kinsman of Red Cloud," "Sharon's Choice," "Napoleon Shave-Tail," "Twenty Minutes for Refreshments," "The Promised Land," revised version of "Hank's Woman," "Padre Ignazio."

Volume 4, *The Virginian*: Incorporates revisions of eight stories: "Em'ly," "Balaam and Pedro," "Where Fancy Was Bred," "Grandmother Stark," "The Game and the Nation," "In a State of Sin," "Superstition Trail," "With Malice Aforethought."

Volume 5, *Members of the Family*: "The Patronage of High Bear" reprinted under title "Happy Teeth," "The Vicious Circle" reprinted under title "Spit-Cat Creek," "How the Energy Was Conserved" reprinted under title "In the Back," "Timberline," "The Gift Horse," "Extra Dry," "Where It Was," "The Drake Who Had Means of His Own."

Volume 6, *When West Was West*: "Sun Road" reprinted under title "Bad Medicine," "Captain Quid," "Once Round the Clock," "The Right Honorable the Strawberries," "Lone Fountain," "Molting Pelican" reprinted under title "Absalom and Moulting [*sic*] Pelican," "Skip to My Loo," "Little Old Scaffold," "At the Sign of the Last Chance."

Electronic editions of *Red Men and White, Lin McLean, The Jimmyjohn Boss and Other Stories*, and *The Virginian* are available online at Project Gutenberg. PDF images of the same books as well as *Members of the Family* are available online at the Hathi Trust.

Several of Wister's western writings have never been collected: "Chalkeye," *American West* 21 (January-February 1984), 37–52; "Among the Cow-Boys—Random Notes of a Tenderfoot and Sportsman in Wyoming," *Philadelphia Times*, April 12, 1892; reprinted in Louis Tanner, "Owen Wister: From History to Myth," *Journal of the West* 37 (April 1998), 64–69; "The Mountain Sheep: His Ways," in *Musk-Ox, Bison, Sheep, and Goat*, eds. George Bird Grinnell and Caspar Whitney (New York: Macmillan, 1904), 167–224; "Concerning the Contents," preface to *Drawings* by Frederic Remington (New York: Russell, 1897); "Preface" to *A Bunch of Buckskins* by Frederic Remington (New York: Russell, 1901); "Introduction" and verses accompanying *Done in the Open* by Frederic Remington (New York: P. F. Collier, 1903); *The Virginian: A Play in Four Acts* [with Kirk La Shelle], ed. N. Orwin Rush (Tallahassee: privately printed, 1958); *Ten Thousand Cattle Straying: Dead Broke* (New York: Witmark, 1904); "Preface" to *A Monograph of the Works of Mellor, Meigs, and Howe* (New York: Architectural Book Publishing Co., 1923); and "Introduction" to *My Pioneer Past* by Guy Waring (Boston: Brice Humphries, 1936), 13–21.

The most complete and reliable listing of Wister's published writings is Gary Scharnhorst, "Owen Wister: A Primary Bibliography," *Resources for American Literary*

Study 36 (2011), 83–105, which cites more than 250 published writings by Wister, more than 100 of them new to scholarship.

The most comprehensive survey of Wister's contemporary reception, based largely on the clippings in Wister's scrapbooks in the Library of Congress, is Sanford E. Marovitz, "Owen Wister: An Annotated Bibliography of Secondary Material," *American Literary Realism* 7 (1974), 1–110.

Two indispensable histories of the Johnson County cattle war in 1892 are Helena Huntington Smith's *The War on Powder River* (New York: McGraw-Hill, 1966) and John W. Davis's *Wyoming Range War: The Infamous Invasion of Johnson County* (Norman: University of Oklahoma Press, 2010). No less indispensable for readers interested in the Wham robbery is Larry D. Ball's *Ambush at Bloody Run: The Wham Paymaster Robbery of 1889: A Story of Politics, Religion, Race, and Banditry in Arizona Territory* (Tucson: Arizona Historical Society, 2000).

Structural analyses of the modern formulaic western are legion. Among the best are the following: John W. Cawelti, *Adventure, Mystery, and Romance* (Chicago: University of Chicago Press, 1976); Cawelti, *Six-Gun Mystique* (Bowling Green: Bowling Green State University Popular Press, 1971); David Brion Davis, "Ten-Gallon Hero," *American Quarterly* 6 (Summer 1954), 111–25; and Marcus Klein, *Easterns, Westerns, and Private Eyes: American Matters, 1870–1900* (Madison: University of Wisconsin Press, 1994). On the psychological source and appeal of the formula, see Barbara Will, "The Nervous Origins of the American Western," *American Literature* 70 (June 1998): 293–316.

On a related note, Jennifer S. Tuttle has authored a trio of essays on Wister, the West Cure, and neurasthenia. These are: "Gilman's *The Crux* and Owen Wister's *The Virginian*: Intertextuality and 'Women's Manifest Destiny,'" in *Charlotte Perkins Gilman and Her Contemporaries*, eds. Cynthia J. Davis and Denise D. Knight (Tuscaloosa: University of Alabama Press, 2004), 127–38; "Indigenous Whiteness and Wister's Invisible Indians," in *Reading The Virginian in the New West*, eds. Melody Graulich and Stephen Tatum (Lincoln: University of Nebraska Press, 2003), 89–112; and "Rewriting the West Cure: Charlotte Perkins Gilman, Owen Wister, and the Sexual Politics of Neurasthenia," in *The Mixed Legacy of Charlotte Perkins Gilman*, eds. Catherine J. Golden and Joanna Schneider Zangrando (Newark: University of Delaware Press, 2000), 103–21.

There are precious few previous biographies of Wister. The most comprehensive one published to date is Darwin Payne's *Owen Wister: Chronicler of the West, Gentleman of the East* (Dallas: Southern Methodist University Press, 1985). John L. Cobbs's *Owen Wister* (Boston: Twayne, 1984) is a reliable introduction to Wister's life and career. G. Edward White's *The Eastern Establishment and the Western Experience: The West of Frederic Remington, Theodore Roosevelt, and Owen Wister* (New Haven: Yale University Press, 1968) is a well-regarded but derivative group biography.

Some details about Wister's life also appear in Hamlin Garland, *Roadside Meetings* (New York: Macmillan, 1931); Ethelbert Talbot, *My People of the Plains* (New York: Harper & Brothers, 1906); and William Webster Ellsworth, *A Golden Age of Authors: A Publisher's Recollections* (Boston: Houghton Mifflin, 1919). Wister is also occasionally mentioned in the letters and biographies of his contemporaries; such as *The Letters of Theodore Roosevelt*, ed. Elting E. Morison et al. (Cambridge: Harvard University Press, 1951–54); *Frederic Remington: Selected Letters*, eds. Allen P. Splete and Marilyn D. Splete (New York: Abbeville Press, 1987); and Peggy Samuels and Harold Samuels, *Frederic Remington: A Biography* (Austin: University of Texas Press, 1985). In addition, Owen Wister's daughter Marina Wister sometimes mentioned her father in letters to her future husband, the New Mexico artist Andrew Dasburg, written while she was visiting Philadelphia in 1935. Scans of these manuscript letters in the Archives of American Art are available online. Finally, Henry Brock, a retired foreman at Apache Tejo in southwestern New Mexico, reminisced in an interview audiotaped on April 13, 1953, about Wister's visit to the ranch in 1895. A microfilmed transcript of the interview is available in the Pioneers Foundation Oral History Collection 1952–1960, Center for Southwest Research, Zimmerman Library, University of New Mexico, Albuquerque.

In the heyday of the so-called "myth and symbol" school in American literary studies, Wister's western fiction was a popular topic. See Mody Boatright, "The American Myth Rides the Range: Owen Wister's Man on Horseback," *Southwest Review* 36 (Summer 1951) 157–63; Sanford E. Marovitz, "Unseemly Realities in Owen Wister's Western/American Myth," *American Literary Realism* 17 (Autumn 1984), 209–15; and Wallace Stegner, "Owen Wister: Creator of the Cowboy Myth," *American West* 21 (January–February 1984), 48–52.

Over the years Wister's fiction, especially *The Virginian*, has also attracted the attention of comparative literature scholars, as in the following essays: Sonya Yvette Alvarado, "Em'ly in the Cuckoo's Nest," *Midwest Quarterly* 38 (Summer 1997), 351–62; John Donahue, "Nature in *Don Segundo Sombra* and *The Virginian*," *Great Plains Quarterly* 7 (Summer 1987), 166–77; Marilyn Francus, "Calamity Jane? Austen and Owen Wister's *The Virginian*," *Persuasions: The Jane Austen Journal* 27 (2005), 219–33; J. C. Furnas, "Transatlantic Twins: Rudyard Kipling and Owen Wister," *American Scholar* 64 (Autumn 1995), 599–606; Kenneth Alan Hovey, "Wister's 'Life Among the Lowly' and Anglocentrism," *Western American Literature* 39 (Winter 2005), 395–419; Sara Humphreys, "'Truer 'n Hell': Lies, Capitalism, and Cultural Imperialism in Owen Wister's *The Virginian*, B. M. Bower's *The Happy Family*, and Mourning Dove's *Cogewea*," *Western American Literature* 45 (Spring 2010), 30–52; and Ben M. Vorpahl,

"'Very Much Like a Fire-Cracker': Owen Wister on Mark Twain," *Western American Literature* 6 (Summer 1971), 83–98. Two essays discuss the relationship of the novel to Shakespeare's *Henry V*: Max Westbrook, "Bazarov, Prince Hal, and the Virginian," *Western American Literature* 24 (August 1989), 103–11; and James T. Bratcher, "Shakespeare and the Cowboy: Prince Hal as the Model for Owen Wister's Virginian," *Journal of the West* 43 (Spring 2004), 72–77. Three scholars focus particularly on Henry James's influence on Wister: Carl Bode, "Henry James and Owen Wister," *American Literature* 26 (May 1954), 250–52; Ben M. Vorpahl, "Henry James and Owen Wister," *Pennsylvania Magazine of History and Biography* 95 (July 1971), 291–338; and Don D. Walker, "Wister, Roosevelt and James: A Note on the Western." *American Quarterly* 12 (Fall 1960), 358–66. Two literary historians also examine Wister's relationship with Theodore Roosevelt: John A. Barsness, "Theodore Roosevelt as Cowboy: The Virginian as Jacksonian Man," *American Quarterly* 21 (Fall 1969), 609–19; and Forrest G. Robinson, "The Roosevelt-Wister Connection," *Western American Literature* 14 (August 1979), 95–114.

Critics continue to debate the structure and coherence of *The Virginian*. Sanford E. Marovitz in "Testament of a Patriot: The Virginian, the Tenderfoot, and Owen Wister," *Texas Studies in Literature and Language* 15 (Fall 1973), 551–75, insists that "the stories have been well integrated into a unified whole through themes and characters that have been developed and interwoven with a great deal of subtlety," and John D. Nesbitt in "Owen Wister's Achievement in Literary Tradition," *Western American Literature* 18 (Fall 1983), 199–208, commends the novel's "organic coherence." But Bernard DeVoto complains that Wister assembled the novel with scissors and paste and "the joints left visible" ("Birth of an Art," *Harper's Monthly*, 211 [December 1955], 8–9, 12–16), and William R. Handley in "Wister's Omniscience and Omissions," in *Reading*

The Virginian in the New West, 39–71, contends that "the novel's narrative structure is the result of Wister's botched attempt to make his previous short stories cohere." Gerald Thompson contends that Wister considered the novel "something of an American Lohengrin," in "Musical and Literary Influences on Owen Wister's *The Virginian*," *South Atlantic Quarterly* 85 (Winter 1986), 40–55. Although Wister certainly alluded to Wagner occasionally in his western journals and letters, there is no reference to Wagner in the novel or in any versions of the stories that it comprises, nor is there external evidence that Wister had Wagner in mind as he was writing it. The tale was less Wagnerian opera than horse opera.

In recent years, under the sway of the "new" American Studies, Wister's western fiction has become fodder for the New Historicists; for example, Christine Bold's "How the Western Ends: Fenimore Cooper to Frederic Remington," *Western American Literature* 17 (Summer 1982), 116–35, and *The Frontier Club: Popular Westerns and Cultural Power 1880–1924* (New York: Oxford University Press, 2013); Jane Kuenz's "The Cowboy Businessman and 'The Course of Empire': Owen Wister's *The Virginian*," *Cultural Critique* 48 (Spring 2001), 98–128; and Gary Scharnhorst's "The Virginian as Founding Father," *Arizona Quarterly* 40 (Autumn 1984), 227–41, and "Wister and the Great Railway Strike of 1894," in *Reading The Virginian in the New West*, 113–25.

More specifically, some recent New Historicist scholarship on Wister and the West has focused on issues of race and gender. Examples include Wendy Pearce Miller, "Domesticating the Cowboy: Owen Wister's *The Virginian* as Validation of Marriage," *Studies in the Western*, 13 (2005), 101–106; Lee Clark Mitchell, "'When You Call Me That . . .': Tall Talk and Male Hegemony in *The Virginian*," *PMLA* 102 (January 1987), 66–77; Louis Owens, "White for a Hundred Years," in *Reading The Virginian in the New*

West, 72–88; and Forrest G. Robinson, "The Virginian and Molly in Paradise: How Sweet Is It?" *Western American Literature* 21 (May 1986), 27–38.

Among the most provocative critical essays on Wister's western writings are a series of articles by Neal Lambert that originated in his 1967 doctoral dissertation. These are: "Owen Wister's 'Hank's Woman': The Writer and His Commitment," *Western American Literature* 4 (Spring 1969) 39–50; "Owen Wister's Lin McLean: The Failure of the Vernacular Hero," *Western American Literature* 5 (Fall 1970), 219–32; "Owen Wister's Virginian: The Genesis of a Cultural Hero," *Western American Literature* 6 (Summer 1971), 99–107; and "The Values of the Frontier: Owen Wister's Final Assessment," *South Dakota Review* 9, i (1971), 76–87.

Of course, many other critical books and articles contain biographical information, including William J. Bogard, "Wister's Journals and *The Virginian*: From Static to Dynamic," *South Dakota Review* 28, ii (1990), 22–33; James T. Bratcher, "The Ennui of Arizona Military Life in 1893–94: Events Behind an Owen Wister Short Story," *Journal of the West* 46 (Spring 2007), 88–92; Robert Murray Davis, "*The Virginian*: Social Darwinist Pastoral," *Acta Litteraria Academiae Scientiarum Hungaricae* 23 (1981), 271–79; Donald E. Houghton, "Two Heroes in One: Reflections Upon the Popularity of *The Virginian*," *Journal of Popular Culture* 4 (Fall 1970), 497–506; Marvin Lewis, "Owen Wister: Caste Imprints in Western Letters," *Arizona Quarterly* 10 (1954), 147–56; David Mogen, "Owen Wister's Cowboy Heroes," *Southwestern American Literature* 5 (1975), 47–61; Stephen L. Tanner, "*The Virginian* as Bildungsroman," *Studies in the Western* 10 (2002), 20–26; Stephen Tatum, "Pictures (Facing) Words," in *Reading The Virginian in the New West*, 1–38; Gerald Thompson, "Owen Wister and His Critics: Realism and Morality in *The Virginian*," *Annals of Wyoming* 64 (Winter 1992), 2–10;

George T. Watkins, "Wister and 'The Virginian,'" *Pacific Northwesterner* 2 (Fall 1958), 49–54; Richard Wattenberg, *Early-Twentieth-Century Frontier Dramas on Broadway: Situating the Western Experience in Performing Arts* (New York: Palgrave Macmillan, 2011); Leslie T. Whipp, "Owen Wister: Wyoming's Influential Realist and Craftsman," *Great Plains Quarterly* 10 (Fall 1990), 245–59; and John I. White, "The Virginian," *Montana: The Magazine of Western History* 16 (October 1966), 2–11.

At Wister's death, obituaries appeared in newspapers throughout the United States and England, including the *New York Times*, p. 17; the *Times* of London, p. 16; and the *Chicago Tribune*, p. 13, all dated July 22, 1938.

Index

Index

Index

lynch law, 19, 68–69, 131–32,
146–47, 157, 162, 168, 169,
175, 176, 182, 199, 209
Lyons, Gretchen, 177

Mabie, Hamilton W., 186
Major, Charles, 154
Manchester Guardian, 113
Marriages of Scipio, The (Wister),
189–90
Maricopa, Ariz., 78, 183
Marovitz, Sanford, 40
Martin, E. S., 65
Mason, Jules, 14, 214
Mather, Frank, 158
Matthews, Brander, 77
McCrea, Joel, 180
McKinley, William, 142
Medicine Bow, Wyo., 11, 129,
138, 139, 149, 168, 169, 170,
171, 190, 219
Melbourne, Frank, 69–70
Melbourne, Will, 70
Members of the Family (Wister), 4,
124, 182, 185, 186, 189, 195,
217–18
Mencken, H. L., 186, 195
Mercer, Harry, 26, 94
Mérimée, Prosper, 25, 186
Miles, Nelson A., 127
Miller, Henry, 108, 109
Millet, Frank, 46
Minneapolis Times-Journal, 126
Mission San Xavier del Bac, 70
Mitchell, Jack, 103, 104
Mitchell, Langdon, 78, 94, 96,
103, 149, 213
Mitchell, S. Weir, 8, 27, 103, 154,
184
Modoc War, 62–63
Mogen, David, 131

Monroe, Harriet, 155
Monroe, Lucy, 158
Montezuma, 45
Montgomery, Ala., 178
Morgan, J. P., 123
Mormons, 81, 83, 84, 108, 208
Mozart, Wolfgang Amadeus, 189
My Darling Clementine, 170
Myrdal, Gunnar, 147

Nabokov, Vladimir, 78
"Napoleon Shave-Tail" (Wister),
103–4
Nasby, Petroleum V., 20
Nation, 68, 77, 155, 187
"National Guard of Pennsylvania,
The" (Wister), 75, 83, 119
Neighbors Henceforth (Wister), 211
Nelson, Henry Loomis, 93
New Haven, Conn., 174
New Orleans, La., 39, 88, 178,
183
New Orleans Picayune, 187
New Rochelle, N.Y., 63, 171
New Swiss Family Robinson, The
(Wister), 12
New York American, 156
New York Express, 95
New York Herald, 158, 177
New York Herald-Tribune, 210
New York Mail and Express, 126
New York Times, 155, 161
New York Tribune, 41, 64, 91,
112, 126, 155, 177, 187
Newark, N.J., 178
Nez Perce, 61
Nogales, Ariz., 84
Norfolk, Va., 178
Norman, George, 13, 14, 214
North American (Philadelphia),
158

239

Index

241

Index

Index

Index

Wister, Owen: illnesses of, 5,
45–46, 89, 181, 182–83, 191,
193, 194, 203; on censorship,
211; on environmentalism,
218; on free silver, 80, 84; on
immigration, 75, 80, 119, 195,
216; on literary style, 5, 55; on
organized labor, 71–76, 77,
83, 118–19, 120, 121, 192; on
populism, 80; on race, 38, 157,
215; on women's suffrage, 44,
217; use of dialect by, 95; work
habits of, 5. *See individual titles
of works*
Wister, Owen (son), 195, 214
Wister, Owen Jones (father), 12,
103
Wister, Sarah Butler (mother), 12,
13, 21, 27, 49, 96, 103, 117,
140, 148, 153, 157, 158, 174,
180
Wister, William (son), 183, 214
"With Malice Aforethought"
(Wister), 109, 137, 138, 147,
151, 152, 153, 171

Wolcott, Frank, 9, 10, 16, 28, 29,
35, 51, 194
women's suffrage, 44, 217
Wood, Leonard, 198, 206–7
World (London), 187
World (New York), 95, 158
Wounded Knee, S.Dak., 60
Wyoming Stock Growers
Association (WSGA), 9, 16,
17, 28, 29, 51, 74, 103

Yellowstone National Park, 11,
14, 15–16, 24, 26, 56, 70,
104, 118, 190, 197, 214,
218–19, 220
York, Lucille, 174
Yosemite National Park, 93
"Young Lochinvar" (Wister),
170
Youth's Companion, 12
Yuma, Ariz., 59, 84, 183, 208

Ziff, Larzer, 144
Zola, Emile, 113, 142